R. Gupta's®

POPULAR MASTER GUIDE

IBPS Specialist Officer

Institute of Banking Personnel Selection

IT Officer

(Scale-I)

Preliminary & Main Exams

by

RPH Editorial Board

2027 EDITION

RAMESH PUBLISHING HOUSE, NEW DELHI

Published by
O.P. Gupta *for* Ramesh Publishing House

Admin. Office
12-H, New Daryaganj Road, Opp. Officers' Mess,
New Delhi-110002 ✆ 23275224, 23245124

E-mail: info@rameshpublishinghouse.com
For Online Shopping: www.rameshpublishinghouse.com

Showroom
• Balaji Market, Nai Sarak, Delhi-110006 ✆ 23282525 📱 9354373464
• 4457, Nai Sarak, Delhi-110006

Book Code: R-912

ISBN: 978-93-86845-71-9

Price: ₹ 920

Printed at: B.K. Offset, Delhi

CONTENTS

❑❑❑

SCHEME OF ONLINE EXAMINATIONS

The structure of the Examinations which will be conducted online are as follows:

A. PRELIMINARY EXAMINATION

Sr. No.	Name of Tests	No. of Questions	Maximum Marks	Medium of Exam	Duration
1.	English Language	50	25	English	40 minutes
2.	Reasoning	50	50	English & Hindi	40 minutes
3.	Quantitative Aptitude	50	50	English & Hindi	40 minutes
	Total	**150**	**125**		

Candidates have to qualify in each of the three tests by securing minimum cut-off marks to be decided by IBPS. Adequate number of candidates in each category as decided by IBPS depending upon requirements will be shortlisted for Online Main Examination.

B. MAIN EXAMINATION

Name of Tests	No. of Questions	Maximum Marks	Medium of Exam	Duration
Professional Knowledge	60	60	English & Hindi	45 minutes

Note:

- **Penalty for Wrong Answers (Applicable to both – Preliminary and Main Examinations):** There will be penalty for wrong answers marked in the Objective Tests. For each question for which a wrong answer has been given by the candidate one fourth or 0.25 of the marks assigned to that question will be deducted as penalty to arrive at corrected score. If a question is left blank, *i.e.* no answer is marked by the candidate, there will be no penalty for that question.
- **Interview:** Candidates who have been shortlisted in the Main examination will be called for an Interview to be conducted by the Participating Organisations and coordinated by the Nodal Banks in each State/UT with the help of IBPS.
- The total marks allotted for Interview are 100. The weightage (ratio) of Online (Main Exam) and interview will be 80:20 respectively.

Previous Years' Paper

Institute of Banking Personnel Selection

IBPS—Specialist (IT) Officer Scale-I

Preliminary & Main Exam 2025*

PRELIMINARY EXAMINATION

ENGLISH LANGUAGE

Directions (Qs. No. 1-10): *Read the following passage and answer the given questions.*

When Company X introduced its online game, the market response was immediate and overwhelming. The very next year, the company earned huge profits and quickly gained users across the globe. Reports revealed that the game generated 50 million dollars worldwide, making it one of the most successful digital launches in recent years. This sudden success was seen as a major **hit**, granting Company X recognition and dominance in the industry.

Yet, beneath the shining surface of profits and popularity, a darker picture began to emerge. Parents started to **raise** concerns over the time children were spending on this game. Many young users became addicted, unable to manage their daily schedules, and their studies suffered significantly. Teachers noticed falling grades, a decline in participation, and a visible drop in discipline. At home, the situation worsened as children grew increasingly irritable, spending less time with family and showing signs of inappropriate behavior.

Roommates, on the other hand, reported that their relationships remained smooth only during gaming sessions. Once the console was turned off, interactions were minimal, and genuine conversations reduced. What was marketed as a tool for entertainment and bonding ironically created isolation and dependency. Parents found themselves struggling to establish healthy routines for their children, often entering into conflicts that left family ties strained.

An independent organisation decided to investigate these growing concerns and carried out a large-scale survey. The data collected and the report submitted revealed an alarming trend. The impact of the game was largely negative, with cases of extreme dependency, reduced academic achievement, and antisocial tendencies being repeatedly recorded. What initially gave the company a **toe hold** in the international gaming market was now turning into a nationwide social concern.

The report strongly emphasized that while the company's financial growth was undeniable, the cost to society was far greater. Addiction had begun to reshape the daily lives of thousands of children, disturbing family harmony and disrupting the overall learning environment. Based on the overwhelming findings, the organisation recommended that the game should be banned in the country. The conclusion was clear: no amount of profit could justify the erosion of discipline, values, and future prospects of the younger generation.

1. What is the primary irony highlighted by the author regarding Company X's online game?
   (*a*) The company's most profitable year was also its most controversial.
   (*b*) A game designed for entertainment and bonding ended up fostering addiction and isolation.
   (*c*) The company grew financially, but its user base started declining soon after.
   (*d*) Parents initially appreciated the game but later demanded it be banned.
   (*e*) While profits surged, the company secretly planned to shut down the game.

2. What negative consequences of the game were observed in children, as per the passage?
   (*a*) Children began losing interest in digital games and preferred outdoor activities instead.
   (*b*) Students became highly disciplined and responsible with their schoolwork and home routines.
   (*c*) Many children showed signs of addiction, poor academic performance, irritability, and spent less time with family members.
   (*d*) Young users formed better relationships with their teachers but struggled with peer pressure.
   (*e*) Children used the game as a stress-relief method and became more independent in their decision-making.

*Based on Memory, 30-08-2025

3. What can be inferred about the survey conducted by the independent organisation?

(*a*) It focused solely on academic performance in urban schools.
(*b*) It revealed mild concerns that were largely exaggerated by the media.
(*c*) It showed that most users balanced gaming and daily life efficiently.
(*d*) It confirmed widespread negative impacts, prompting a ban recommendation.
(*e*) It offered technical fixes for the game's issues but no regulatory suggestions.

4. According to the passage, what role did roommates play in revealing the social effects of the game?

(*a*) They actively tried to prevent gaming in their homes.
(*b*) They became addicted and dropped out of college.
(*c*) They used the game as a bonding tool but lacked real interaction otherwise.
(*d*) They encouraged younger players to limit their screen time.
(*e*) They often fought over gaming equipment, causing tension.

5. Why did Company X's game gain global popularity so quickly after its launch?

(*a*) The game was unique and had no competitors in the digital market.
(*b*) The company launched a global advertising campaign supported by educational institutions.
(*c*) The game quickly attracted millions of users and earned substantial profits, establishing the company's position in the gaming industry.
(*d*) Parents and teachers encouraged children to use the game for both fun and learning.
(*e*) The company offered the game free of cost to users during the initial launch phase.

6. How did teachers contribute to the concern about the game's impact?

(*a*) They partnered with the company to create school-safe gaming tools.
(*b*) They observed and reported a consistent decline in student behavior and academic performance.
(*c*) They welcomed the game, saying it helped students with teamwork.
(*d*) They banned the use of computers in classrooms due to gaming.
(*e*) They noticed students becoming physically stronger due to eye-hand coordination practice.

7. Fill in the blank with the most appropriate option:

(*a*) downfall (*b*) shortcut
(*c*) toe hold (*d*) decline
(*e*) conclusion

8. Choose the option that is the **closest in meaning** to the word **"hit"** as used in the passage:

(*a*) Blow (*b*) Success
(*c*) Punch (*d*) Trial
(*e*) Drama

9. Choose the word that is the **opposite in meaning** to **"raise"** as used in the passage:

(*a*) Boost (*b*) Improve
(*c*) Lower (*d*) distribute
(*e*) Elevate

10. What was the main recommendation made by the independent organisation after analyzing the impact of the game?

(*a*) The organisation suggested that the game should be modified to include educational content.
(*b*) The organisation recommended that the game should be banned due to its harmful effects on children and society.
(*c*) The organisation advised parents to install stricter internet filters to monitor their children's gaming habits.
(*d*) The organisation proposed that the game be used as a tool for team building and school collaboration.
(*e*) The organisation recommended offering rewards to children who limit their gaming time.

Directions (Qs. No. 11-16): *In the following question, few sentences are given. Choose and mark the sentence which contains no grammatical or contextual error in it. If all the sentences are grammatically and contextually incorrect, mark "All are incorrect" option as the answer choice.*

11. (*a*) He insisted to go to the market even though he was not feeling well.
(*b*) She said she would rather stay home than going to the party.
(*c*) The manager along with his team were present at the conference.
(*d*) The players were congratulated for their outstanding performance.
(*e*) All are incorrect.

12. (*a*) If he will call me, I will inform you immediately.
(*b*) The police is investigating the matter seriously.
(*c*) The meeting has been rescheduled due to unavoidable circumstances.
(*d*) Everyone must submitted their reports by tomorrow without fail.
(*e*) All are incorrect.

13. (*a*) He told me that he is living in Delhi since 2010.
   (*b*) The data show a remarkable increase in productivity this year.
   (*c*) Either the principal or the teachers is responsible for this confusion.
   (*d*) The book that you gave me are very interesting.
   (*e*) All are incorrect.

14. (*a*) He did not attend the meeting, nor he informed anyone about his absence.
   (*b*) The new policy aims at improving efficiency across departments.
   (*c*) She is one of the student who always complete their homework.
   (*d*) The company have decided to expand its operations abroad.
   (*e*) All are incorrect.

15. (*a*) Neither of the brothers were willing to take responsibility for the mistake.
   (*b*) The committee have submitted its report to the higher authorities.
   (*c*) She denied to have taken any money from the locker.
   (*d*) The workers demanded that their wages be increased immediately.
   (*e*) All are incorrect.

16. (*a*) If I was you, I would accept the offer immediately.
   (*b*) She congratulated him on his promotion to the post of manager.
   (*c*) Each of the boys are responsible for cleaning the classroom.
   (*d*) The results of the survey has been published in today's newspaper.
   (*e*) All are incorrect.

Directions (Qs. No. 17-22): *In the following question, a passage is provided with few blanks. Choose the most suitable word from the given options to fill the respective blank.*

The nation has recently __**(A)**__ a surge in fake bomb threats targeting trains and flights, creating panic among passengers and disrupting essential travel services. Anonymous calls and messages falsely claimed the __**(B)**__ of explosives, forcing authorities to carry out emergency checks. These incidents led to delays, cancellations, and inconvenience for thousands of travelers. Union government ministers confirmed that detailed information about the threats had been __**(C)**__ and stressed that such false alarms are treated as serious crimes. They noted that spreading fake information not only causes fear but also __**(D)**__ security resources and diverts attention from genuine concerns.

Investigations are underway to __**(E)**__ the sources of these false alerts. Early indications point to organized attempts to spread chaos. Officials assured that once the responsible organization is identified, strict punishment will be __**(F)**__ under existing laws. The government has also directed railways and aviation authorities to step up security measures and verify all suspicious communications without delay.

While no actual explosives have been discovered, the gravity of the threats cannot be ignored. Passengers are advised to remain calm and cooperate with security checks, as the government reiterated its commitment to ensuring safety and penalizing those spreading fake threats.

17. Which of the following is most suitable to fill the blank A?
   (*a*) faced (*b*) created
   (*c*) ignored (*d*) welcomed
   (*e*) imagined

18. Which of the following is most suitable to fill the blank B?
   (*a*) growth (*b*) presence
   (*c*) function (*d*) arrival
   (*e*) reason

19. Which of the following is most suitable to fill the blank C?
   (*a*) invented
   (*b*) ignored
   (*c*) delayed
   (*d*) destroyed
   (*e*) received

20. Which of the following is most suitable to fill the blank D?
   (*a*) saves (*b*) collects
   (*c*) wastes (*d*) builds
   (*e*) increases

21. Which of the following is most suitable to fill the blank E?
   (*a*) confuse (*b*) mislead
   (*c*) identify (*d*) replace
   (*e*) hide

22. Which of the following is most suitable to fill the blank F?
   (*a*) ignored
   (*b*) enforced
   (*c*) avoided
   (*d*) delayed
   (*e*) reduced

Directions (Qs. No. 23-25): *In the question given below two sentences are given which are grammatically correct and meaningful. Connect them with the most suitable word given below the statements in the best possible way without changing the intended meaning. Choose the answer accordingly from the options to form a correct coherent sentence.*

23. I. She saved money for several months;
II. She finally bought a new laptop.
(*a*) although (*b*) so
(*c*) however (*d*) despite
(*e*) moreover

24. I. He prepared well for the interview;
II. He did not get selected for the job.
(*a*) yet (*b*) because
(*c*) therefore (*d*) moreover
(*e*) hence

25. I. The shop was closed;
II. We could not buy any groceries.
(*a*) although (*b*) therefore
(*c*) yet (*d*) despite
(*e*) moreover

Directions (Qs. No. 26-27): *Rearrange the following five sentences (A), (B), (C), (D) and (E) in the proper sequence to form a meaningful paragraph and then answer the question given below.*

26. A. The development of the electronic computer began in the 20th century, with machines like ENIAC marking a significant leap.
B. Early computing devices such as the abacus and mechanical calculators laid the foundation for modern machines.
C. Over time, computers evolved rapidly, moving from bulky machines to compact, powerful personal computers.
D. In the 19th century, Charles Babbage conceptualized the Analytical Engine, often regarded as the first mechanical computer design.
E. This evolution continued into the 21st century, leading to innovations like smartphones and cloud computing.
(*a*) BDACE (*b*) CBADE
(*c*) DCBAE (*d*) CBEAD
(*e*) DBAEC

27. A. Glucose, commonly referred to as blood sugar, is the primary source of energy for the body's cells.
B. When blood sugar levels drop too low, a person may experience dizziness, confusion, and even loss of consciousness.
C. Such regulation is vital for maintaining stable blood sugar, ensuring overall health and the proper functioning of organs.
D. Conversely, consistently high blood sugar can lead to serious health issues such as nerve damage, vision problems, and diabetes.
E. The body carefully regulates these glucose levels through hormones like insulin, which enable cells to absorb sugar from the bloodstream.
(*a*) BCADE (*b*) ADCBE
(*c*) DBCAE (*d*) AECBD
(*e*) DACBE

Directions (Qs. No. 28-29): *In the given question, few sentences are given. Also, sentence (D) is fixed as the fourth sentence. Rearrange the remaining four sentences in the proper sequence to form a meaningful paragraph.*

28. A. Wheat thrives on a cool growing season, followed by a warm, dry period for harvest.
B. In many parts of the world, wheat is a staple food crop, cultivated extensively for its adaptability and nutritional value.
C. With the help of modern techniques like mechanized irrigation and improved seed varieties, wheat production has seen significant growth.
D. After harvesting, the grains are cleaned, stored in dry conditions, and distributed for consumption or further processing.
E. Given these requirements, farmers select suitable soils and time their sowing to secure a healthy yield.
(*a*) CEADB (*b*) AEBDC
(*c*) ABCDE (*d*) AECDB
(*e*) BAEDC

29. A. Technology has become a defining force of modern life, reshaping domains from communication to healthcare and beyond.
B. While it brings convenience and efficiency, it also raises concerns about privacy, mental health, and dependency.
C. As innovations continue to emerge, society must learn to balance technological advancement with human values.
D. These developments have deeply influenced human behavior, altering habits, routines, and even attention spans.
E. This rapid pace of change has introduced both opportunities and challenges into daily routines.
(*a*) CEADB (*b*) AEBDC
(*c*) EACDB (*d*) EABDC
(*e*) ACEDB

Directions (Qs. No. 30-32): *In the following question, a word is highlighted in the sentence given. Followed by few sentences are given using that word. Identify the sentences that have use the given word in the same meaning as used in the question statement.*

30. The teacher asked the students to ***show*** their homework notebooks.

A. They went to see a ***show*** at the theatre.
B. His paintings are on ***show*** at the gallery.
C. The wound did not ***show*** any sign of infection.

(*a*) Only B (*b*) Both B and C
(*c*) Only C (*d*) Only A
(*e*) All A, B, C

31. He ate the ***whole*** cake by himself.

A. The ***whole*** matter was discussed in the meeting.
B. she is missed terribly and her death has left a ***whole*** in all our lives.
C. The ***whole*** class was present during the lecture.

(*a*) Only B (*b*) Both A and C
(*c*) Only C (*d*) Only A
(*e*) All A, B, C

32. She has a ***firm*** belief in honesty.

A. He started his own law ***firm*** in the city.
B. The ground was ***firm*** after the heavy rain.
C. The manager took a ***firm*** decision against corruption.

(*a*) Only B (*b*) Both A and C
(*c*) Only C (*d*) Only A
(*e*) All A, B, C

Directions (Qs. No. 33-37): *In each of the questions given below, six words have been highlighted. These six words may or may not have been placed in their correct positions. The sentence is then followed by options with the correct combination of words that should replace each other in order to make the sentence grammatically and contextually correct. Find the correct combination of the words that should replace each other. If the sentence is correct as it is, then select option "No interchange required" as your choice.*

33. The manager's **missing (A)** question about the **unexpected (B)** report seemed to abash him **completely (C)**, leaving him **speechless (D)** and visibly **uncomfortable (E)** in front of **colleagues (F)**.

(*a*) B-F (*b*) A-B
(*c*) A-B & C-D (*d*) A-F & B-E
(*e*) No interchange required

34. After (A) hours of **relentless (B)** rain, the storm **abate (C)** to **began (D)**, allowing residents to **cautiously (E)** step outside and **assess (F)** the flood damage.

(*a*) C-D (*b*) A-B
(*c*) A-B & C-D (*d*) A-F & B-E
(*e*) No interchange required

35. The monarch **while (A)** to **abdicate (B)** his throne, choosing a **immense (C)** life of service, **decided (D)** his **successor (E)** prepared for **quieter (F)** responsibility.

(*a*) B-F (*b*) A-B
(*c*) A-D & C-F (*d*) C-F & B-E
(*e*) No interchange required

36. The sudden **collapse (A)** of a strong financial **institution (B)** was **considered (C)** an **aberration (D)**, shaking investor **confidence (E)** and disrupting the otherwise **stable (F)** market.

(*a*) B-F (*b*) B-D
(*c*) A-B & C-D (*d*) A-F & B-E
(*e*) No interchange required

37. Many voters **chose (A)** to **abstain (B)** from the election, citing **participation (C)** with both **candidates (D),** which significantly **reduced (E)** overall turnout and **dissatisfaction (F)** rates.

(*a*) C-F (*b*) D-F
(*c*) A-B & C-D (*d*) A-F & B-E
(*e*) No interchange required

Directions (Qs. No. 38-42): *In each of the following sentences, a part of the sentence has been bold. Below are given alternatives to the bold part which may improve the sentence. Choose the correct alternative. Wherever no improvement is needed, choose 'No replacement required' as the answer.*

38. Five years later, **I was eating** this same dish at the same restaurant.

(*a*) will have been eating
(*b*) has been eating
(*c*) am eating
(*d*) had been eating
(*e*) No replacement required

39. I **have been yet** to go to the flower exhibition at Delhi University.

(*a*) have yet being (*b*) have yet
(*c*) have yet been (*d*) had been yet
(*e*) No replacement required

40. I had **not only helped her by** giving hints but also with providing her links.

(*a*) helped her not only by
(*b*) helped her not by
(*c*) helped her only by
(*d*) helped not only her by
(*e*) No replacement required

41. This secret will remain **between you and I**.

(*a*) between you and me
(*b*) between I and you
(*c*) between you
(*d*) among you and I
(*e*) No replacement required

42. The train **left before I reached** the station.

(*a*) left before I had reached
(*b*) left before I reach
(*c*) left before I have reached
(*d*) had left before I reached
(*e*) No replacement required

Directions (Qs. No. 43-50): *Read the following passage and answer the given questions.*

Lakes are crucial freshwater reserves that support aquatic life, agriculture, and human needs. Their long-term health depends greatly on internal chemical processes. Two significant ones are phosphorus reactions and the chloride + water reaction.

Phosphorus, though essential for growth, becomes harmful when it enters lakes in excess through fertilizers, detergents, or untreated sewage. These phosphorus reactions trigger algal blooms that block sunlight and reduce oxygen. As algae decompose, oxygen levels in the lake **lower**, suffocating fish and disrupting biodiversity. Since phosphorus can remain trapped in sediments for years, its negative effects often persist long after the external supply is reduced.

The chloride + water reaction influences lakes differently. Chloride, introduced through road salts, mining, or industrial effluents, steadily raises salinity. This alters water density and circulation, stressing species adapted to freshwater. Overtime, plant diversity declines, fish populations shrink, and the water often acquires a taste unsuitable for drinking or irrigation.Lake water naturally contains several elements vital for ecological balance. Oxygen is essential for aquatic organisms, calcium supports shell-forming species like mollusks, while sodium and magnesium maintain mineral stability. When levels of elements such as chloride or phosphorus rise unnaturally, however, the lake's chemistry shifts in ways that damage both ecosystems and human use.

Monitoring these chemical reactions helps prevent major damage. Tracking phosphorus levels makes it possible to predict algal blooms, while chloride studies guide alternatives to road salt, such as sand or organic compounds. Establishing buffer zones around farms and improving wastewater treatment can also reduce nutrient flow into lakes.

Yet, implementing such measures often demands high costs or changes in established practices. Farmers may resist reducing fertilizer use, while cities in snowy regions rely heavily on road salts for safety. Balancing ecological preservation with economic and practical needs remains a challenge. If ignored, these reactions can leave lakes unsuitable for consumption, raising the risk of dehydration in communities dependent on them. Protecting the chemical balance of lakes is therefore vital not only for biodiversity but also for ensuring safe and reliable freshwater for human survival.

43. Why the effects of phosphorus on lake ecosystems are difficult to reverse?

(*a*) Phosphorus is continually supplied by natural sources like aquatic plants.
(*b*) Phosphorus boosts oxygen production, which leads to microbial overgrowth.
(*c*) Phosphorus reactions are neutralized quickly, masking their long-term impact.
(*d*) Even after external inputs are reduced, phosphorus trapped in sediments continues to affect the ecosystem.
(*e*) Chloride presence intensifies the impact of phosphorus, making it a dual threat to aquatic life.

44. Why is the chloride + water reaction considered particularly disruptive to lake biodiversity?

(*a*) It reduces calcium levels, thereby weakening shell-forming species.
(*b*) It causes rapid pH fluctuations that kill algae and fish.
(*c*) It increases water salinity, which affects circulation and freshwater-adapted species.
(*d*) It directly interacts with oxygen, accelerating eutrophication.
(*e*) It combines with magnesium to form harmful mineral clusters.

45. Which of the following measures is NOT mentioned as a strategy to mitigate chemical imbalance in lakes?

(*a*) Creating buffer zones around farms
(*b*) Improving wastewater treatment systems
(*c*) Substituting road salts with organic alternatives
(*d*) Using oxygenation devices to prevent fish suffocation
(*e*) Monitoring chloride and phosphorus levels regularly

46. Which of the following statements is/are CORRECT based on the passage?

I. The chloride + water reaction can affect the drinkability of lake water.
II. High chloride concentration leads to biodiversity decline and poor irrigation quality.
III. Phosphorus boosts plant diversity in lake ecosystems.

(*a*) Only (I) (*b*) Both (I) and (II)
(*c*) Only (III) (*d*) Both (I) and (III)
(*e*) All (I), (II) and (III)

47. Which of the following statements is INCORRECT according to the passage?
(*a*) Road salts are a significant source of chloride in lakes.
(*b*) Phosphorus comes solely from industrial sources and has no agricultural links.
(*c*) Excess phosphorus can lead to oxygen depletion in water bodies.
(*d*) Freshwater species can suffer due to changing water density.
(*e*) Socioeconomic barriers can impede ecological reforms.

48. Based on the passage, how does the chemical balance in lakes impact the survival of aquatic plants and animals?
(*a*) Species in lakes can adapt quickly to chemical imbalances caused by human intervention.
(*b*) Minor fluctuations in chemicals like chloride or phosphorus help sustain aquatic food chains.
(*c*) Disruptions in chemical balance can cascade through the ecosystem, affecting biodiversity and human utility.
(*d*) Human influence on chemical levels in lakes has negligible impact on species survival.
(*e*) Lakes with higher oxygen and chloride content support a broader range of aquatic species.

49. According to the passage, why is it difficult to protect lakes from harmful chemical changes?
(*a*) Governments lack awareness about freshwater preservation.
(*b*) Road salts have no viable alternatives in snow-heavy regions.
(*c*) Human reluctance and economic dependency hinder ecological practices.
(*d*) Farming practices naturally prevent phosphorus runoff.
(*e*) Chloride has more environmental benefits than drawbacks.

50. Choose the word that is opposite in meaning to "lower" as used in the passage:
(*a*) intensify (*b*) improve
(*c*) raise (*d*) filter
(*e*) enhance

REASONING

Directions (Qs. No. 51-55): *A number and word arrangement machine, when given an input, rearranges the words and the numbers following a particular set of rules. An illustration is given below of it.*

Input: 53 Quashing 59 Crusader 75 Stipulate 48 Enactment 22 Plummet 34 Resentment
Step I: Resentment 53 Quashing 59 Crusader 75 Stipulate 48 Enactment Plummet 34 22
Step II: Plummet Resentment 53 Quashing 59 Crusader Stipulate 48 Enactment 34 22 75
Step III: Enactment Plummet Resentment 53 Quashing 59 Crusader Stipulate 48 22 75 34
Step IV: Crusader Enactment Plummet Resentment 53 Quashing Stipulate 48 22 75 34 59
Step V: Stipulate Crusader Enactment Plummet Resentment 53 Quashing 22 75 34 59 48
Step VI: Quashing Stipulate Crusader Enactment Plummet Resentment 22 75 34 59 48 53
Input: 43 Purview 68 Chronic 73 Dismantle 47 Incumbent 38 Relegating 56 Doughty

51. What is the position of "Incumbent" in Step VI from the left end?
(*a*) Fourth (*b*) Fifth
(*c*) None of these (*d*) Second
(*e*) Third

52. How many numbers are to the left of "Doughty" in Step III?
(*a*) Two
(*b*) Three
(*c*) One
(*d*) Four
(*e*) None of these

53. Which of the following numbers will be 2nd to the left of the 3rd number from the right end in step V?
(*a*) 38 (*b*) 73
(*c*) 47 (*d*) 68
(*e*) None of these

54. In which of the following step "Purview 68 47" exists in the same order?
(*a*) Step I (*b*) Step II
(*c*) Step III (*d*) Step IV
(*e*) None of these

55. What is the sum of the numbers at the odd position in Step IV from the right end?
(*a*) 118 (*b*) 126
(*c*) 120 (*d*) 134
(*e*) None of these

Directions (Qs. No. 56-58): *Study the following alphanumeric-symbol series carefully and answer the questions based on it.*

F M 9 0 * Y 7 U F G % $ 3 2 O
6 @ N X 4 # L 1 & Z R 6 * V S

56. Which of the following element is fourth to the right of 12th element from the left end?

(*a*) @ (*b*) O
(*c*) X (*d*) 6
(*e*) 2

57. How many such consonants are there each of which is immediately preceded by a symbol and immediately followed by a number?

(*a*) One (*b*) Four
(*c*) Two (*d*) None
(*e*) Five

58. What will be the sum of 3rd odd number from left end and 2nd number from right end?

(*a*) 3 (*b*) 4
(*c*) 8 (*d*) 7
(*e*) 6

Directions (Qs. No. 59-62): *Each of the questions below consists of a question and two statements numbered I and II given below it. You have to decide whether the data provided in the statement are sufficient to answer the question. Read both the statements and Give answer:*

(*a*) If the data in statement I alone are sufficient to answer the question, while the data in statement II alone are not sufficient to answer the question.
(*b*) If the data in statement II alone are sufficient to answer the question, while the data in statement I alone are not sufficient to answer the question.
(*c*) If the data either in statement I alone or in statement II alone are sufficient to answer the question.
(*d*) If the data even in both statements I and II together are not sufficient to answer the question.
(*e*) If the data in both statements I and II together are necessary to answer the question.

59. Seven people-A, B, C, D, E, F and G-live on different floors of a 7-floor building but not necessarily in the same order. The ground floor is numbered 1, the floor just above it is numbered 2, and so on. Who lives three floors below A.

Statement I: A lives on an even-numbered floor. E lives immediately above A. B lives on floor number 4. There are as many persons live above A as below G.

Statement II: D lives on a floor immediately above G. F does not live on the topmost floor. C lives on floor number 5 below A.

60. In a row of children facing North, where does Rajat stand in the row?

Statement I: Jyoti stands 3rd from left end and 2nd to the left of Rajat who stands immediate left of the one who is 10th from the right end of the row.

Statement II: There are 19 children between Rajat and Meena, and Meena is 15th from one of the ends of the row.

61. In four family members, how is Rohan related to Meena?

Statement I: Rohan's father is the only brother of Meena's mother.

Statement II: Meena's mother is the sister of the father of Rohan's sister.

62. Eight boxes-P, Q, R, S, T, U, V, and W-are stacked above each other but not necessarily in the same order.

Statement I: Box P is immediately above box Q. Box S is immediately above box R, which is not at the bottommost position.

Statement II: Box T is above box U but below box V. Box W is at the bottommost position. Box P is not at the topmost position.

Directions (Qs. No. 63-67): *Study the following information carefully and answer the given questions.*

Seven Boxes i.e. A, B, C, D, E, F and G placed one above the other and all are of different colours viz. Yellow, Brown, Pink, Green, Red, Black and Blue but not necessarily in the same order. Each box contains different items i.e., Balls, Pencils, Chocolate, Juice, Berry, Toys and Bottles but not necessarily in the same order.

Box A is placed three places above the brown colour. More than three boxes placed between box B and the box of yellow colour. Blue colour box placed below the box which is contains Bottles and placed above the box which contains Balls. The box contains Chocolate placed just above box B. Two boxes placed between box B and box E which contains Juice. Box C is of red colour and placed 2 places above box E. Brown colour box contains Pencil but that is not box B. Box F is placed above the box of yellow colour. Black colour box contains Toy's and placed below box D. Green colour box contains Berry.

63. How many boxes placed between black colour box and green colour box?

(*a*) As many boxes placed below box D
(*b*) As many boxes placed between A and B
(*c*) As many boxes placed above yellow colour box
(*d*) As many boxes placed between D and G
(*e*) None of these

106. The total number of chains sold by shop I is 20% less than the total number of rings sold by shops II and IV together. If the ratio of the total number of chains sold by shop I to II is 4 : 7, respectively, then find the total number of chains and bracelets sold by shop II.

(*a*) 293 (*b*) 288
(*c*) 272 (*d*) 267
(*e*) 291

Directions (Qs. No. 107-111): *Read the following line chart carefully and answer the questions given below. The line chart shows the number of people who purchased two different types of dishes from four different hotels.*

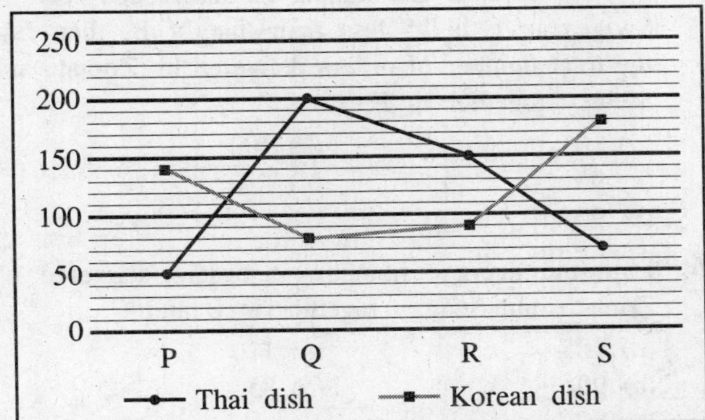

107. The number of people who purchased a Thai dish from P and R together is what percentage of the number of people who purchased a Korean dish from Q?

(*a*) 266.67% (*b*) 235%
(*c*) 275% (*d*) 225%
(*e*) 250%

108. Find the ratio of the number of people who purchased a Thai dish from S to the number of people who purchased a Korean dish from P.

(*a*) 1 : 2 (*b*) 2 : 1
(*c*) 1 : 3 (*d*) 3 : 2
(*e*) 2 : 5

109. The number of people who purchased a Korean dish from T is 3/5 of the number of people who purchased a Thai dish from R. If the number of people who purchased a Thai dish from T is 33.33% more than the number of people who purchased a Korean dish from S, then find the number of people who purchased a Korean and Thai dish together from T.

(*a*) 300 (*b*) 320
(*c*) 330 (*d*) 310
(*e*) 340

110. Find the average number of people who purchased Thai and Korean dishes together from P, Q, and S.

(*a*) 220 (*b*) 310
(*c*) 240 (*d*) 250
(*e*) 290

111. The number of people who purchased a Thai dish and a Korean dish together from R is what percentage more or less than the number of people who purchased a Thai dish from P and Q together?

(*a*) 4% (*b*) 2.5%
(*c*) 5% (*d*) 3%
(*e*) 6%

112. The efficiency of B is two times of the efficiency of A. Both started work together and after x days A left the work. If B completed 25% of the remaining work alone in 4 days, then find the value of x?

(*a*) 12 (*b*) 3
(*c*) 8 (*d*) 4
(*e*) 6

113. The cost price of a watch is Rs. 750 and a bag is Rs. 840. A shopkeeper sold the watch at profit of 20% and the bag at loss of 15%. Find the overall profit or loss received by the shopkeeper (in Rs.)?

(*a*) 30 (*b*) 12
(*c*) 36 (*d*) 24
(*e*) 48

114. The upstream speed of a boat is 15 km/hr and the ratio of time taken by the boat to cover 105 km upstream and 108 km downstream 7 : 6 respectively. Find the speed of stream (in km/hr)?

(*a*) 3 (*b*) 5
(*c*) 4 (*d*) 7
(*e*) 1

115. Two cars A and B started from point X & Y respectively, and the distance between these two points is 660 km. Both cars started at 10 AM and meet at 3 PM. If speed of car A is 12 km/hr more than that of B, then find the speed of car A (in km/hr)?

(*a*) 60 (*b*) 72
(*c*) 84 (*d*) 102
(*e*) 90

116. Abhi and Bhushan started a business with capital of Rs. 2000 & Rs. 3000 respectively. At the end of 8 months, Divya joined the business with capital of Rs. 4000. At the end of a years, the profit share of Divya is Rs. 6000. Find the total profit share of Abhi and Bhushan (in Rs.)?

(*a*) Rs. 20500 (*b*) Rs. 21500
(*c*) Rs. 22500 (*d*) Rs. 27500
(*e*) Rs. 25000

117. The ratio of area of a rectangle to a square is 7 : 6 and the perimeter of the square is 96 cm. If the ratio of length to breadth of the rectangle is 21 : 8, then find the perimeter of the rectangle (in cm)?

(*a*) 232 (*b*) 58
(*c*) 116 (*d*) 174
(*e*) 46

118. A vessel contains 72 liters mixture of milk and water in the ratio of 5 : 3 respectively. 40 liters mixture is taken out and x liters of pure added in the remaining mixture. If the quantity of milk becomes 7 times of the water in the final mixture, then find the value of *x*?

(*a*) 72 (*b*) 48
(*c*) 68 (*d*) 60
(*e*) 64

Directions (Qs. No. 119-124): *Read the following information carefully and answer the questions given below. The information is about the total number of orders delivered by Zomato and Swiggy in three different cities.*

The average number of orders delivered by Zomato in all three cities is $43\frac{1}{3}$. The total number of orders delivered by Swiggy in A and Zomato in B is in the ratio of 5:3, respectively. The number of orders delivered by Swiggy in C is 20 more than the orders delivered by Zomato in B. The number of orders delivered by Zomato in A and Swiggy in B is the same. The number of orders delivered by Zomato in C is 20% of the number of orders delivered by Swiggy in A. The total number of orders delivered by Zomato and Swiggy together in A is 150.

119. The total number of orders delivered by Zomato in A is how many more or less than the total number of orders delivered by Swiggy in C.

(*a*) 30 (*b*) 20
(*c*) 10 (*d*) 15
(*e*) 25

120. Find the ratio of the number of orders delivered by Zomato in C to the number of orders delivered by Swiggy in A.

(*a*) 1 : 5 (*b*) 2 : 7
(*c*) 3 : 4 (*d*) 4 : 1
(*e*) 3 : 8

121. The number of orders delivered by Swiggy in B is what percentage of the total number of orders delivered by Zomato and Swiggy tighter in C?

(*a*) 33.33% (*b*) 50%
(*c*) 12.5% (*d*) 66.67%
(*e*) 75%

122. The number of orders delivered by Swiggy in D is average of the number of orders delivered by Zomato in A and C. If the total number of orders delivered by Zomato and Swiggy together in D is 90% more than the number of orders delivered by Zomato in B, then find the number of orders delivered by Zomato in D.

(*a*) 78 (*b*) 97
(*c*) 79 (*d*) 98
(*e*) 74

123. The number of orders delivered by Zomato in F is 25% less than the number of orders delivered by Swiggy in C. If the number of orders delivered by Swiggy in F is 15 less than that of B, then find the total number of orders delivered by Zomato and Swiggy together in F.

(*a*) 105 (*b*) 100
(*c*) 95 (*d*) 120
(*e*) 90

124. Find the average number of orders delivered by Zomato and Swiggy together in B and C.

(*a*) 105 (*b*) 110
(*c*) 90 (*d*) 85
(*e*) 80

Directions (Qs. No. 125-130): *Read the following table carefully and answer the questions given below.*

The table shows the total number of people, the ratio of males to females, and the number of graduates people out of the total people in five different towns.

Towns	Total number of people	Males : Females	Number of graduates people out of the total
A	400	3 : 5	290
B	250	11 : 14	130
C	180	5 : 4	120
D	360	11 : 7	245
E	550	6 : 5	305

Note: Total people = Males + Females
Total people = Number of people graduates + Number of people non-graduates.

125. Find the difference between the number of non-graduate people in A and D together and the number of females in E.

(*a*) 25
(*b*) 20
(*c*) 35
(*d*) 40
(*e*) 45

126. The non-graduate people in C are what percentage of the difference between the number of males in D and E?

(*a*) 35% (*b*) 80%
(*c*) 75% (*d*) 50%
(*e*) 70%

127. If 40% of the number of graduates are male in A, then find the difference between the number of non-graduate males and the number of graduate females in A.

(*a*) 110 (*b*) 100
(*c*) 140 (*d*) 120
(*e*) 130

128. The total number of people in F is 60% that of B, and the number of females in F is 40% less than that of C. Find the average number of males in F and D.

(*a*) 124 (*b*) 192
(*c*) 178 (*d*) 161
(*e*) 143

129. The ratio of non-graduate males to females in B is 7 : 5, respectively. The number of male graduates in B is what percentage of the total number of people in A?

(*a*) 5% (*b*) 25%
(*c*) 20% (*d*) 15%
(*e*) 10%

130. Find the ratio between the total number of females in A, D and E together to the total number of non-graduates in B and C together.

(*a*) 33 : 7 (*b*) 32 : 9
(*c*) 31 : 4 (*d*) 34 : 5
(*e*) 36 : 11

131. A vessel contains 180 liters mixture of milk to water is 5 : 1. 40% of the mixture taken out and x liters of pure milk added in the mixture. If the ratio of milk to water in resultant mixture becomes 7 : 1, then find value of x?

(*a*) 32 (*b*) 60
(*c*) 48 (*d*) 36
(*e*) 40

132. The length of train A is $x + 10$ meters and length of train B is $x + 20$ meters respectively. Both trains cross each other is 11/2 seconds and speed of train A is 90 km/hr. The speed of train B is 40% more than that of train A, then find the time taken by the train B to cross a 110 meters long platform (in seconds)?

(*a*) 10 (*b*) 12
(*c*) 8 (*d*) 6
(*e*) 16

133. A borrowed a sum of money from B at the rate of 8% per annum on simple interest for the first four years, 10% per annum for the next six years and 12% per annum for the period beyond ten years. If he pays a total of Rs. 12160 as interest only at the end of 15 years, then how much money did A borrowed?

(*a*) Rs. 8000 (*b*) Rs. 10000
(*c*) Rs. 12000 (*d*) Rs. 9000
(*e*) Rs. 6000

134. The ratio of present age of Amit is to Manish is 3 : 2, while five years ago, Amit's age was two times of Manish's age at that time. Five years hence, the sum of ages of Manish and Amit is equal to Lalit's age at that time, then find present age of Lalit?

(*a*) 35 (*b*) 40
(*c*) 20 (*d*) 25
(*e*) 30

135. The area of a rectangle is equal to area of a right-angle triangle. The breadth of the rectangle is 18 cm and the base of the triangle is 8 cm more than the length of the rectangle and height of the triangle is 3 cm more than length of the rectangle. Find length (in cm) of the rectangle (length > breadth)

(*a*) 36 (*b*) 24
(*c*) 21 (*d*) 12
(*e*) 40

Directions (Qs. No. 136–138): *Each question is followed by two statement I & II. You have to determine which statement (s) is/are necessary/sufficient to answer the question and mark answer accordingly.*

(*a*) Only statement II alone is sufficient to answer.
(*b*) Either statement I or statement II alone is sufficient to answer.
(*c*) Both statement I & II together are necessary to answer.
(*d*) Only statement I alone is sufficient to answer.
(*e*) Neither statement I nor statement II is sufficient to answer.

136. What is speed of train?

I. The train can cross 100 m long platform in 10 sec & a trees in 5 sec.
II. The train can cross another train of same length coming from opposite direction at same speed in 20 sec.

137. In what time the tank will be filled by inlet pipes A, B & C together?

I. B alone takes 10 min to fill the tank. Part of Tank filled by A in 4 min is equal to part of tank filled by C in 8 min.

II. A alone & B alone can fill the tank in 10 & 12 min respectively. B & C when working together can fill tank in 6 min.

138. What is probability of drawing 2 red balls from the bag?

I. there are 10 balls in the bag of which 3 are green balls which are 1 more than pink balls.

II. if there would be 2 more pink balls in the bag then number of pink balls will be equal to number red balls in the bag.

Directions (Qs. No. 139-144): *Find the approximate value of (?) in the following questions.*

139. 189.98 + 49.96% of 539.98 + ? = 630.03

(*a*) 190 (*b*) 170
(*c*) 120 (*d*) 240
(*e*) 200

140. $\frac{276.02}{12.03} \times \frac{79.99}{115.01} \times ? = 31.99\%$ of 199.98.

(*a*) 4 (*b*) 16
(*c*) 30 (*d*) 8
(*e*) 24

141. (284.02 + 184.001 ÷ 3.997) ÷ (594.01 ÷ 9.02) = ?

(*a*) 25 (*b*) 15
(*c*) 20 (*d*) 5
(*e*) 10

142. 684.03 + 2171.999 ÷ 5.98 + 49.98 × 5.02 = $?^2$

(*a*) 42 (*b*) 36
(*c*) 24 (*d*) 26
(*e*) 16

143. (79.97% of 250.02) of 4.99 ÷ $(4.97)^2$ = ?

(*a*) 40 (*b*) 70
(*c*) 90 (*d*) 60
(*e*) 20

144. $\frac{24.89\% \text{ of } 624.09}{19.7\% \text{ of } 994.89} \times 397.97 - 19.78 = ?^3 - 19.14 \times 23.06.$

(*a*) 9 (*b*) 13
(*c*) 4 (*d*) 19
(*e*) 11

Directions (Qs. No. 145-150): *In each of these questions a number series is given. In each series only one number is wrong. Find out the wrong number.*

145. 17, 35, 71, 143, 287, 575, 1150

(*a*) 17 (*b*) 1150
(*c*) 35 (*d*) 143
(*e*) 287

146. 128, 32, 96, 240, 840, 3780, 20790

(*a*) 32 (*b*) 96
(*c*) 240 (*d*) 840
(*e*) 3780

147. 91, 235, 163, 199, 181, 190, 187.5

(*a*) 91 (*b*) 235
(*c*) 163 (*d*) 187.5
(*e*) 199

148. 15, 75, 129, 191, 243, 309, 357

(*a*) 15 (*b*) 75
(*c*) 309 (*d*) 243
(*e*) 357

149. 103, 145, 190, 247, 313, 388

(*a*) 103 (*b*) 313
(*c*) 247 (*d*) 190
(*e*) 145

150. 473, 406, 335, 262, 183, 99, 11

(*a*) 99 (*b*) 183
(*c*) 335 (*d*) 406
(*e*) 473

ANSWERS

1	2	3	4	5	6	7	8	9	10
(*b*)	(*c*)	(*d*)	(*c*)	(*c*)	(*b*)	(*c*)	(*b*)	(*c*)	(*b*)
11	**12**	**13**	**14**	**15**	**16**	**17**	**18**	**19**	**20**
(*d*)	(*c*)	(*b*)	(*b*)	(*d*)	(*b*)	(*a*)	(*b*)	(*e*)	(*c*)
21	**22**	**23**	**24**	**25**	**26**	**27**	**28**	**29**	**30**
(*c*)	(*b*)	(*b*)	(*a*)	(*b*)	(*a*)	(*d*)	(*e*)	(*b*)	(*b*)
31	**32**	**33**	**34**	**35**	**36**	**37**	**38**	**39**	**40**
(*b*)	(*c*)	(*b*)	(*a*)	(*c*)	(*e*)	(*a*)	(*e*)	(*b*)	(*a*)
41	**42**	**43**	**44**	**45**	**46**	**47**	**48**	**49**	**50**
(*a*)	(*d*)	(*d*)	(*c*)	(*d*)	(*b*)	(*b*)	(*c*)	(*c*)	(*c*)
51	**52**	**53**	**54**	**55**	**56**	**57**	**58**	**59**	**60**
(*a*)	(*b*)	(*a*)	(*e*)	(*e*)	(*d*)	(*c*)	(*b*)	(*e*)	(*a*)

61	**62**	**63**	**64**	**65**	**66**	**67**	**68**	**69**	**70**
(c)	*(d)*	*(a)*	*(d)*	*(a)*	*(b)*	*(c)*	*(a)*	*(b)*	*(c)*
71	**72**	**73**	**74**	**75**	**76**	**77**	**78**	**79**	**80**
(c)	*(b)*	*(b)*	*(b)*	*(c)*	*(c)*	*(d)*	*(d)*	*(a)*	*(b)*
81	**82**	**83**	**84**	**85**	**86**	**87**	**88**	**89**	**90**
(d)	*(c)*	*(a)*	*(c)*	*(d)*	*(d)*	*(d)*	*(e)*	*(e)*	*(b)*
91	**92**	**93**	**94**	**95**	**96**	**97**	**98**	**99**	**100**
(d)	*(b)*	*(c)*	*(e)*	*(a)*	*(c)*	*(c)*	*(a)*	*(e)*	*(d)*
101	**102**	**103**	**104**	**105**	**106**	**107**	**108**	**109**	**110**
(b)	*(b)*	*(d)*	*(c)*	*(e)*	*(c)*	*(e)*	*(a)*	*(c)*	*(c)*
111	**112**	**113**	**114**	**115**	**116**	**117**	**118**	**119**	**120**
(a)	(*)	*(d)*	*(e)*	*(b)*	*(c)*	*(c)*	*(e)*	*(a)*	*(a)*
121	**122**	**123**	**124**	**125**	**126**	**127**	**128**	**129**	**130**
(b)	*(c)*	*(c)*	*(a)*	*(a)*	*(c)*	*(c)*	*(d)*	*(e)*	*(b)*
131	**132**	**133**	**134**	**135**	**136**	**137**	**138**	**139**	**140**
(d)	*(c)*	*(a)*	*(e)*	*(b)*	*(d)*	*(a)*	*(c)*	*(b)*	*(a)*
141	**142**	**143**	**144**	**145**	**146**	**147**	**148**	**149**	**150**
(d)	*(b)*	*(a)*	*(a)*	*(b)*	*(a)*	*(d)*	*(c)*	*(e)*	*(a)*

EXPLANATORY ANSWERS

1. The passage explicitly states that the game was promoted as a source of entertainment and bonding, but in reality it led to isolation, dependency, and addiction, which is presented as the central irony by the author.

2. The passage clearly describes children becoming addicted, suffering academically, turning irritable, and distancing themselves from family, all of which are fully covered in this option.

3. The independent organisation's large-scale survey revealed alarming and repeated negative consequences of the game, leading directly to the recommendation that it should be banned.

4. Roommates reported that relationships functioned smoothly only during gaming sessions, while real conversations and interactions declined once gaming stopped, matching this option exactly.

5. The passage states that the game gained global users rapidly, generated 50 million dollars, and brought recognition and dominance to Company X, which explains its quick global popularity.

6. Teachers noticed falling grades, reduced participation, and a drop in discipline among students, and these observations contributed significantly to concerns about the game's impact.

7. The phrase "gave the company a toe hold in the international gaming market" correctly uses "toe hold" to mean an initial secure position, making this option the most appropriate fit.

8. In the passage, the term "hit" is used to describe the game's sudden popularity and achievements, clearly indicating success rather than any physical or negative meaning.

9. The word "raise" in "raise concerns" means to increase or bring up concerns, and its opposite in this context is "lower", which means to reduce.

10. After analysing the data, the organisation concluded that the social and educational harm caused by the game outweighed its profits and therefore recommended a complete ban.

11. This sentence is grammatically and contextually correct. The passive construction is proper, the verb agrees with the subject, and the preposition "for" is correctly used with "congratulated". All other options contain errors in verb form, agreement, or parallel structure.

12. This sentence is fully correct. The tense is appropriate, subject–verb agreement is correct, and the phrase "due to unavoidable circumstances" is idiomatically and contextually sound.

13. "Data" is correctly treated as a plural noun here, taking the verb "show." The sentence is grammatically accurate and contextually meaningful.

14. The verb "aims" correctly agrees with the singular subject "policy," and the gerund form "improving" after "aims at" is grammatically correct.

15. This sentence correctly uses the subjunctive form "be increased" after "demanded that",w which is the proper grammatical structure in formal English.

16. The verb "congratulated" is correctly followed by the preposition "on", and the sentence is both grammatically correct and contextually appropriate.

17. The phrase "has recently faced a surge" is grammatically correct and contextually appropriate, as it conveys that the nation has encountered or experienced an increase in fake bomb threats. Other options do not fit the meaning or tone of the sentence.

18. Fake threats usually claim the presence of explosives, not growth, function, arrival, or reason. "Presence of explosives" is the standard and contextually accurate expression.

19. The sentence states that ministers confirmed detailed information about the threats had been received, which logically fits official communication and investigation procedures. Other options contradict the context.

20. Spreading fake information wastes security resources by forcing authorities to divert manpower and attention from real threats. The other options convey meanings opposite or irrelevant to the context.

21. Investigations are conducted to identify the sources of false alerts. This verb directly matches the purpose of investigations mentioned in the passage.

22. Once the responsible organization is identified, punishment will be enforced under existing laws. This is the correct legal and contextual usage; other options do not align with the intended meaning.

23. Sentence I shows the cause (she saved money for several months) and Sentence II shows the result (she finally bought a new laptop). The connector "so" correctly links cause to outcome: "She saved money for several months, so she finally bought a new laptop."

24. The two sentences present a contrast: despite preparing well, he was not selected. The connector "yet" best expresses this unexpected result: "He prepared well for the interview, yet he did not get selected for the job."

25. Sentence I gives the reason (the shop was closed) and Sentence II gives the consequence (we could not buy any groceries). "Therefore" correctly shows cause → effect: "The shop was closed; therefore, we could not buy any groceries."

26. The paragraph should start with the earliest devices (abacus, mechanical calculators) as the foundation (B), then move to Babbage's 19th-century Analytical Engine (D), then the 20th-century electronic computer like ENIAC (A), then rapid evolution to personal computers (C), and finally continue into the 21st century with smartphones and cloud computing (E). This sequence is logically chronological and coherent.

27. It begins by defining glucose and its importance (A), then explains regulation through hormones like insulin (E). After mentioning regulation, it states why such regulation is vital (C). Then it describes problems when blood sugar drops too low (B), followed by the contrasting case of consistently high blood sugar and its harms (D). This order builds meaning smoothly: definition → control → importance → low vs high effects.

28. The paragraph logically begins by introducing wheat as a staple crop grown worldwide (B). It then explains the climatic requirements needed for wheat cultivation (A). Based on these requirements, farmers choose suitable soil and sowing time (E). Sentence (D) is correctly fixed as the fourth sentence, describing post-harvest handling. Finally, the paragraph concludes with modern techniques contributing to increased wheat production (C), making BAEDC the correct sequence.

29. The paragraph starts by stating the broad role of technology in modern life (A). It then highlights the rapid pace of technological change and its impact on daily routines (E). This is followed by concerns arising from technology, such as privacy and dependency (B). Sentence (D), fixed as the fourth sentence, explains how these developments influence human behavior. The paragraph ends by stressing the need to balance technological progress with human values (C). Thus, AEBDC is the correct order.

30. In the question sentence, "show" means to display or reveal. Sentence B uses "show" in the sense of display ("on show at the gallery"), and sentence C uses it in the sense of reveal ("did not show any sign"), both matching the core meaning used in the question.

31. In the question, "whole" means entire or complete. Sentence A ("The whole matter") and sentence C ("The whole class") both use "whole" in the same sense of entirety. Sentence B uses "whole" incorrectly instead of "hole", so it does not match.

32. In the question, "firm" means strong or steadfast. Sentence C ("a firm decision") uses "firm" with the same meaning of being resolute. Sentence A uses "firm" as a noun (business), and sentence B uses it to describe physical hardness, so only C matches.

33. The original sentence is contextually incorrect because a "missing question" does not logically explain why the manager would be abashed or speechless. After interchanging A (missing) and B (unexpected), the sentence correctly reads: "The manager's unexpected question about the missing report..." This creates a clear and logical cause–effect relationship, where a sudden question regarding a lost report reasonably leads to embarrassment, speechlessness, and discomfort in front of colleagues. All other highlighted words are already placed correctly and do not require any change.

34. The error lies in the verb phrase "the storm abate to began". The correct structure should be "the storm began to abate". Hence, words at positions C (abate) and D (began) need to be interchanged to make the sentence grammatically correct.

35. The phrase "The monarch while to abdicate" is incorrect; "while" should be replaced with "decided", and "decided" should move to position A, requiring A–D interchange. Also, "a immense life of service" is incorrect; "immense" should describe "responsibility," while "quieter" should describe "life", so C and F need to be interchanged.

36. The sentence is correct in meaning and structure. "Sudden collapse", "aberration", and "disrupting the otherwise stable market" are all contextually and grammatically sound, so no interchange is needed.

37. The phrase "citing participation with both candidates" is contextually incorrect. It should be "citing dissatisfaction with both candidates". Therefore, the words at positions C (participation) and F (dissatisfaction) must be interchanged to convey the correct meaning.

38. The sentence is grammatically correct. "Five years later" sets a past time reference, and "I was eating" is an acceptable past continuous construction to describe an action occurring at that later past point. No tense correction is necessary.

39. The correct idiomatic structure is "have yet to + verb." Replacing the bold part with "have yet" makes the sentence read correctly as "I have yet to go to the flower exhibition at Delhi University."

40. In the correlative construction "not only ... but also," the placement of "not only" must immediately follow the main verb to maintain parallelism. Replacing the bold part with "helped her not only by" results in a grammatically balanced and correct sentence.

41. After the preposition "between", an object pronoun is required. "Me" is the correct object form, not "I", so this replacement corrects the grammatical error.

42. When two past actions are described and one is completed before the other, the earlier action should be in the past perfect tense. "The train had left before I reached the station" correctly reflects this sequence.

43. The passage clearly states that phosphorus can remain trapped in lake sediments for years, so its harmful effects persist long after fertilizers or sewage inputs are reduced, making reversal difficult.

44. The chloride + water reaction is described as steadily raising salinity, altering water density and circulation, and stressing species adapted to freshwater, leading to biodiversity loss.

45. The passage mentions monitoring phosphorus and chloride levels, creating buffer zones, improving wastewater treatment, and substituting road salts, but it does not mention oxygenation devices.

46. The passage states that increased chloride makes water unsuitable for drinking or irrigation (supporting I and II) and causes biodiversity decline. Statement III is incorrect because excess phosphorus harms ecosystems rather than boosting plant diversity.

47. This statement is incorrect because the passage explicitly mentions fertilizers (agriculture), detergents, and untreated sewage as phosphorus sources.

48. The passage explains that unnatural rises in phosphorus or chloride damage ecosystems, disrupt biodiversity, and reduce suitability of water for human consumption and irrigation.

49. The passage highlights resistance from farmers, reliance on road salts by cities, and high costs as major challenges in implementing protective measures.

50. In the passage, "lower" is used in the sense of reducing oxygen levels. The direct opposite in meaning is "raise", which means to increase.

(For Qs No. 51–55)

From the original illustration, the machine works as follows:

- Words are arranged in reverse alphabetical order, one per step, added from the left
- Numbers are arranged in ascending order, one per step, added from the right
- At each step, one word (highest alphabetically among remaining) moves to the extreme left

- At each step, one smallest remaining number moves to the extreme right

Input for Q.51–55

43 Purview 68 Chronic 73 Dismantle 47 Incumbent 38 Relegating 56 Doughty

Step-wise Arrangement (CORRECT)

Step I

Word (reverse alpha): Relegating

Smallest number: 38

Relegating 43 Purview 68 Chronic 73 Dismantle 47 Incumbent 56 Doughty 38

Step II

Next word: Purview

Next smallest number: 43

Purview Relegating 68 Chronic 73 Dismantle 47 Incumbent 56 Doughty 38 43

Step III

Next word: Incumbent

Next smallest number: 47

Incumbent Purview Relegating 68 Chronic 73 Dismantle 56 Doughty 38 43 47

This matches your corrected logic that numbers appear before Doughty

Step IV

Next word: Doughty

Next smallest number: 56

Doughty Incumbent Purview Relegating 68 Chronic 73 Dismantle 38 43 47 56

Step V

Next word: Dismantle

Next smallest number: 68

Dismantle Doughty Incumbent Purview Relegating Chronic 73 38 43 47 56 68

Step VI

Next word: Chronic

Next smallest number: 73

Chronic Dismantle Doughty Incumbent Purview Relegating 38 43 47 56 68 73

51. Incumbent in Step VI:

1. Chronic 2. Dismantle
3. Doughty 4. Incumbent

52. Numbers to the left of Doughty in Step III: 68, 73, 56 → 3 numbers.

53. Step V numbers (right → left): 68, 56, 47, 43, 38, 73
3rd number from right = 47
2nd to the left of 47 = 38.

54. Sequence "Purview 68 47" does not appear consecutively in any step

55. Step IV numbers at odd positions from right: 56 (1st), 47 (3rd), 38 (5th)
Sum = 56 + 47 + 38 = 141
141 is not listed, hence None of these.

56. The 12th element from the left end is $ (... F G % $ ...). The 4th element to the right of $ is: 1st = 3, 2nd = 2, 3rd = O, 4th = 6.

57. Consonants that are immediately preceded by a symbol and immediately followed by a number are Y (preceded by * and followed by 7) and L (preceded by # and followed by 1). Hence, total = 2.

58. Odd numbers from the left are 9 (1st), 7 (2nd), 3 (3rd), 1 (4th). The 2nd number from the right is 1 (numbers from right: 6 is 1st, 1 is 2nd). So sum = 3 + 1 = 4.

59. From Statement I: A is even and E is immediately above A; with B on floor 4, A cannot be 2 or 4, so A = 6 and E = 7. Also, "as many above A as below G" gives 1 above A ⇒ 1 below G ⇒ G = 2. From Statement II: D is immediately above G ⇒ D = 3, and C is 5 floors below A ⇒ C = 1. Then 3 floors below A (6 − 3 = 3) is D, which is uniquely determined only when both statements are used.

60. Statement I fixes Rajat as 2nd to the right of Jyoti who is 3rd from left ⇒ Rajat is 5th from the left, so the position is directly known. Statement II alone gives a distance relation with Meena and her end-position but does not uniquely fix Rajat's exact position without knowing which end Meena is counted from and the total length.

61. Statement I makes Rohan's father the only brother of Meena's mother ⇒ Rohan is Meena's cousin. Statement II says Meena's mother is sister of Rohan's father (father of Rohan's sister = Rohan's father) ⇒ same relationship ⇒ Rohan is Meena's cousin. Each statement alone is sufficient.

62. The specific question to be answered about the stack (e.g., "which box is at the top/third from bottom," etc.) is not provided here, so even after combining both statements, a definite answer to an unstated query cannot be concluded.

63. Black colour box is F and green colour box is B. Positions are F-6 and B-2, so boxes between them are at positions 3, 4, 5 = 3 boxes. Boxes below D (position 4) are 5, 6, 7 = 3 boxes, so the required match is (a).

64. Actual arrangement gives C at position 3 and D at position 4, so C is just above D, not below. Hence statement (d) is not true.

65. If A (position 1) and E (position 5) are interchanged, then A moves to position 5. Boxes above position 5 are positions 1, 2, 3, 4 = 4 boxes, so the answer is Four.

66. In the given arrangement, D is immediately below C, and C contains Bottles; similarly F is immediately below E, and E contains Juice. So the pattern is: a box is related to the item in the box immediately above it. Since Chocolate is in A, the box immediately below A is B, so B is related to Chocolate.

67. The pink colour box is A, and it is at the topmost position (1). There is no box above it, so the number of boxes above the pink box is 0, i.e., None.

68. R is the parent of N (because R is the parent of L's son-in-law, and L's son-in-law is N). So, if R has a daughter, she will be N's sister. N's spouse (wife/husband of N) will therefore be the sister-in-law of R's daughter.

69. E's paternal aunt is N's spouse, so E's cousin (from the paternal side) is the child of N and N's spouse (i.e., V). H is the child of R and R is also parent of N, so H is N's sibling; since H is male, H is the uncle of V, and thus H is uncle with respect to E's cousin.

70. A is the only nephew of N's spouse, so A is the son of N's spouse's brother (i.e., E's father). Also, A's parent is G and L is A's paternal grandparent, so G is A's father. E's father is the same brother of N's spouse, and P is the mother of E's sibling (hence P is E's mother). Therefore, A (a son of E's father) has mother P.

71. V is N's child (V is the child of N's spouse, and N's child is stated to be of the opposite gender to G and H; with G and H same gender, N's child is the other gender). If V is married to S, then S becomes the spouse of N's child, so S is N's son-in-law.

72. A "course of action" means a recommended step/ solution. Among the given statements, only II suggests what should be done ("a wide-ranging transformation... could pull ecosystems..."). Statements I, III, and IV describe impact/condition and do not propose a direct action.

73. The statement says marathon training reverses ageing of major blood vessels, implying blood vessels are a meaningful component in the ageing process, so III follows. I is too absolute ("Only first-time..."), and II is unrelated/unsupported by the statement.

74. The person from Hyderabad is D. The one sitting immediate left of D is E. The one sitting second to the left of E is G.

75. In the arrangement, A is opposite the person from Mumbai, and E is opposite the person from Pune. So the relation is "sits opposite to that city-person." F sits opposite C, and C is from Jaipur.

76. The one from Delhi is F. H is positioned second to the left of F (considering F's facing direction at the corner facing inside).

77. F, H, C, and the one from Hyderabad all sit at corners (facing inside). The one from Mumbai sits at a middle-side position (facing outside), so it does not belong to the group.

78. From the final seating and city allocation, E is the person who belongs to Bengaluru.

79. The government announced a special relief package specifically for affected farmers, which assumes that floods have severely impacted farmers (their crops/livelihood), making them a key group needing targeted relief.

80. The decision to impose stricter vehicle emission norms assumes that vehicles are a major source of air pollution in cities; otherwise tightening vehicle norms would not meaningfully reduce pollution.

81. From the arrangement, O is 4th from the left and M sits at position 14. The number of persons between them is 14 – 4 – 1 = 9.

82. M is at position 14, so the 7th to the left of M is position 14 – 7 = 7. The person at position 7 is B.

83. The final valid arrangement satisfies all conditions only when the total number of persons in the row is 15 (with O at 4, V at 2, G at 11, K at 12, H at 15, M at 14, and B at 7).

84. "Alphabetical order from the right end" means the smallest letter goes to the extreme right, next smallest just left of it, and so on (so the left end becomes reverse-alphabetical). CONCEPTUAL → letters in reverse-alphabetical order from left: U T P O N L E C C A. Comparing with original C O N C E P T U A L, no position matches, so 0 letters remain unchanged.

85. From MUD → FYS and BAT → VEH, the rule is: reverse the word, then shift letters by +2, +4, +6 respectively. HAN → reverse N A H; N + 2 = P, A + 4 = E, H + 6 = N ⇒ PEN (meaningful).

86. From H > U ≥ E > N ≥ P, we definitely get H > P (I true). Also P ≤ K ≤ R < S gives P < S, and whenever P < S, it is always true that P ≤ S (II true). Hence, both conclusions follow.

87. Given M = O and O = T, so M = T. Also R > O and R < H ⇒ H > R > O (= M), hence H > M (I true). And P ≥ M with M = T ⇒ P ≥ T (II true).

88. From T ≤ Z we get Z ≥ T; from J = N ≥ T we get J ≥ T. But this does not fix whether Z ≥ J (I not definite). Also, there is no definite link that forces R < S (R is only compared with K and J; S is only compared with W and T), so II is also not definite.

89. From Y = A ≥ R < V, A's exact relation with V is not fixed; and from I = B ≤ V, B's relation with A/Y is also not fixed. So A ≥ I is not definite, and Y < B is not definite either.

90. 435673538 → digits <6 subtract 2, digits ≥6 subtract 1 ⇒ 4 → 2, 3 → 1, 5 → 3, 6 → 5, 7 → 6, 3 → 1, 5 → 3, 3 → 1, 8 → 7 ⇒ 213561317. Repeated digits are 1 and 3, remove all repeated digits ⇒ remaining digits 2, 5, 6, 7. Sum of odd digits = 5 + 7 = 12, sum of even digits = 2 + 6 = 8, difference = 12 – 8 = 4.

91. From the unique arrangement: A is on floor 5, so floors above A = 8 – 5 = 3. We need "floors above A" = "floors below (required subject)" + 1 ⇒ floors below = 2 ⇒ that person must be on floor 3. The person on floor 3 likes Biology, so it fits: 3 = 2 + 1.

92. From the final arrangement, F likes English.

93. G is on floor 2 and the one who likes Philosophy is on floor 8, so the exact middle floor is 5. The person on floor 5 likes Science, hence the one exactly between them is the one who likes Science.

94. In the final arrangement, D likes Mathematics, so only this pair is correct among the options.

95. I is true because E is on floor 3 and D is on floor 1, so E is above D. II is false because B likes Chemistry (not Science). III is true because H is on the topmost floor 8, so nobody is above H. Therefore only statement II is false.

96. The pattern is: (alphabetical position of first letter + alphabetical position of last letter) – (number of letters in the word). PLAYER → (P = 16 + R = 18) – 6 = 34 – 6 = 28, NOISE → (N = 14 + E = 5) – 5 = 19 – 5 = 14, so HOCKEY → (H = 8 + Y = 25) – 6 = 33 – 6 = 27.

97. Take M as reference. Q is 6 m east of M, so R (midpoint of M and Q) is 3 m east of M. S is 6 m south of R, so S is 3 m east and 6 m south of M. T is 7 m east of S, so T is 10 m east and 6 m south of M ⇒ direction is South-east.

98. L is 15 m south of M. Since R is 3 m east of M, S is 3 m east and 6 m south of M. So relative to L (at 0 east, 15 south), S is 3 m east and 9 m north of L. Shortest distance SL = $\sqrt{(3^2 + 9^2)}$ = $\sqrt{(9 + 81)}$ = $\sqrt{90}$ m.

99. In (a) M→S is east + south (South-east). In (b) O → L is also east + south (South-east). In (c) S → U is east + south (South-east). In (d) Q → T is east + south (South-east). But (e) O → T is only east (same north–south level), so it does not follow the same direction pattern.

100. Total distance along the defined chain R → M → L → N → O: RM = 3 m (midpoint gives 3 m), ML = 15 m, LN = 13 m, NO = 9 m. Sum = 3 + 15 + 13 + 9 = 40 m.

101. Total rings & bracelets = 440.

Shop I = 25% → 110,

Shop III = 10% → 44.

Rings total = 200 → Shop I rings = 18% of 200 = 36, Shop III rings = 7% of 200 = 14.

Bracelets: Shop I = 110 – 36 = 74,

Shop III = 44 – 14 = 30.

Bracelets (I + III) = 74 + 30 = 104.

Rings sold by Shop IV = 40% of 200 = 80.

Difference = 104 – 80 = 24.

102. Bracelets sold by Shop II = 132 – 70 = 62.

Bracelets sold by Shop IV = 154 – 80 = 74.

Total = 62 + 74 = 136.

Rings & bracelets sold by Shop I = 110.

Percentage difference = $\frac{136-110}{110} \times 100$

≈ 23.6% ≈ 24%.

103. Bracelets: Shop I = 74, Shop III = 30.

Average = $\frac{74+30}{2} = 52$

Rings: Shop II = 70, Shop IV = 80.

Difference = 10.

Required ratio = 52 : 10 = 26 : 5.

104. Rings sold by Shop IV = 80

⇒ Shop V rings = 20% more = 96.

Bracelets ratio (Shop II : Shop V) = 31 : 29.

Shop II bracelets = 62

⇒ 1 part = 2 ⇒ Shop V bracelets = 58.

Total Shop II = 70 + 62 = 132.
Total Shop V = 96 + 58 = 154.
Difference = 154 − 132 = 22.

105. Shop III rings = 14, bracelets = 30.

Revenue = 14 × 275 + 30 × (X + 180) = 10150.

3850 + 30X + 5400 = 10150

⇒ 30X = 900 ⇒ X = 30.

106. Rings sold by Shops II & IV = 70 + 80 = 150.
Chains sold by Shop I = 20% less = 120.
Ratio chains (I : II) = 4 : 7

⇒ Shop II chains = $120 \times \frac{7}{4} = 210$

Bracelets sold by Shop II = 62.
Total chains & bracelets sold by Shop II = 210 + 62 = 272.

107. Thai dish from P = 50
Thai dish from R = 150
Total Thai from P and R = 50 + 150 = 200
Korean dish from Q = 80

Required percentage = $\frac{200}{80} \times 100 = 250\%$.

108. Thai dish from S = 70
Korean dish from P = 140
Ratio = 70 : 140 = 1 : 2.

109. Thai dish from R = 150

Korean dish from T = $\frac{3}{5} \times 150 = 90$

Korean dish from S = 180
Thai dish from T = 33.33% more than 180

Thai from T = $180 + \frac{1}{3} \times 180 = 240$

Total from T = 240 + 90 = 330.

110. Total dishes sold:

P = 50 + 140 = 190
Q = 200 + 80 = 280
S = 70 + 180 = 250

Average = $\frac{190 + 280 + 250}{3} = \frac{720}{3} = 240$.

111. Total dishes from R = 150 + 90 = 240
Thai dishes from P and Q = 50 + 200 = 250
Difference = 250 − 240=10

Percentage = $\frac{10}{250} \times 100 = 4\%$.

So, the number from R is 4% less than Thai dishes from P and Q together.

112. Let A's efficiency = a and B's efficiency = $2a$.
In x days together, work done = $3ax$,
so remaining work = $1 - 3ax$.
After A leaves, B alone does 25% of the remaining work in 4 days:

$$2a \times 4 = \frac{25}{100}(1 - 3ax)$$

$$8a = \frac{1}{4}(1 - 3ax)$$

$$\Rightarrow \quad 32a = 1 - 3ax$$

This gives

$$x = \frac{1 - 32a}{3a}$$

Since a (A's daily work rate) is not fixed by any other condition, multiple values of x are possible. Hence, no single option is guaranteed.

113. Watch: CP = 750, profit 20%

⇒ SP = $750 \times \frac{120}{100} = 900$

Bag: CP = 840, loss 15%

⇒ SP = $840 \times \frac{85}{100} = 714$

Total CP = 750 + 840 = 1590,
Total SP = 900 + 714 = 1614.
Overall profit = 1614 − 1590 = 24.

114. Upstream speed = 15 km/hr
Time for 105 km upstream:

$$t_u = \frac{105}{15} = 7 \text{ hours}$$

Given ratio of upstream time to downstream time = 7 : 6, so downstream time:

$$t_d = 6 \text{ hours}$$

Downstream speed:

$$v_d = \frac{108}{6} = 18 \text{ km/hr}$$

Let speed of boat in still water = b and speed of stream = s.

$$b - s = 15, \; b + s = 18$$

Adding:

$$2b = 33 \Rightarrow b = 16.5$$

Then:

$$s = 18 - 16.5 = 1.5 \text{ km/hr}$$

Hence, the speed of the stream is 1.5 km/hr.

115. Time = 10 AM to 3 PM = 5 hours.
Let speed of B = v, then A = $v + 12$.
$(v + 12 + v) \times 5 = 660$
$(2v + 12) = 132 \Rightarrow 2v = 120 \Rightarrow v = 60$
So A's speed = 60 + 12 = 72 km/hr.

116. Capital–time investments:

Abhi: $2000 \times 12 = 24000$

Bhushan: $3000 \times 12 = 36000$

Divya (joins after 8 months, works 4 months):

$4000 \times 4 = 16000$

Profit ratio:

$24000 : 36000 : 16000 = 6 : 9 : 4$

Divya's 4 parts = ₹ 6000

$$1 \text{ part} = \frac{6000}{4} = 1500$$

Total profit:

$(6 + 9 + 4) \times 1500 = 19 \times 1500 = 28500$

Profit of Abhi and Bhushan:

$28500 - 6000 =$ ₹ 22500.

117. Perimeter of square = 96 cm

$$\text{Side} = \frac{96}{4} = 24$$

Area of square $= 24^2 = 576$

Area ratio (rectangle : square) = 7 : 6

$$\text{Area of rectangle} = \frac{7}{6} \times 576 = 672$$

Let rectangle dimensions be $21k : 8k$:

$21k \times 8k = 168k^2 = 672$

$k^2 = 4 \Rightarrow k = 2$

Length = 42, Breadth = 16

Perimeter: $2(42 + 16) = 116$.

118. Initial mixture = 72 L, milk : water = 5 : 3

$$\text{Milk} = 72 \times \frac{5}{8} = 45, \text{ Water} = 27$$

40 L removed $\Rightarrow$ remaining = 32 L (same ratio):

$$\text{Milk} = 32 \times \frac{5}{8} = 20, \text{ Water} = 12$$

Let x liters of pure milk be added.

Final condition:

Milk = 7 × Water

$20 + x = 7 \times 12 = 84$

$x = 64$.

119. First find all required orders.

Average Zomato orders in A, B, C $= 43\frac{1}{3}$

$\Rightarrow$ total Zomato $= 43\frac{1}{3} \times 3 = 130$.

Let Swiggy (A) : Zomato (B) = 5 : 3

$\Rightarrow$ SA = $5k$, ZB = $3k$.

Also ZC = 20% of SA = $\frac{1}{5}$ SA = k.

So ZA + ZB + ZC = ZA + $3k + k$

= ZA + $4k$ = 130

$\Rightarrow$ ZA = $130 - 4k$.

Given ZA + SA = 150 $\Rightarrow (130 - 4k) + 5k = 150$

$\Rightarrow k = 20$.

Hence, ZA = 50, ZB = 60, ZC = 20.

Swiggy(C) = ZB + 20 = 80.

Now compare ZA = 50 with SC = 80:

Zomato in A is 30 less than Swiggy in C, so the required difference is 30.

120. From above,

ZC = 20 and SA = 100.

Ratio ZC : SA = 20 : 100 = 1 : 5.

121. Swiggy (B) = ZA = 50

(given ZA and Swiggy in B are same).

Total orders in C = ZC + SC

= 20 + 80 = 100.

$$\text{Percentage} = \frac{\text{SB}}{\text{ZC} \times \text{SC}} = \frac{50}{100} \times 100 = 50\%.$$

122. Swiggy (D) is average of Zomato (A) and Zomato (C):

$$\text{SD} = \frac{50 + 20}{2} = 35.$$

Total in D = ZD + SD is 90% more than Zomato (B) = 60:

ZD + SD = $60 \times 1.9 = 114$.

So, ZD = $114 - 35 = 79$.

123. Zomato (F) is 25% less than Swiggy (C) = 80:

ZF = $80 \times 0.75 = 60$.

Swiggy (F) is 15 less than Swiggy (B) = 50:

SF = $50 - 15 = 35$.

Total in F = ZF + SF = 60 + 35 = 95.

124. Total in B = ZB + SB = 60 + 50 = 110.

Total in C = ZC + SC = 20 + 80 = 100.

$$\text{Average} = \frac{110 + 100}{2} = 105.$$

125. Non-graduates in A:

$400 - 290 = 110$

Non-graduates in D:

$360 - 245 = 115$

Together:

$110 + 115 = 225$

Females in E (M : F = 6 : 5):

$$\frac{5}{11}\times 550 = 250$$

Difference:

$$250 - 225 = 25.$$

126. Non-graduates in C:

$$180 - 120 = 60$$

Males in D (11 : 7):

$$\frac{11}{18}\times 360 = 220$$

Males in E (6 : 5):

$$\frac{6}{11}\times 550 = 300$$

Difference:

$$300 - 220 = 80$$

Percentage:

$$\frac{60}{80}\times 100 = 75\%.$$

127. Males in A (3 : 5):

$$\frac{3}{8}\times 400 = 150$$

Graduate males in A:

$$40\% \times 290 = 116$$

Graduate females:

$$290 - 116 = 174$$

Non-graduate males:

$$150 - 116 = 34$$

Difference:

$$174 - 34 = 140.$$

128. Total people in F:

$$60\% \times 250 = 150$$

Females in C:

$$\frac{4}{9}\times 180 = 80$$

Females in F (40% less):

$$60\% \times 80 = 48$$

Males in F:

$$150 - 48 = 102$$

Males in D: 220

Average:

$$\frac{102 + 220}{2} = 161.$$

129. Non-graduates in B:

$$250 - 130 = 120$$

Non-graduate males (7 : 5):

$$\frac{7}{12}\times 120 = 70$$

Total males in B:

$$\frac{11}{25}\times 250 = 110$$

Graduate males:

$$110 - 70 = 40$$

Percentage of total people in A:

$$\frac{40}{400}\times 100 = 10\%.$$

130. Females in A: 250

Females in D:

$$\frac{7}{18}\times 360 = 140$$

Females in E: 250

Total females:

$$250 + 140 + 250 = 640$$

Non-graduates in B: 120

Non-graduates in C: 60

Total non-graduates:

$$120 + 60 = 180$$

Ratio:

$$640 : 180 = 32 : 9.$$

131. Total mixture = 180 L, milk : water = 5 : 1

$$\text{Milk} = 180\times\frac{5}{6} = 150,$$

$$\text{Water} = 180\times\frac{1}{6} = 30$$

40% of mixture removed ⇒ 60% remains:

Milk remaining = 150 × 0.6 = 90,

Water remaining = 30 × 0.6 = 18

After adding x liters of pure milk:

Milk = 90 + x, Water = 18

Given, final ratio = 7 : 1:

$$\frac{90 + x}{18} = 7 \Rightarrow 90 + x = 126$$

$$\Rightarrow \quad x = 36.$$

132. Speed of train A:

90 km/hr = 25 m/s

Speed of train B (40% more):

126 km/hr = 35 m/s

Time to cross each other: $\frac{11}{2}s$

Total length crossed:

$$(25 + 35)\times\frac{11}{2} = 60 \times 5.5 = 330$$

$$(x + 10) + (x + 20) = 2x + 30 = 330$$

$$\Rightarrow \quad x = 150$$

Length of train B:

$x + 20 = 170$ m

Time to cross 110 m platform:

$$\frac{170+110}{35} = \frac{280}{35} = 8s.$$

133. Simple interest calculation:

First 4 years at 8%:

$0.08 \times 4 = 0.32P$

Next 6 years at 10%:

$0.10 \times 6 = 0.60P$

Next 5 years at 12%:

$0.12 \times 5 = 0.60P$

Total interest:

$(0.32 + 0.60 + 0.60)P = 1.52P$

Given: $1.52P = 12160 \Rightarrow P = 8000.$

134. Present age ratio:

Amit : Manish = 3 : 2

Let, Amit = $3k$, Manish = $2k$

Five years ago:

$3k - 5 = 2(2k - 5) \Rightarrow k = 5$

Present ages:

Amit = 15, Manish = 10

Five years hence: $(15 + 5) + (10 + 5) = 35$

So, Lalit's present age:

$35 - 5 = 30.$

135. Let rectangle length = L, breadth = 18

Area rectangle = 18L

Triangle:

Base = L + 8, Height = L + 3

$$\text{Area triangle} = \frac{1}{2}(L+8)(L+3)$$

Equating areas:

$$18L = \frac{1}{2}(L+8)(L+3)$$

$$36L = L^2 + 11L + 24$$

$\Rightarrow L^2 - 25L + 24 = 0$

$(L - 24)(L - 1) = 0$

Since $L > 18$:

$L = 24.$

136. Statement I gives two equations in L and v:

$L + 100 = 10v,\ L = 5v$

$\Rightarrow 5v + 100 = 10v \Rightarrow v = 20$ m/s

So, speed is uniquely obtained from I alone.

Statement II gives only $L/v = 20$, which cannot uniquely determine v.

137. Statement I gives $B = \frac{1}{10}$ and $A = 2C$, but no absolute value of A or C, so total rate A + B + C cannot be fixed.

Statement II gives:

$$A = \frac{1}{10},\ B = \frac{1}{12},$$

$$B + C = \frac{1}{6} \Rightarrow C = \frac{1}{12}$$

So, A + B + C and hence the time are fully determined from II alone.

138. Statement I gives: total = 10, green = 3, pink = 2, so red + others = 5 ⇒ red is not uniquely fixed.

Statement II gives: $p + 2 = r$ but no values for p or total ⇒ insufficient alone.

Combining: from I, $p = 2$, so from II $r = 4$.

Now total and red are fixed, so probability of 2 reds is determined.

Hence, both statements together are necessary.

139. Approximate the values:

$189.98 \approx 190$

$49.96\% \approx 50\%,\ 539.98 \approx 540$

50% of 540 = 270

So the equation becomes:

$190 + 270 + ? \approx 630$

$460 + ? \approx 630$

$? \approx 630 - 460 = 170$

Hence, the approximate value of ? is 170.

140. Approximate each term:

$$\frac{276.02}{12.03} \approx \frac{276}{12} = 23$$

$$\frac{79.99}{115.01} \approx \frac{80}{115} \approx 0.7$$

So LHS: $23 \times 0.7 \times ? \approx 16.1 \times ?$

RHS: 31.99% of 199.98 ≈ 32% of 200 = 64

Now: $16.1 \times ? \approx 64 \Rightarrow ? \approx 64/16.1 \approx 4.$

Hence, the approximate value of ? is 4.

141. Given expression:

$(284.02 + 184.001 \div 3.997) \div (594.01 \div 9.02)$

Approximate values:

$284.02 \approx 284,\ 184.001 \div 3.997 \approx 184 \div 4 = 46$

Numerator:

$284 + 46 = 330$

Denominator:

$594.01 \div 9.02 \approx 594 \div 9 = 66$

Final calculation:

$330 \div 66 = 5$

17. 1. Should you need a visa you must submit an application along with your Passport and a copy of income tax returns.
2. Unless you do not submit an application along with your passport and "copy of income tax returns, you will not get visa".
3. If you submit your application along with your passport and a copy of income tax returns you do not need visa.

A. (1) and (2) B. (2) and (3)
C. (1) and (3) D. All the three
E. All different

18. 1. The judge remarked that not all the accused were really guilty.
2. The judge remarked that some of the accused were guilty while others were not.
3. The judge remarked that all those who are accused include some who are not really guilty.

A. (1) and (2)
B. (2) and (3)
C. (1) and (3)
D. All the three
E. None of these

Directions (Qs. 19 to 23): *In each of these questions a set of 3 or 4 sentences which convey an idea is given. Of these, one or two is/are suppressed. To fill up the spaces of the suppressed sentence(s) two possible fillers as (1) and (2) are given. Find out which one, two or none can fill up the space of the suppressed sentence(s) to make the paragraph meaningful and mark your answer accordingly.*

Caution : While making your answer please also consider the sequence of the sentences if both the sentences are required to fill up the spaces.

19. As far as aircraft maintenance procedures are concerned, they are rigorous. (.........). Such cases may end-up in disastrous results, though exceptionally.
1. All problems are immediately corrected on almost every occasion.
2. Only due to urgency or want of aircraft for substitution, certain ones are overlooked.

A. (1) and (2) B. (2) and (1)
C. only 1 D. only 2
E. None

20. The interrogation lasted for about nine full working days. (.........). The judge observed that he was impressed with the outcome as the involvement of the accused in the crime was crystal clear.
1. Hardly anything worth the name came out of such a marathon interrogation.
2. The prosecution lawyer, though in van, had relentlessly applied all his wit to expose the accused.

A. (1) and (2) B. (2) and (1)
C. only 1 D. only 2
E. None

21. Auto riding is a very fascinating hobby. (.........). It is obvious that they consider the hobby more important than anything else.
1. Low or even middle income group people can't afford it.
2. I know many people who had missed many important cases or opportunities for participating in auto riding.

A. (1) and (2) B. (2) and (1)
C. only 1 D. only 2
E. None of these

22. There is no doubt that we must be fair and honest in all our dealings. (.........). What you really are is less important than what you are perceived by people around you.
1. It means that perception assumes greater importance than reality.
2. But even more important is how you are perceived by others.

A. (1) and (2) B. (2) and (1)
C. only 1 D. only 2
E. None of these

23. The admiration for those who fight against corruption in high places has always been very spontaneous amongst the common people in India. (.........). They unhesitantly appreciate such acts but are afraid of openly doing so for fear of the higher ups.
1. They hold such people in high esteem who make sacrifices on principles and moral issues.
2. They make verbose speeches of admiration and appreciation of such acts.

A. (1) and (2) B. (2) and (1)
C. only 1 D. only 2
E. None of these

17. E	**18.** D	**19.** A	**20.** E	**21.** D	**22.** B	**23.** C

Directions (Qs. 24 to 30): *Which of the phrases (A), (B), (C) and (D) given below should replace the phrase given in* **bold** *in the following sentence to make the sentence grammatically correct. If the sentence is correct as it is and no correction is required, mark (E) as the answer.*

24. The military has highly sophisticated simulators **on which soldiers train**.
A. which soldiers training on
B. on which soldiers have trains
C. which the soldiers do train
D. on which the soldiers have been train
E. No correction required

25. Any policy of social welfare **will be likely to face** resistance from vested interests.
A. would be like facing
B. will be likely facing
C. is likely to face
D. is likely to be facing with
E. No correction required

26. The key to a competitive economy is **its investment regime**.
A. in its invested regime
B. in its investment regime
C. investment of its regime
D. investment in its regime
E. No correction required

27. The honourable court had taken a lenient view because the accused **have not previous conviction**.
A. had no previous conviction
B. had not previously convicted
C. had not been previous convictions
D. had no previously convicted
E. No correction required

28. Our foreign exchange reserves **have increased substantial**.
A. have been increased substantially
B. have increased substantially
C. have substantially increasing
D. have been substantial in increase
E. No correction required

29. As it was a dark and stormy night, Lata was **too scared to** go home alone,
A. very scary to
B. much scared to
C. as scared to
D. to scare too
E. No correction required

30. Since, it was her engagement party, Riya was **dress to kill**.
A. dresses to kill
B. dressed to kill
C. dressed to killings
D. dressing to killed
E. No correction required

Directions (Qs. 31 to 35): *Each sentence below has two blanks, each blank indicating that something has been omitted. Choose the words that best fit the meaning of the sentence as a whole.*

31. The proposal has been .... and will be sent to the cabinet for final ....
A. designed, process
B. drafted, approval
C. amend, sanction
D. said, objection
E. mentioned, figure

32. The fake diesel factory was being .... under the .... of a dairy.
A. operated, operation
B. captured, array
C. functioned, alias
D. run, garb
E. activated, control

33. The moment, the staff opened the office, unidentified ...., ... weapons entered and asked the cashier to hand over the keys to the vault.
A. miscreants, brandishing
B. object, carrying
C. persons, had
D. people, associating
E. man, lifting

34. The singer, who has been very .... about his faith in the party, also .... at the grand event.
A. vocal, performed
B. strong, sang
C. open, dance
D. loud, came
E. creative, present

24. E	**25.** C	**26.** B	**27.** A	**28.** B	**29.** E	**30.** B	**31.** B	**32.** D	**33.** A	**34.** A

35. Over the years, the town has .... popularity as the best .... for paragliding and pilot from across the world visit it.
A. acquired, spot
B. claim, one
C. gained, destination
D. sought, wonder
E. sent, place

Directions (Qs. 36-40): *In the following questions, read each sentence to find out whether there is any grammatical error in it. The error, if any, will be in one part of the sentence. Mark the part with the error as your answer. Ignore the errors of punctuation, if any.*

36. Many citizens are gravitating (A)/ towards the nation's (B)/ second-largest State because it offer (C)/ ample job opportunities. (D)/ No error (E)

37. Most African nations were largely (A)/ shielded from the 2008 financial crisis (B)/ by China's insatiable demand (C)/ for natural resources. (D)/ No error (E)

38. Skeptics worries that the devaluation (A)/ of the country's currency is (B)/ a desperate move to (C)/ bail out struggling exporters. (D) No error (E)

39. Consumers are constantly been (A)/ encouraged to take (B)/ advantage of the (C)/ lowered interest rates. (D)/ No error (E)

40. Emerging economies are (A)/ dominating the news (B)/ but for (C)/ all the wrong reasons. (D)/ No error (E)

Directions (Qs. 41-50): *In the following questions, read the following passage carefully and answer the questions given below it. Certain words/phrases are given in* **bold** *to help you locate them while answering some of the questions.*

Over the past few days alone, the China's central bank has pumped extra cash into the financial system and cut interest rates. The aim is to **free** more cash for banks to lend and provide boost for banks seeking to improve the return on their assets. The official data, though, suggested that bad loans make up only 1.4% of their balance sheets. How to explain the discrepancy? One possible answer is that bad loans are a **tagging** indicator, i.e. it is only after the economy has struggled for a while that borrowers began to suffer. Looked at this way, China is trying to anticipate problems, keeping its banks in good health by susteining economic growth of nearly 7% year on year. Another more worrying possibility is that bad loans are worse than official data indicate. This does not look to be the cause for China's biggest banks, which are managed conservatively and largely focus on the country's biggest value and quality borrowers. But there is **mounting** evidence that when it comes to smaller banks, especially those yet to list on the stock market, bad loans piling up. That is important because unlisted lenders account for just over a third of the Chinese banking sector, making them as big as Japan's entire banking industry.

Although, non-performing loans have edged up slowly, the increase in special-mention loans (a category that includes those overdue but not yet classified as impaired loans) has been much bigger. Special-mention loans are about 2% at most of China's big listed banks, suggesting that such loans must be much higher at their smaller, unlisted peers. Many of these loans are simple bad debts which banks have not yet admitted to. Another troubling fact is that fifteen years ago, the government created asset-management companies (often referred to as bad-banks) to take on the non-performing loans of the lenders. After the initial transfer these companies had little to pay. But, last year, Cinda, the biggest of the bad banks, bought nearly 150 billion Yuan ($24 billion) of distressed assets last year, two-thirds more than in 2013. These assets would have raised the banks bad-loans ratio by a few tenths of a percentage point. Although such numbers do not seem very alarming, experts who reviewed last year's results for 158 banks, of which only 20 are listed, found that "shadow loans", loans recorded as investments which may be a disguise for bad loans have grown to as much as 5.7 billion Yuan, or 5% of the industry's assets. These are heavily concentrated on the balance sheets of smaller-unlisted banks, and at the very least, all this **points** to a need for recapitalization of small banks.

41. Choose the word which is most nearly the same in meaning as the word 'TAGGING' given in bold as used in the passage.
A. delayed
B. breaking
C. stopping
D. protecting
E. tying

35. C	**36.** C	**37.** B	**38.** A	**39.** A	**40.** E	**41.** E

42. Choose the word which is opposite in meaning to the word FREE given in bold as used in the passage.

A. expensive
B. secret
C. complimentary
D. restrict
E. charged

43. According to the passage, which of the following can be said about China's large banks?

(*a*) These are cautiously run
(*b*) Their clients are mainly high-value
(*c*) 2 percent of their loans have been classified as overdue but not impaired

A. only (*b*)
B. only (*a*)
C. all (*a*), (*b*) and (*c*)
D. only (*a*) and (*c*)
E. only (*b*) and (*c*)

44. Which of the following is the central idea of the passage?

A. small banks should be permitted to become listed on the stock exchange.
B. The government should do away with asset management companies.
C. China's financial crisis is not as serious as it is being made out to be.
D. China's central bank has failed to predict and stop the decline of its banks.
E. There is trouble brewing in China's small unlisted banks.

45. Choose the word which is most nearly the same in meaning to the word 'POINTS' given in bold as used in the passage.

A. peaks
B. moments
C. arguments
D. indicates
E. plugs

46. Which of the following is true in the context of the passage?

A. China has not implemented any resources to help its banking sector in recent times.
B. Approximately 32% of China's banking sector is unlisted.
C. China's stock market has plummeted in recent times.
D. Japan's banking industry is experiencing a boom unlike that of China.
E. None of the given option is true in the context of the passage.

47. What does the example of Cinda convey?

A. Many of the loans given by China's banks are in trouble.
B. Many such large Chinese asset management companies are failing.
C. China's economy is overly dependent on large banks.
D. China is the ideal destination for small banks to flourish.
E. Such companies have become obsolete.

48. Choose the word which is opposite in meaning to the word MOUNTING given in bold as used in the passage.

A. melting
B. accumulating
C. removing
D. submerging
E. decreasing

49. Which of the following best describes experts' findings regarding shadow loans?

A. Shadow loans have been steadily falling and are negligible at present.
B. These are growing substantially and indicate the need for reform of small banks.
C. Shadow loans are unfairly being passed on to asset management companies.
D. These loans are inconsequential for the health of banks.
E. The findings are faulty as if only includes few listed banks.

50. What is the author's view regarding small banks?

A. These have a better loan portfolio than large banks.
B. These are in good health helping to sustain economic growth of 7 percent.
C. These should be merged with large banks to bail them out of trouble.
D. Regulations governing these banks should be relaxed.
E. Other than those given as options

42. D	**43.** E	**44.** E	**45.** D	**46.** E	**47.** B	**48.** E	**49.** B	**50.** E

REASONING

Directions (Qs. No. 51-55): *Read the following comprehension and answer the following questions carefully.*

Eight people P, Q, R, S, T, U, V, and W are sitting on a circular table facing inside. R is sitting second to the right of T. Only two people are sitting between R and Q. S is sitting second to the left of Q. Only three people are sitting between S and V. V is sitting second to the left of U. One person is sitting between T and W. P is not a neighbour of Q.

51. Who is sitting second to the right of V?

A. S
B. R
C. U
D. P
E. T

52. Who is sitting infront of R?

A. W
B. S
C. Q
D. P
E. U

53. How many people are sitting between W and V when counting from right of V?

A. Five
B. Two
C. Three
D. None
E. Four

54. Who is sitting third to the left of T?

A. W
B. S
C. P
D. U
E. V

55. As many people are sitting between Q and V sitting between Q and _______?

A. W
B. U
C. S
D. T
E. P

Directions (Qs. No. 56-58): *Study the following information carefully and answer the below questions:*

A family consists of seven members– L, M, N, P, I, S, and T. There are two married couples in the family. N is the sister-in-law of S who is the daughter of M. N is the wife of L. S has a sister. L is the only son of P. I is the son of S's only brother. P is the father of T. M is the spouse of P.

56. How many male members are there in the family?

A. One
B. Five
C. Two
D. Four
E. Three

57. How T is related to I?

A. Mother
B. Sister
C. Father
D. Uncle
E. Aunt

58. If T is married to R, then R is _________ of P.

A. Son in law
B. Daughter in law
C. Father in law
D. Mother in law
E. None of the above

Directions (Qs. No. 59-61): *In the question below are given three statements followed by two conclusions I and II. You have to take the given statements to be true even if they seem to be at variance from commonly known facts. Read all the conclusions and then decide which of the given conclusions logically follows from the given statements disregarding commonly known facts.*

59. Statements:

All fruits are healthy.
Some vegetables are not healthy.
Only a few fruits are sweet.

Conclusions:

I. Some sweet things are healthy.
II. Some vegetables are healthy.

A. Only I follows.
B. Only II follows.
C. Either I or II follows.
D. Neither I nor II follows.
E. Both I and II follows.

60. Statements:

Some wood are steel.
Some steel are not iron.
Only a few irons are copper.

Conclusions:

I. Some iron are not steel.
II. All copper being steel is a possibility.

A. Only I follows
B. Only II follows
C. Either I or II follows
D. Neither I nor II follows
E. Both I and II follow

51. C	**52.** A	**53.** E	**54.** B	**55.** C	**56.** E	**57.** E	**58.** A	**59.** A	**60.** B

61. Statement:
Only a few books are notebooks.
Some notebooks are notepads.

Conclusion:
I. All books can be notepads.
II. Some books are notepads.
A. Only I follows
B. Only II follows
C. Either I or II follows
D. Neither I nor II follows
E. Both I and II follow

Directions (Qs. No. 62-66): *Study the following information to answer the following questions.*

In a certain code,
"Ram goes to school" is written as "rx gw ts mh"
"He goes hospital" is written as "ez gw lp"
"He studies in school" is written as "ez yr ga mh"
"Ram works in hospital" is written as "rx kt ga lp"

62. What is code for word "school"?
A. rx B. mh
C. lp D. kt
E. Cannot be determined

63. What is code for word "goes hospital"?
A. kt lp B. rx gw
C. ez lp D. gw lp
E. yr mh

64. What is code for word "studies"?
A. gw B. ez
C. yr D. rx
E. Cannot be determined

65. What is code for word "works"?
A. kt B. qa
C. yr D. ez
E. Cannot be determined

66. What is code for word "Ram"?
A. gw B. mh
C. ts D. rx
E. Cannot be determined

67. How many such pairs of digits are there in the number '6315784' each of which has as many digits as between them in the number as are there in the general numerical order?
A. One B. Two
C. Three D. Four
E. Five

68. How many meaningful four-letter words (Not ending with F) can be made with the alphabets N, R, E and F each being used only once in each word?
A. One B. Two
C. Three D. More than three
E. None of these

Directions (Qs. No. 69-73): *Study the following information and answer the given questions.*

Eight candidates have exam on 5th and 20th of four months among March, May, June and July. H is one of the candidates. Two candidates have exam between A and B. C has exam on 20th May and immediate before A. E's exam is immediately after D's exam. F's exam is immediately after G's exam but not in same month. D has exam in the month, which has 30 days.

69. Who has exam on 5th July?
A. A B. B
C. C D. D
E. E

70. How many persons have exam after C?
A. Three B. Four
C. One D. Five
E. Two

71. Find odd one.
A. H B. None
C. G D. E
E. F

72. How many persons have exam between H and the one who has exam on 5th July?
A. Five B. Four
C. Three D. Two
E. None

73. ___ has exam on ___ of ___.
A. H – 20 – June B. E – 5 – March
C. A – 20 – July D. F – 5 – June
E. D – 20 – June

Directions (Qs. No. 74-77): *Study the following arrangement and answer the given question carefully.*

B # M I N E & > G P * F $ X R % A ? @ D ! Q

74. In the given arrangement, how many alphabets are there which are immediately preceded by a symbol?
A. Three B. Four
C. Five D. Six
E. Seven

61. A	**62.** B	**63.** D	**64.** C	**65.** A	**66.** D	**67.** B
68. A	**69.** E	**70.** B	**71.** C	**72.** A	**73.** E	**74.** E

75. How many symbols are there which are immediately preceded by a vowel?

A. None B. One
C. Two D. Three
E. Four

76. If we drop all the symbols from the above arrangement, then which is the 7th element from the left end?

A. G B. P
C. E D. F
E. X

77. How many symbols are there between 4th element from the right end and E?

A. Four B. Six
C. Five D. Three
E. Seven

Directions (Qs. No. 78-80): *Read the following comprehension carefully and answer the questions given below.*

Six people—A, B, C, D, E and F have different heights. B is taller than only C. A has less height than F who is less height than E. Only two people are there in between D and A. The person who has the third lowest height is 140 cm taller. E is 20 cm taller than A.

78. What is the posssible height of F?

A. 166 cm B. 170 cm
C. 156 cm D. 139 cm
E. 125 cm

79. Who is the tallest among of all?

A. E B. F
C. A D. D
E. C

80. Who is the third tallest?

A. A B. D
C. F D. B
E. C

Directions (Qs. No. 81-85): *Study the following information carefully and answer the questions given below:*

Six persons - P, Q, R, S, T, and U visited different countries - Russia, Canada, Japan, Netherlands, France, and China. They attended a meeting on two different dates either 11 or 22 of three different months- September, October, and November of the same year. All the information is not necessarily in the same order.

P attended two persons before the one who visited Japan. At least three persons attended after P. Only two persons attended between P and S. The number of persons who attended before S is the same as the number of persons who attended the meeting after the one who visited Russia. U attended immediately after the one who visited China. U neither visited Japan nor the Netherlands. R attended on an odd number date but after P. T neither visited Russia nor Japan. Q attended immediately before the one who visited France.

81. Who among the following person attended the meeting on September 22?

A. Q
B. The one who visited China
C. The one who visited France
D. U
E. R

82. Which of the following statement is/are correct?

A. P attended two persons before U.
B. Only two persons attended between Q and U.
C. No one attended after R.
D. Both (A) and (B)
E. Both (B) and (C)

83. In which of the following countries did R visit?

A. Netherlands B. Russia
C. France D. Japan
E. Canada

84. How many persons attended before the one who visited China?

A. Two B. Three
C. Four D. One
E. None

85. Which of the following Month and Date did S attend the meeting?

A. October 11 B. September 22
C. September 11 D. December 11
E. December 22

Directions (Qs. No. 86-90): *Study the following information carefully and answer the questions given below:*

Six persons viz. A, B, C, D, E, and F are sitting around a circular table facing towards the center. All of them like different fruits viz. Mango, Apple, Orange, Banana, Guava, and Grapes. All the information is not necessarily in the same order.

75. C	76. B	77. B	78. C	79. D	80. C	81. C	82. B	83. D	84. A	85. E

Only one person sits between the one who likes Grapes and Banana. The one who likes Guava doesn't sit adjacent to the one who likes Mango. E sits facing towards D, who likes Apple. B sits second to the right of C, who likes Mango. The one who likes Apple doesn't sit adjacent to the one who likes Grapes. Neither B nor E likes Guava. The person who likes Grapes sits immediately right of the one who sits opposite to F.

86. Four of the following five are alike in a certain way and hence form a group. Which of the following one that does not belong to that group?
A. B - Grapes
B. A - Apple
C. F - Banana
D. E - Mango
E. D - Guava

87. Who among the following person sits third to the right of the one who likes Mango?
A. The one who likes Guava
B. The one who likes Banana
C. F
D. Both (A) and (B)
E. Both (A) and (C)

88. Which of the following statement/s is/are not true with respect to the final arrangement?
A. A sits second to the right of the one who likes Guava.
B. The one who likes Mango sits to the immediate left of the one who likes Grapes.
C. The one who likes Apple sits second to the left of C.
D. The one who likes Banana sits facing towards E.
E. All are true

89. What is the position of B with respect to the one who likes Guava?
A. Third to the right
B. Immediate left
C. Second to the left
D. Third to the left
E. Immediate right

90. Who among the following person likes Banana?
A. F
B. The one who sits to the immediate left of D
C. A
D. Both (A) and (B)
E. Both (B) and (C)

Directions (Qs. No. 91-93): *Study the following information carefully and answer the questions given below:*

In a certain code language:
"work is worship" is coded as "jk rt pq"
"work hard always" is coded as "jk mn uv"
"always do worship" is coded as "uv st pq"
"hard time passes" is coded as "mn ab ef"

91. Which among the following words is coded as "rt"?
A. work
B. is
C. hard
D. time
E. None of these

92. Which among the following words is coded as "ab"?
A. time
B. passes
C. is
D. Either (A) or (B)
E. None of these

93. Which of the following words is correctly matched with its code?
A. word - rt
B. is - jk
C. worship - mn
D. do - rt
E. hard - mn

Directions (Qs. No. 94-96): *Read the following information and answer the questions accordingly.*

Seven boys P, Q, R, S, T, U and V have different weights. V is heavier than Q. P is heavier than only three people. Q is heavier than P. T is heavier than S but lighter than R. U is heavier than R but lighter than Q.

94. How many boys are lighter than U?
A. Five
B. Four
C. Two
D. Three
E. None of these

95. Who is the third lightest boy?
A. T
B. U
C. R
D. P
E. None of these

96. How many boys are there between Q and T?
A. Three
B. One
C. More than three
D. Two
E. None of these

Directions (Qs. No. 97-100): *Study the following information and answer the following questions.*

Eight person named E, F, G, H, I, J, K and L are sitting in a row. Some of them are facing north and some of them are facing south direction. Not more than two persons sitting next to each other are facing the same

86. C	**87.** E	**88.** D	**89.** B	**90.** C	**91.** B	**92.** D	**93.** E	**94.** B	**95.** C	**96.** A

direction. E sits 2nd to the right of F. F and J face the same direction. The number of persons sitting to the right of G is the same as to the left of H. I faces north. L sits 4th to the right of J and both of them are facing opposite directions. K sits 3rd to the left of L. H sits 2nd to the right of K. Both the immediate neighbours of H face opposite directions.

97. Who sits second to the left of I?
A. K
B. The person who sits 2nd to the right of F.
C. H
D. J
E. The person who sits 2nd to the left of G.

98. How many persons are facing South?
A. One B. Two
C. Three D. Four
E. Five

99. How many persons are sitting between F and K?
A. Six
B. Five
C. Four
D. Three
E. Two

100. Which of the following is false?
A. The person sitting between J and G is facing the same direction as J.
B. The person sitting between F and E is facing the same direction as E.
C. The person sitting between H and E is facing the same direction as H.
D. The person sitting between L and I is facing the same direction as L.
E. The person sitting between H and K is not facing the same direction as K.

QUANTITATIVE APTITUDE

Directions (Qs. No. 101-106): *Read the following directions carefully and answer the following question.*

Line graph represents the total number of population visited in Museum A, B and C on Sunday.

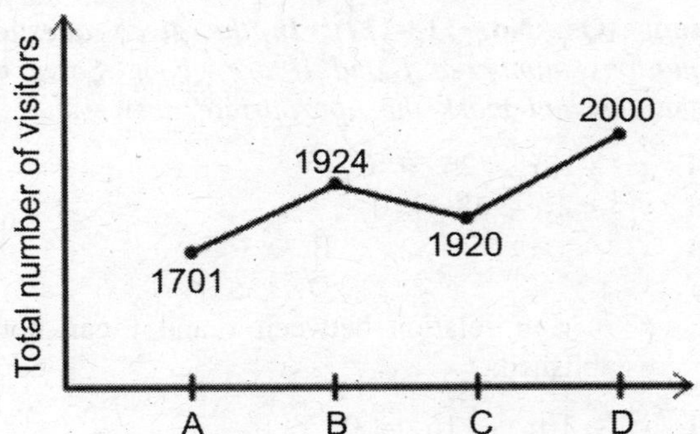

Table represent the number of male visited in Museum out of total population.

Museum	Number of Male out of total people who visited in Museum
A	2/9
B	11/13
C	13/16
D	19/50

101. If the number of male and number in Museum E are 7.69% more than the number of male who visited in Museum C and the number of female are 300 less than the number of Male visited in Museum B. Then find the difference between the number of male and female who visited Museum E?
A. 600 B. 560
C. 628 D. 678
E. 700

102. Museum A is in village Rampur where the number of population was 1,24,000 and the ratio of male and female 15 : 16. Then, find the percentage of total female on Sunday in Rampur village to the total number of male in Museum B?
A. More than 4043%
B. Between 3508% to 4040%
C. Less than 3886%
D. Both option (A) and (C)
E. None of these

103. What are the difference between male who visited museum B and C together to the average of female who visited museum A, B and C together? (approx value)
A. 1962 B. 1700
C. 1882 D. 1688
E. None of these

97. E	**98.** D	**99.** B	**100.** B	**101.** C	**102.** B	**103.** D

104. If the cost price of male ticket and the female ticket is ₹ X and ₹ (X-5). And the museum B get the revenue ₹ 94720. Find the total revenue getting from male ticket from museum A?

A. 18900 B. 20800
C. 20600 D. 18700
E. None of these

105. Find the average number of visitors in B, C and D?

A. 1176 B. 2096
C. 1556 D. 1948
E. None of these

106. The number of population of village Mowar was increased by *p*% on Sunday due to the number visitors visited at museum D. On Sunday there were total female 30% of the population on that day and the number of male population on that day was 4200. Find the value of P?

A. 200 B. 150
C. 300 D. 100
E. None of these

Directions (Qs. No. 107-112): *Read the following instruction and answer the following question.*

Tabular graph shows the number of article sold by shop Pesto.

Months	Average of article sold by (A, B & C)	% of article sold by A out of total	Article sold by C
April	100	20%	160
May	120	25%	70
June	72	50%	65

107. Find the difference between the number of article sold by C sold by pesto in June and April months?

A. 86 B. 55
C. 95 D. 42
E. 36

108. The price of article sold by B is ₹ 180 and in the month of June they offer discount of *p*% and the company will get ₹ 12420. Find the *p*?

A. 40 B. 50
C. 75 D. 60
E. 35

109. If out of the total number of products sold by A in June, 25% were returned due to defects, then find the ratio of non defective products sold by A in June and the number of products sold by C in April?

A. 25 : 31 B. 27 : 32
C. 21 : 32 D. 8 : 5
E. None of these

110. In April, if person B sold two types of products *i.e.* TV and Refrigerator in the ratio of 7 : 5, then find the difference between the total number of TVs sold by B in April and total number of products sold by B in June.

A. 50 B. 70
C. 80 D. 55
E. None of these

111. Find the average of number of products sold by B in May and that by C in June?

A. 116 B. 120
C. 118 D. 124
E. None of these

112. If 1/3rd of the products sold by B in June were sold to females then find the sum of number of products sold by B to males in June and the number of products sold by A in May?

A. 112 B. 108
C. 98 D. 118
E. None of these

Directions (Qs. No. 113-117): *In the given questions, two equations numbered I and II are given. Solve both the equations and mark the appropriate answer.*

113. I. $x^2 + 2x - 35 = 0$
II. $y^2 - 2y - 48 = 0$

A. $x > y$ B. $x < y$
C. $x \geq y$ D. $x \leq y$
E. $x = y$ or relation between x and y can not be established.

114. I. $x^2 - 10x + 16 = 0$
II. $y^2 - 5y - 24 = 0$

A. $x > y$ B. $x < y$
C. $x \geq y$ D. $x \leq y$
E. $x = y$ or relation between x and y can not be established.

115. I. $x^2 - 52x + 51 = 0$
II. $y^2 - 57y + 56 = 0$

A. $x > y$ B. $x < y$
C. $x \geq y$ D. $x \leq y$
E. $x = y$ or relation between x and y can not be established.

104. A	**105.** D	**106.** A	**107.** C	**108.** A	**109.** B
110. B	**111.** A	**112.** D	**113.** E	**114.** E	**115.** E

116. I. $x^2 - 3x + 2 = 0$
II. $y^2 + 12y + 36 = 0$
A. $x > y$ B. $x < y$
C. $x \geq y$ D. $x \leq y$
E. $x = y$ or relation between x and y can not be established.

117. I. $x^2 + 2x - 8 = 0$
II. $y^2 - 8y + 12 = 0$
A. $x > y$ B. $x < y$
C. $x \geq y$ D. $x \leq y$
E. $x = y$ or relation between x and y can not be established.

Directions (Qs. No. 118-120): *Read the following information carefully and answer the questions based on it.*

The number of products sold by A in 2015 is 1.5 times of the number of products sold by B in that year. Number of Products sold by A in 2017 is 14 more than that in 2015. In 2016 A sold 10% less products as compared to 2017. The Ratio of number of products sold by B in 2015 to that in 2017 is 3 : 8. Total number of products sold by B in all the three years is 1 less than the number of products sold by A and B together in 2017. The number of products sold by B in 2016 is 1 more than that sold by it in 2015.

118. In 2017, A and B sold 40% and 64% of their respective products, then find the difference between the number of unsold products of A and B in 2017.
A. 39 B. 18
C. 25 D. 21
E. None of these

119. If the number of products sold by C in 2017 is 25% more than the number of products sold by A in 2015, then find the sum of number of products sold by C in 2017 and that by B in 2016.
A. 92 B. 104
C. 1101 D. 112
E. 70

120. In 2016, if 40% of the number of products sold by A were sold in the local market and rest were transported to outside. Find the total number of products sold by A outside.
A. 27 B. 30
C. 35 D. 25
E. None of these

121. A invested ₹ 5000 in a business and after 6 months, B also joined him. At the end of year, B received ₹ 2700 profit out of ₹ 8700. Find the investment of B.
A. ₹ 4000 B. ₹ 5400
C. ₹ 4800 D. ₹ 4500
E. None of these

122. If the marked price of a laptop is ₹ 24,000 which is 20% more than the cost price. The laptop is sold at a profit of ₹ 1000. Find the discount%.
A. 12.5% B. 21.5%
C. 22.5% D. 25%
E. 50%

123. T alone can complete the work in 12 days. T and U together worked on a piece of work and completed one-third work in 3 days. In how many days can U alone complete the same piece of work?
A. 36 days B. 40 days
C. 25 days D. 30 days
E. 34 days

124. The cost price of the two articles A and B are ₹ 500 and ₹ 600 respectively. If both the articles were sold at the same price and the profit earned by both the articles were $2x$% and x% respectively, then find the selling price of article A.
A. ₹ 550 B. ₹ 650
C. ₹ 750 D. ₹ 850
E. ₹ 950

125. The marked price of an article is 50% above its cost price. If the marked price is ₹ 600, and the profit is 30%. Find the selling price of the article?
A. ₹ 525 B. ₹ 515
C. ₹ 510 D. ₹ 530
E. None of these

Directions (Qs. No. 126-130): *Answer the questions based on the information given below.*

The table given below illustrates the number of bikes sold by four distinct companies in two different consecutive years 2021 and 2022.

Company	Number of bikes sold in 2021	Number of bikes sold in 2022
A	240	160
B	1120	800
C	960	480
D	640	160

116. A **117.** D **118.** A **119.** E **120.** A **121.** D **122.** A **123.** A **124.** C **125.** E

126. If the number of bikes sold by company 'X' in 2022 is 50% of that by company 'B' in the same year then what is the respective ratio between the number of bikes sold by company 'X' and company 'B' together in 2022 and that by company 'C' and company 'D' together in the same year?

A. 5 : 4 B. 13 : 16
C. 15 : 8 D. 21 : 16
E. 25 : 8

127. If the respective ratio of the number of bikes sold by company 'Y' in 2021 to that by company 'D' in the same year is 7:8 then what is the average number of bikes sold by companies 'Y', 'A', 'B', and 'C' together in 2021?

A. 720 B. 760
C. 780 D. 800
E. 820

128. The total number of bikes sold by company 'B' in 2021 and 2022 together is what percent more/less than the total number of bikes sold by company 'C' in 2021 and 2022 together?

A. 25%
B. 33.33%
C. 50%
D. 66.66%
E. 83.33%

129. What is the average number of bikes sold by company 'C' and company 'D' together in the year 2023, if the number of bikes sold by in 2023 is 75% less for company 'C' and 60% less for company 'D' compared to their respective sales in 2021?

A. 238 B. 240
C. 244 D. 248
E. 250

130. If company 'D' priced each bike sold in 2021 at ₹ 40000 and each bike sold in 2022 at ₹ 48000 then what is the average per bike revenue generated by company 'D' when considering the sales from both 2021 and 2022 together?

A. ₹ 41600 B. ₹ 42400
C. ₹ 43200 D. ₹ 44400
E. ₹ 45600

Directions (Qs. No. 131-145): *What value will come in the place of the question mark '?' in the following questions?*

131. (1700 + 1800 – 1300 + 1800) ÷ ? = 200 + $(5)^2$ + 25

A. 21 B. 16
C. 18 D. 22
E. 24

132. 250 × 24 ÷ 12 + 6 + 2 of 3 of 18 = ?

A. 416 B. 612
C. 614 D. 610
E. 510

133. 2400 ÷ 12 – {26 × 6 + (32 – 5 × 6)} = ?

A. 45 B. 54
C. 42 D. 40
E. 39

134. 125% of 120 + 50% of 460 – 21 ÷ 7 = 250% of 180 + ?

A. 70 B. 72
C. 73 D. 75
E. –73

135. $\sqrt[3]{512} - \sqrt{361} + 7^2 = 19 \times \sqrt{?}$

A. 2 B. 4
C. 8 D. 16
E. 7

136. 25% of 40% of 60% of 3000 = ? × 2

A. 90 B. 35
C. 20 D. 10
E. 55

137. $256^{1/2} + 343^{1/3} + 21^2$ = ? – 16% of 800

A. 616 B. 692
C. 512 D. 592
E. 716

138. 360 × 9 ÷ 3 + 120 + 900 ÷ 5 = ?

A. 1426 B. 1286
C. 1380 D. 1275
E. 1180

139. 260 ÷ ? + 60 × 4 + 10 = 315 + 65 × 3

A. 5 B. 8
C. 1 D. 3
E. 4

140. 15% of 800 + 35 × 4 = ? + 150 ÷ 3

A. 210 B. 110
C. 240 D. 150
E. 190

141. 52 + 65 – 25 – 40 = ? × 4

A. 14 B. 13
C. 22 D. 26
E. 16

126. C	127. A	128. B	129. D	130. A	131. B	132. C	133. C
134. E	135. B	136. A	137. D	138. C	139. C	140. A	141. B

142. 50% of 170 + 60% of 180 + 110 = ? + 10
A. 293
B. 273
C. 313
D. 413
E. 253

143. 15 × ? + 20% of 450 = 360 + 15× 8
A. 18
B. 16
C. 26
D. 20
E. 12

144. (54/6) × 5 + 12 × (17/2) = ?% of 700
A. 20
B. 21
C. 35
D. 25
E. 11

145. (12.5 + 10) ÷ (108 ÷ 36) = ? + $\sqrt{25}$ – 2.5
A. 7 B. 6
C. 4 D. 5
E. None of these

Directions (Qs. No. 146-150): *Find the wrong term in the following series.*

146. 100, 91, 81, 70, 60, 45
A. 91 B. 81
C. 60 D. 70
E. 45

147. 98, 128, 162, 200, 242, 266
A. 98 B. 266
C. 162 D. 128
E. 200

148. 42, 54, 66, 78, 90, 100
A. 100 B. 90
C. 78 D. 66
E. 42

149. 27, 25, 22, 17, 10, 1
A. 27 B. 25
C. 22 D. 10
E. 1

150. 34, 17, 17, 25.5, 50, 127.5
A. 50 B. 34
C. 17 D. 127.5
E. 25.5

EXPLANATORY ANSWERS

For Qs. No. (51-55): From given direction

8 people are sitting on a circular table facing inside.

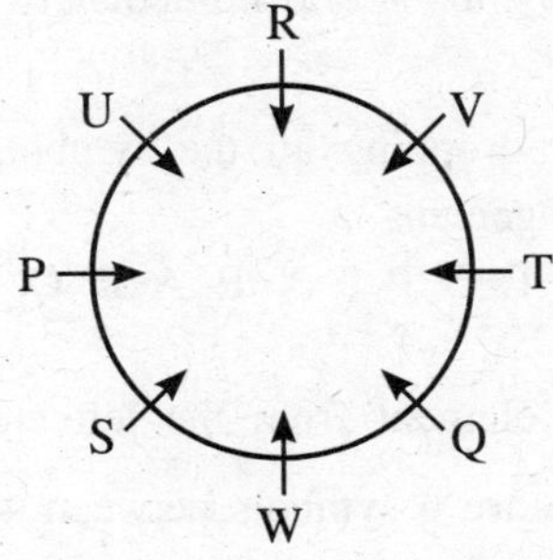

51. (C): U is sitting second to the right of V.

52. (A): W is sitting in front of R.

53. (E): 4 people are sitting between W and V when counting from right of V.

54. (B): S is sitting third to the left of T.

55. (C): As many people are sitting between Q and V sitting between Q and S.

For Qs. No. (56-58) From given information.

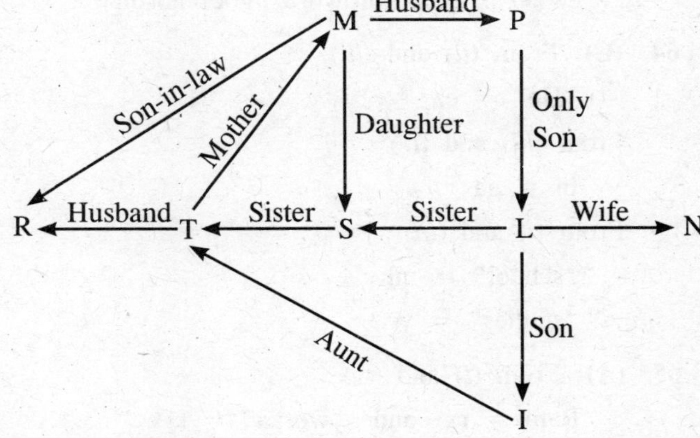

56. (E): There are 3 male members (P, L, I) in the family.

57. (E): T is the Aunt of I.

58. (A): Given, T is married to R
Then, T is son-in-law of P.

142. A	143. C	144. B	145. D	146. C	147. B	148. A	149. E	150. A

61. (A): From given statement.

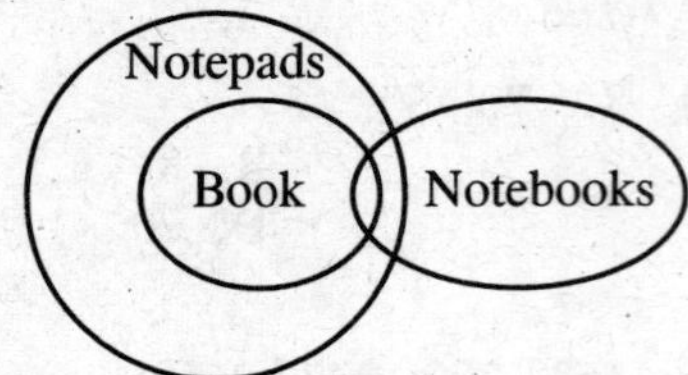

Conclusion: I. All books can be notepads. (True)
II. Some books are notepads. (False)

Hence, only I follows.

For Qs. No. (62-66)

From given direction

In a certain code,

"Ram goes to school" = "rx gw ts mh" ...(*i*)

"He goes hospital" = "ez gw lp" ...(*ii*)

"He studies in school" = "ez yr ga mh" ...(*iii*)

"Ram works in hospital" = "rx kt ga lp" ...(*iv*)

62. (B): From (*i*) and (*iii*), we obtain,

"School" = mh

63. (D): From (*i*) and (*ii*)

"goes" = "gw"

From (*ii*) and (*iv*)

"hospital" = lp

∴ gw lp is code for word "goes hospital".

64. (C): From (*ii*) and (*iii*)

"He" = ez

From (*iii*) and (*iv*)

in = ga

From (*i*) and (*iii*)

"school" = mh

∴ "studies" = yr.

65. (A): From (*i*) and (*iv*)

Ram = rx and "works" = kt

66. (D): From (*i*) and (*iv*)

"Ram" = rx

67. (B): Given,

'6 3 1 5 7 8 4'

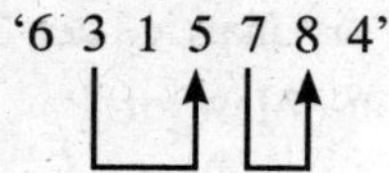

There are 2 such pair of digits (3&5, 7&8) in the given number, according to general numerical order.

68. (A): Meaningful four-letter word = FERN (a plant).

For Qs. No. (69-73)

From given information,

March		May		June		July	
5th	20th	5th	20th	5th	20th	5th	20th
H	G	F	C	A	D	E	B

8 candidates have exam on 5th and 20th of four months among March, May, June and July.

69. (E): E has exam on 5th July.

70. (B): 4 persons have exam after C.

71. (C): (A) H — 5th March
(C) G — 20th March
(D) E — 5th July
(E) F — 5th May

As H, E & F have exam on 5th of every month & only G has on 20th of the month.

Hence, option (C) is the odd one.

72. (A): 5 persons have exam between H and the one who has exam on 5th July (E).

73. (E): D - 20 - June.

74. (E): In the given arrangement.

M, > G, * F, $ X, % A, @ D, ! Q

Here, 7 alphabets are immediately preceded by a symbol.

75. (C): E &, A ?

Here, 2 symbols are immediately preceded by a vowel.

76. (B): After dropping all the symbols,

New arrangement =

B M I N E G P F X R A D Q
↑ (P)

Here, 7th element from the left end = P.

77. (B): There are 6 symbols between 4th element from right end (@) and E.

For Qs. No. (78-80)

From given directions,

6 people have different heights

D > E > F > A > B > C

(E: 160 cm, A: 140 cm)

78. (C): 156 cm is the possible height of F.

⇒ (E > F > A)

⇒ (160 > 156 > 140).

79. (D): D is the tallest among of all.

80. (C): F is the third tallest.

For Qs. No. (86-90):

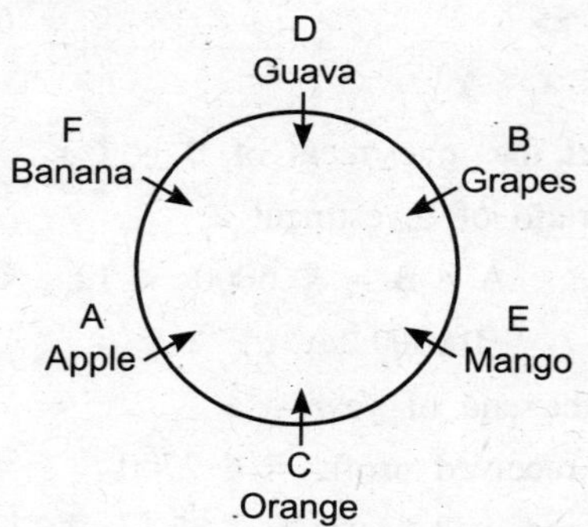

86. (C) **87. (E)** **88. (D)**

89. (B) **90. (C)**

For Qs. No. (91-93):

In a certain code language.
"Work is worship" is coded as "jk rt pq"
"Work hard always" is coded as "jk mn uv"
"always do worship" is coded as "uv st pq"
"hard time passes" is coded as "mn ab ef"

91. (B): 'is' word is coded as "rt".

92. (D): Either 'time' or 'passes' word is coded as "ab".

93. (E): hard-mn word is correctly matched with its code.

For Qs. No. (94-96):

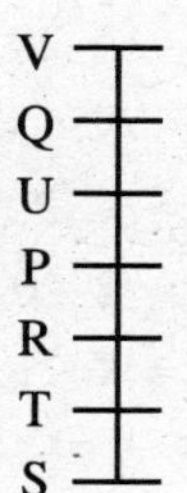

94. (B): There are four boys lighter then U.

95. (C): R is the third lightest boy.

96. (A): There are three boys between Q and T.

For Qs. No. (97-100):

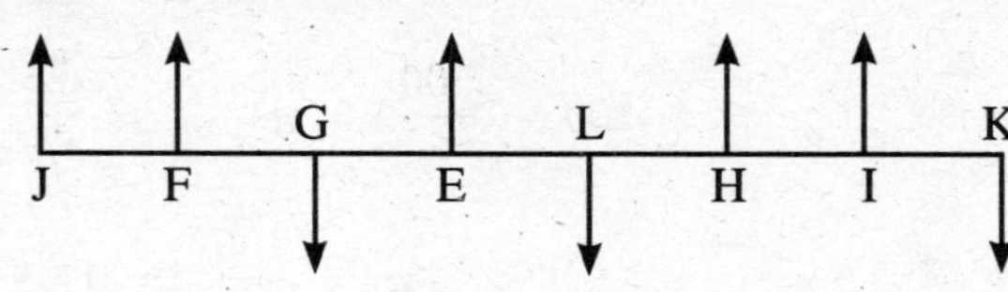

97. (E) **98. (D)** **99. (B)**

100. (B)

102. (B): Number of female was in Rampur before Sunday

$$= \frac{16}{31}\times 124000 = 64000$$

Total no. of female population in village Rampur on Sunday

$$= 64000 + 1323 = 65323$$

$$\text{Required \%} = \frac{65323}{1628}\times 100 = 4012.46\%.$$

104. (A): $\because$ Revenue generating by male in museum B

$$= 1628 \times x$$

Revenue generating by female in museum B

$$= 296(x - 5)$$

Total revenue $= 1628x + 296(x - 5) = 94720$

$\Rightarrow 1628x + 296x - 1480 = 94720$

$\Rightarrow \quad 1924x = 94720 + 1480 = 96200$

$\Rightarrow \quad x = \frac{96200}{1924} = 50$

$\therefore$ Total revenue getting from male ticket from museum A $= 378 \times 50 =$ ₹ 18900.

105. (D): Total number of visitors in B, C and D

$$= 1924 + 1920 + 2000 = 5844$$

Average number of visitors $= \frac{5844}{3} = 1948.$

106. (A): Population of village Mowar was increased by P% on Sunday at museum D

No. of visitors visited in D = 2000

Population increased $= \frac{P}{100}\times 2000 = 20P$

Total population after increased $= 20P + 2000$

Female Population $= \frac{30}{100}(20P + 2000)$

$$= 6P + 600$$

And the number of male population

$$= 20P + 2000 - 6P - 600$$
$$= 14P + 1400$$

According to the question

$14P + 1400 = 4200$

$\Rightarrow \quad P + 100 = 300$

$\Rightarrow \quad P = 200$

Hence, the value of P = 200.

113. (E): I. $x^2 + 2x - 35 = 0$

$\Rightarrow \quad x^2 + 7x - 5x - 35 = 0$

$\Rightarrow \quad x(x + 7) - 5(x + 7) = 0$

$\Rightarrow \quad (x + 7)(x - 5) = 0$

$\Rightarrow \quad x = 5 \text{ or } -7$

II. $y^2 - 2y - 48 = 0$

$\Rightarrow \quad y^2 - 8y + 6y - 48 = 0$

$\Rightarrow \quad y(y - 8) + 6(y - 8) = 0$

$\Rightarrow \quad (y - 8)(y + 6) = 0$

$\Rightarrow \quad y = 8, -6$

Clearly, relation between x and y can not be established.

114. (E): I. $x^2 - 10x + 16 = 0$

$\Rightarrow \quad x^2 - 2x - 8x + 16 = 0$

$\Rightarrow \quad x(x - 2) - 8(x - 2) = 0$

$\Rightarrow \quad (x - 2)(x - 8) = 0$

$\Rightarrow \quad x = 2, 8$

II. $y^2 - 5y - 24 = 0$

$\Rightarrow \quad y^2 - 8y + 3y - 24 = 0$

$\Rightarrow \quad y(y - 8) + 3(y - 8) = 0$

$\Rightarrow \quad (y - 8)(y + 3) = 0$

$\Rightarrow \quad y = 8, -3$

Relation between x and y can not be established.

115. (E): I. $x^2 - 52x + 51 = 0$

$\Rightarrow \quad x^2 - x - 51x + 51 = 0$

$\Rightarrow \quad x(x - 1) - 51(x - 1) = 0$

$\Rightarrow \quad (x - 1)(x - 51) = 0$

$\Rightarrow \quad x = 1, 51$

II. $y^2 - 57y + 56 = 0$

$\Rightarrow \quad y^2 - y - 56y + 56 = 0$

$\Rightarrow \quad y(y - 1) - 56(y - 1) = 0$

$\Rightarrow \quad (y - 1)(y - 56) = 0$

$\Rightarrow \quad y = 1, 56$

Relation between x and y can not be established.

116. (A): I. $x^2 - 3x + 2 = 0$

$\Rightarrow \quad x^2 - x - 2x + 2 = 0$

$\Rightarrow \quad x(x - 1) - 2(x - 1) = 0$

$\Rightarrow \quad (x - 1)(x - 2) = 0$

$\Rightarrow \quad x = 1, 2$

II. $y^2 + 12y + 36 = 0$

$\Rightarrow \quad y^2 + 6y + 6y + 36 = 0$

$\Rightarrow \quad y(y + 6) + 6(y + 6) = 0$

$\Rightarrow \quad (y + 6)(y + 6) = 0$

$\Rightarrow \quad y = -6, -6$

Clearly, $x > y$.

117. (D): I. $x^2 + 2x - 8 = 0$

$\Rightarrow \quad x^2 + 4x - 2x - 8 = 0$

$\Rightarrow \quad x(x + 4) - 2(x + 4) = 0$

$\Rightarrow \quad (x - 2)(x + 4) = 0$

$\Rightarrow \quad x = 2, -4$

II. $y^2 - 8y + 12 = 0$

$\Rightarrow \quad y^2 - 6y - 2y + 12 = 0$

$\Rightarrow \quad y(y - 6) - 2(y - 6) = 0$

$\Rightarrow \quad (y - 6)(y - 6) = 0$

$\Rightarrow \quad y = 6, 2$

Clearly, $x \leq y$.

121. (D): Let the investment of B is ₹ x

Then, ratio of investment

A : B = ₹ 5000 × 12 : ₹ x × 6

$\Rightarrow$ 10,000 : x

∵ At the end of year

B received profit = ₹ 2700

∴ A received profit = ₹ 8700 – ₹ 2700 = ₹ 6000

Hence, 10,000 : x = 6000 : 2700

$\Rightarrow \quad 6000 \times x = 10{,}000 \times 2700$

$\Rightarrow \quad x = \frac{10 \times 2700}{6}$

$= \frac{9000}{2} = ₹\ 4500$

Hence, the investment of B = ₹ 4500.

122. (A): Given, Marked price of a laptop = ₹ 24,000

Let cost price = ₹ x

Then, $x \times \frac{120}{100} = 24{,}000$

$\Rightarrow \quad x \times \frac{6}{5} = 24{,}000$

x = ₹ 20,000

Given, Profit = ₹ 1,000

∴ Selling price = C.P. + profit

= ₹ 20,000 + ₹ 1,000

= ₹ 21,000

Let discount = $a\%$

Then, ₹ 24,000 × $\frac{(100 - a)}{100}$ = ₹ 21,000

$\Rightarrow \quad 240 \times (100 - a) = 21{,}000$

$\Rightarrow \quad 100 - a = \frac{21{,}000}{240} = \frac{700}{8}$

$\Rightarrow \quad 100 - \frac{700}{8} = a$

$\Rightarrow \quad a = \frac{100}{8} = 12.5$

$\Rightarrow \quad a = 12.5\%$.

123. (A): T's 1 day's work $= \frac{1}{12}$

and (T + U)'s 1 day's work $= \frac{1}{3} \times \frac{1}{3} = \frac{1}{9}$

∴ U's 1 day's work $= \frac{1}{9} - \frac{1}{12}$

$= \frac{4-3}{36} = \frac{1}{36}$

Hence, U alone can complete the same piece of work in 36 days.

125. (E): Let the cost price of an article = ₹ x

Then, $x \times \frac{100+50}{100} = 600$

$\Rightarrow \frac{3}{2}x = 600$

$\Rightarrow x = 400$

$\Rightarrow$ C.P. = 400

Given profit = 30%

∴ The S.P. of the article $= 400 \times \frac{130}{100}$ = ₹ 520.

No options matches with ₹ 520, except option (E) i.e., None of these.

126. (C): From the given table,

The number of bikes sold by X in 2022

$= 800 \times \frac{50}{100} = 400$

∴ The number of bikes sold by X and B together in 2022

= 400 + 800 = 1200

and the number of bikes sold by C and D together in the same year

= 480 + 160 = 640

Hence, required ratio = 1200 : 640 = 15 : 8.

127. (A): From given table:

Y : 640 = 7 : 8

$\Rightarrow Y = \frac{640 \times 7}{8}$

= 80 × 7 = 560

∴ The average number of bikes sold by companies

$= \frac{Y+A+B+C}{4}$

$= \frac{560+240+1120+960}{4}$

$= \frac{2880}{4} = 720.$

128. (B): From given table

The total number of bikes sold by B in 2021 and 2022 together

= 1120 + 800 = 1920

and the total number of bikes sold by C in 2021 and 2022 together

= 960 + 480 = 1440

B's selling is more than C = 1920 – 1440 = 480

∴ Selling percentage (more) $= \frac{480}{1440} \times 100$

$= \frac{4800}{144} = \frac{400}{12}$

$= \frac{100}{3} = 33.33\%.$

129. (D): From given table,

The number of bikes sold by C and D together in 2023

$= 960 \times \frac{100-75}{100} + 640 \times \frac{100-60}{100}$

$= 960 \times \frac{1}{4} + 640 \times \frac{2}{5}$

= 240 + 256 = 496

Hence, the average number of bikes sold

$= \frac{496}{2} = 248.$

130. (A): From given table

The average per bike revenue generated by company D

$= \frac{640 \times ₹\,40000 + 160 \times ₹\,48000}{640+160}$

$= \frac{25600000+7680000}{800}$

$= \frac{33280000}{800}$ = ₹ 41600.

132. (C): 250 × 24 ÷ 12 + 6 + 2 of 3 of 18

= 250 × 24 ÷ 12 + 6 + 108

= 250 × 2 + 6 + 108

= 500 + 114 = 614.

133. (C): 2400 ÷ 12 – {26 × 6 + (32 – 5 × 6)}

= 2400 ÷ 12 – {26 × 6 + 2}

$= 2400 \div 12 - \{156 + 2\}$
$= 2400 \div 12 - 158$
$= 200 - 158 = 42.$

135. (B): $\sqrt[3]{512} - \sqrt{361} + 7^2 = 19 \times \sqrt{?}$
$\Rightarrow (8^3)^{1/3} - (19^2)^{1/2} + 49 = 19 \times \sqrt{?}$
$\Rightarrow 8 - 19 + 49 = 19 \times \sqrt{?}$
$\Rightarrow 57 - 19 = 19 \times \sqrt{?}$
$\Rightarrow 38 = 19 \times \sqrt{?}$
$\Rightarrow \sqrt{?} = 2$
$\Rightarrow ? = 4$

136. (A): 25% of 40% of 60% of 3000 = ? × 2
$\Rightarrow 3000 \times \frac{60}{100} \times \frac{40}{100} \times \frac{25}{100} = ? \times 2$
$\Rightarrow 30 \times 6 \times 4 \times \frac{1}{4} = ? \times 2$
$\Rightarrow 180 = ? \times 2$
$\Rightarrow ? = 90.$

137. (D): $256^{1/2} + 343^{1/3} + 21^2 = ? - 16\%$ of 800
$\Rightarrow (16^2)^{1/2} + (7^3)^{1/3} + 441 = ? - 800 \times \frac{16}{100}$
$\Rightarrow 16 + 7 + 441 = ? - 8 \times 16$
$\Rightarrow 464 = ? - 128$
$\Rightarrow ? = 464 + 128$
$\Rightarrow ? = 592$

138. (C): $360 \times 9 \div 3 + 120 + 900 \div 5 = ?$
$\Rightarrow 360 \times 3 + 120 + 180 = ?$
$\Rightarrow 1080 + 120 + 180 = ?$
$\Rightarrow ? = 1080 + 300$
$\Rightarrow ? = 1380.$

139. (C): $260 \div ? + 60 \times 4 + 10 = 315 + 65 \times 3$
$\Rightarrow 260 \div x + 60 \times 4 + 10 = 315 + 195$
$\Rightarrow \frac{260}{x} + 240 + 10 = 510$
$\Rightarrow \frac{260}{x} = 510 - 250$
$\Rightarrow \frac{260}{x} = 260$
$\Rightarrow x = 1$
$\Rightarrow ? = 1$

140. (A): 15% of 800 + 35 × 4 = ? + 150 ÷ 3
$\Rightarrow 800 \times \frac{15}{100} + 140 = ? + 50$
$\Rightarrow 120 + 140 = ? + 50$
$\Rightarrow ? = 260 - 50$
$\Rightarrow ? = 210.$

141. (B): $52 + 65 - 25 - 40 = ? \times 4$
$\Rightarrow 117 - 65 = ? \times 4$
$\Rightarrow 52 = ? \times 4$
$\Rightarrow ? = 13.$

142. (A): 50% of 170 + 60% of 180 + 110 = ? + 10
$\Rightarrow 170 \times \frac{50}{100} + 180 \times \frac{60}{100} + 110 = ? + 10$
$\Rightarrow 85 + 108 + 110 = ? + 10$
$\Rightarrow 303 = ? + 10$
$\Rightarrow ? = 303 - 10$
$\Rightarrow ? = 293.$

145. (D): $(12.5 + 10) \div (108 \div 36) = ? + \sqrt{25} - 2.5$
$\Rightarrow (22.5) \div (3) = ? + 5 - 2.5$
$\Rightarrow 22.5 \times \frac{1}{3} = ? + 2.5$
$\Rightarrow 7.5 = ? + 2.5$
$\Rightarrow ? = 7.5 - 2.5$
$\Rightarrow ? = 5.$

147. (B):

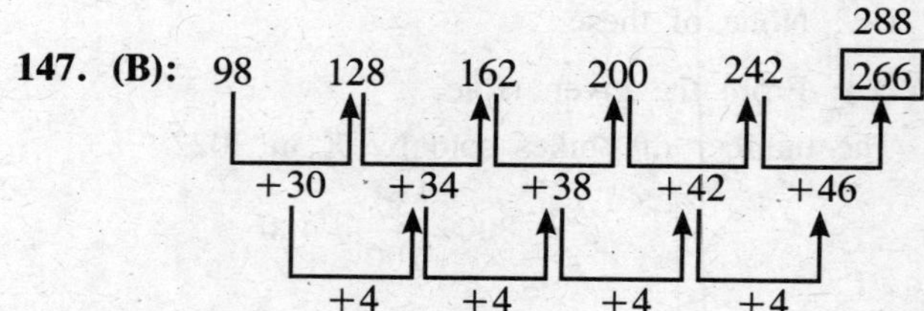

Here, in the place of 266, it should be 288
∴ The wrong term = 266.

148. (A):

Here, in the place of 100 it should be 102.

150. (A):

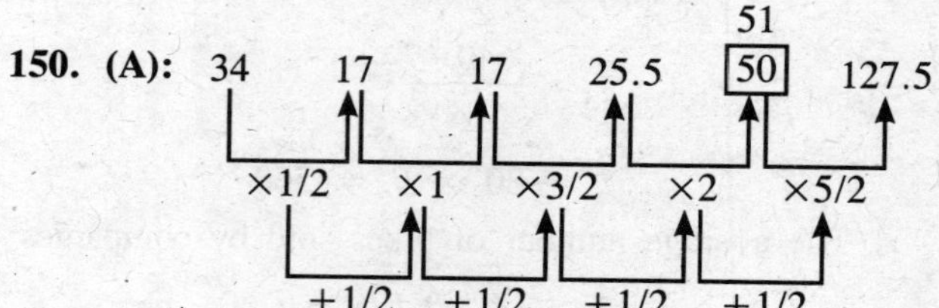

Here, in the place of 50 it should be 51
∴ The wrong term = 50.

MAIN EXAMINATION

PROFESSIONAL KNOWLEDGE (COMPUTER)

1. Which are specially designed computer chips that reside inside other devices, such as your car or your electronic thermostat?
   A. Servers
   B. Embedded computers
   C. Robotic computers
   D. Mainframes
   E. None of these

2. Which of the following number system has base-16?
   A. Unary number system
   B. Binary number system
   C. Octal number system
   D. Hexadecimal Number System
   E. None of the above

3. Which of the following Program are often delivered to a PC through an email attachment and are often designed to do harm?
   A. Spam
   B. Portals
   C. Viruses
   D. Ransomware
   E. None of these

4. Softcopy is the intangible output, so then what is hardcopy?
   A. The physical parts of the computer
   B. The printed parts of the computer
   C. The printed output
   D. The physical output devices
   E. None of the above

5. What is a Firewall in Computer Network?
   A. The physical boundary of Network
   B. An operating System of Computer Network
   C. A system designed to prevent unauthorized access
   D. A web browsing Software
   E. None of these

6. Who is the creator of PASCAL language?
   A. Dennis Ritchie
   B. Brendan Eich
   C. James Gosling
   D. Niklaus Wirth
   E. None of these

7. Which of the following is the shortcut key for hides the selected rows?
   A. Ctrl+D
   B. Ctrl+H
   C. Ctrl+9
   D. Ctrl+10
   E. None of these

8. Integrated Circuit (IC) chips used in computers are made with ______.
   A. Silicon
   B. Copper
   C. Aluminium
   D. Gold
   E. None of these

9. If you wished to limit what you would see on an Excel worksheet, what data function would you see?
   A. Data analysis
   B. Sort
   C. Filter
   D. Conditional format
   E. None of these

10. Which of the memories has the shortest access time?
    A. Cache memory
    B. Magnetic bubble memory
    C. Magnetic core memory
    D. RAM
    E. None of these

11. Harmful programs used to disrupt computer operation, gather sensitive information, or gain access to private computer systems are commonly referred to as:
    A. Adware
    B. Malware
    C. Computer viruses
    D. Spyware
    E. None of these

12. A ______ typically connects personal computers within a very limited geographical area, usually within a single building.
    A. LAN
    B. FAN
    C. TAN
    D. WAN
    E. VPN

13. What database key uniquely identifies a record within a table?
    A. Primary key
    B. Foreign key
    C. Secondary key
    D. Relational key
    E. None of these

14. What is the maximum Zoom Percent allowed in Microsoft PowerPoint 2007?
    A. 100%
    B. 200%
    C. 300%
    D. 400%
    E. None of these

1. B	**2.** D	**3.** C	**4.** C	**5.** C	**6.** D	**7.** C
8. A	**9.** C	**10.** A	**11.** B	**12.** A	**13.** A	**14.** D

15. ISDN stands for ______.
A. Integrated Services Digital Network
B. Integrated Services Data Network
C. Integrated Security Digital Network
D. Integrated Security Data Network
E. None of these

16. What type of resource is most likely to be a shared common resource in a computer network?
A. Keyboards B. Speakers
C. Floppy disk drives D. Printers
E. None of these

17. The most widely used type of database management system is the:
A. Flat database B. Network database
C. Relational database D. Hierarchical database
E. None of the above

18. Managers use sophisticated tool to combat cyberslacking, especially involving the internet. Such tools include ______.
A. Web filters B. Surveillance Software
C. Proxy Server D. Packet Sniffer
E. All of the above

19. What is the full form of DBMS?
A. Database Maintain System
B. Desktop Marketing System
C. Database Management System
D. Durable Management System
E. None of these

20. PROM Stands for ______.
A. Programmable random-on memory
B. Picture random memory
C. Process read-only memory
D. Programmable read-only memory
E. None of these

21. COBOL is used for which of the following purpose?
A. Scientific calculation
B. Business and Finance
C. Application development
D. Network Security
E. None of these

22. Convert Binary number $(111001)^2$ to decimal number ______.
A. $(38)_{10}$ B. $(57)_{10}$
C. $(55)_{10}$ D. $(47)_{10}$
E. None of these

23. Which of the following is the most common tool used to restrict access to a computer system?
A. User logins
B. Computer keys
C. Access-control Software
D. Passwords
E. None of these

24. Photo-editing, spreadsheet and word processing were the examples of:
A. Application software.
B. System software.
C. Operating system software.
D. Platform software.
E. None of these

25. Which among the following key can be used as a shortcut to rename a folder in Microsoft Windows 8 and higher versions?
A. F2 B. F4
C. F6 D. F9
E. F11

26. In order to move from one worksheet to another in MS-Excel workbook. One should click ______.
A. active cell B. scroll bar
C. sheet tab D. tab button
E. None of these

27. Which shortcut key is used to check spelling and grammar in MS-Word?
A. F1 B. F2
C. F7 D. F9
E. F10

28. An image editing software in which we can draw and edit images is?
A. PageMaker B. MS-Paint
C. Coral Draw D. Photo Image
E. Front page

29. Which of the following can be used to select the entire document?
A. Ctrl+A B. Alt+F5
C. Shift+A D. Ctrl+K
E. Ctrl+H

30. Which of the following shortcut key is used to minimize all open windows and display the desktop?
A. Windows logo+D B. Alt+Shift+C
C. Ctrl+fn D. Tab+Shift+C
E. None of these

15. A	**16.** D	**17.** C	**18.** E	**19.** C	**20.** D	**21.** B	**22.** B
23. D	**24.** A	**25.** A	**26.** C	**27.** C	**28.** C	**29.** A	**30.** A

31. Which of the following kind of devices allows the user to add components and capabilities to a computer system?
A. System boards B. Storage devices
C. Input devices D. Output devices
E. Expansion slots

32. Which of the following is a windows utility program that locates and eliminates unnecessary fragments and rearranges filed and unused disk space to optimize operations?
A. Backup B. Disk cleanup
C. Disk defragmenter D. Restore
E. None of these

33. What is the technology used to read pencil or pen marks on a multiple-choice answer sheet called?
A. OMR B. MICR
C. OCR D. CPU
E. FTP

34. Which among the following is a type of error that a compiler can check?
A. Syntax Error B. Power Failure
C. Network Failure D. All of the above
E. None of the above

35. A special, high-speed storage area within the CPU in which all data must be represented before it can be processed is called ______.
A. BIOS B. Cache
C. RAM D. Register
E. None of these

36. In Power Point, the Header & Footer button can be found on the Insert tab in what group?
A. Illustrations group B. Object group
C. Text group D. Tables group
E. None of these

37. Which of the following is generally used for selecting or highlighting?
A. Icon B. Keyboard
C. Mouse D. Floppy Disk
E. None of these

38. The ability of an operating system to run more than one application at a time is called ______.
A. Multi-tasking
B. Object-oriented programming
C. Multi-user computing
D. Real-Time
E. None of the above

39. The process of checking all the peripheral units by the OS during the time of booting is known as ______.
A. BIOS B. POST
C. BUS D. Chkdsk
E. None of these

40. A handheld device that allows you to control your computer without typing instructions from a keyboard is known as ______.
A. Tablet B. PDA
C. Mouse D. Mike
E. None of these

41. When you save a Microsoft Access project, what file format do you use?
A. .adp B. .Xml
C. .mbd D. All of the above
E. None of the above

42. Which of the following topologies has the highest reliability?
A. Star topology
B. Bus topology
C. Ring topology
D. Mesh topology
E. None of these

43. Which among the following term is used for: Unauthorized copying of software to be used for personal gain instead of personal backups?
A. program thievery
B. data snatching
C. software piracy
D. program looting
E. data looting

44. EDBIC code can support how many different representation of characters?
A. 256 B. 149
C. 1024 D. 64
E. 16

45. What is a hyperlink?
A. It is a text or image that you can click on to jump to a new document/page.
B. It is an input type for multimedia files.
C. It is a collection or directory of web pages.
D. It is the home page of a site.
E. None of the above

31. E	**32.** C	**33.** A	**34.** A	**35.** D	**36.** C	**37.** C	**38.** A
39. B	**40.** C	**41.** A	**42.** D	**43.** C	**44.** A	**45.** A	

46. What is a technique used to gain unauthorized access to computers, whereby the intruder sends messages to a computer with an address indicating that the message is coming from a trusted host?
A. Identity Theft B. Forging
C. IP Spoofing D. Pharming
E. Phishing

47. Internet access by transmitting digital data over the wires of a local telephone network is provided by:
A. leased line
B. digital subscriber line
C. digital signal line
D. MODEM
E. None of the above

48. What type of web technology creates an online community where people can make statements and others can read and respond to those statements?
A. I-Journal B. Podcast
C. ASP D. Blog
E. None of the above

49. What is the use of "," symbol in Ms-EXCEL?
A. allows you to make one reference for multiple cells located between 2 cells
B. is used to separate arguments in Excel spreadsheet formulas
C. it is an intersection operator
D. for Sum of two cells
E. None of these

50. What are programs such as Microsoft Edge that serve as navigable windows into the Web called as?
A. Hypertext B. Web browsers
C. Internet D. Networks
E. Windows Navigator

51. Which among the following is a self-contained step-by-step set of operations to be performed?
A. System Software B. Algorithm
C. Network topology D. Application software
E. Utility software

52. Which of the following is an intersection of a row and column in a spreadsheet?
A. Formula B. Worksheet
C. Address D. Cell
E. None of these

53. There is a small-sized type of volatile computer memory that provides high-speed data access to a processor and stores frequently used computer programs, applications and data. Which among the following is a type of memory used to hold frequently used data?
A. Microprocessor B. Cache
C. ROM D. ALU
E. Control

54. Which among the following is a small set of data holding place that is a part of the computer processor and may hold an instruction, a storage address, or any kind of data?
A. Register B. WAN
C. Bus D. Address
E. Processor

55. In a keyboard, left-right-up-down set of keys facilitates which among the following function?
A. Deleting Data or Modification
B. Page Scrolling to view a Document
C. Launching Start Menu
D. Initiating Search and Help
E. Controlling RAM or process execution

56. Which among the following is a term for the initial or main web page of a website or a browser?
A. URL B. Domain
C. Google D. Search Engine
E. Home Page

57. Which among the following is the smallest unit in an image in a computer screen?
A. Unit B. Pixel
C. Array D. Resolution
E. Clip

58. Which unit is a combinational digital electronic circuit that performs arithmetic and bitwise operations on integer binary numbers?
A. BOU B. AEU
C. CPU D. ALU
E. UPS

59. A software program that add functionality to your computer or help your computer perform better is called as:
A. Utility program B. function program
C. specialized program D. manufacturer program
E. compiling program

60. Which unit of computer helps in communication between the memory and the arithmetic logical unit.
A. CMU B. CCU
C. UPS D. CPU
E. ALU

46. C	**47.** B	**48.** D	**49.** B	**50.** B	**51.** B	**52.** D	**53.** B
54. A	**55.** B	**56.** E	**57.** B	**58.** D	**59.** A	**60.** D	

Previous Paper (Solved)

Institute of Banking Personnel Selection

IBPS–Specialist (IT) Officer Scale-I

Preliminary & Main Exam 2021-22*

Preliminary Exam held on - 26 December, 2021

Main Exam held on - 30 January, 2022

PRELIMINARY EXAMINATION

ENGLISH LANGUAGE

Directions (Qs. No. 1-6): *Read the passage carefully then answer the questions given below.*

People have long circulated news via word-of-mouth, and as language evolved into writing and literacy—and governments played larger roles in people's lives—sharing information became a necessity. However, **disseminating** news and information on paper presented significant challenges. When each copy had to be handwritten, mass distribution was impossible. They were first chiseled in stone or metal; later, they were handwritten and distributed in public forums or read from scrolls by town criers. Though both ancient Romans and Chinese—as well as other ancient civilizations—had early forms of news media, they do not qualify as newspapers because they could not be mass-distributed.

The first true newspapers arrived after Johannes Gutenberg introduced his movable type printing press to the European world around 1440. Though printing presses with movable type had existed in eastern Asia for around two centuries, they never made it to Europe; furthermore, Gutenberg's version made it significantly faster to mass produce documents. By 1500, the printing press had made its way throughout Europe, and news sheets (or news books) were mass-distributed.

The first weekly newspaper was published in Germany by Johann Carolus in 1604. Called Relation aller Fürnemmen und gedenckwürdigen Historien, the publication satisfied the four tenets of a "true" newspaper: Accessibility by the public, Published at a regular interval (daily, weekly, monthly, etc.), Information is current, Covers a variety of topics (politics, events, entertainment, sports, etc.) Despite meeting the requirements for a newspaper, there is some debate as to whether The Relation qualifies as the world's first newspaper since it was printed in quarto, not folio, size. It's worth noting the World Association of Newspapers considers T Relation the first true newspaper.'

Other German newspapers followed, and in 1618 t world's first broadsheet newspaper printed in folio size w published in Amsterdam, called Courante uyt Itali Duytslandt, &c. The newspaper format soon spre throughout Europe, with newspapers published in Spa France, and Sweden. The first English newspaper w published in 1665 in Oxford, England. Known as t Oxford Gazette, the newspaper moved to London in 16 and was renamed the London Gazette. It's still bei published today. Soon after, the newspaper became a stap in all major European countries. It then made its way to t New World.

1. Which of the following options is satisfying t condition for being a tenant of a "true newspaper"

A. A newspaper which is accessible to only Asi readers.

B. A newspaper which was published once in month.

C. A newspaper which was printed in quarto, not fol size

D. A newspaper which covers historic developmer leading to various events.

E. A newspaper which is printed in press and is r handwritten.

2. Which of the following options is false according the passage?

A. The relation was not the first newspaper as it d not meet all the required conditions.

B. Information on paper was only possible after t introduction of press.

C. The concept of newspaper was rejected in Euro earlier.

* *Based on Memory*

D. London Gazette is the first newspaper to be published in the multiple languages.

E. All are incorrect.

3. What paved the way for the "true newspapers"?

A. The world's first broadsheet newspaper printed in folio size.

B. The invention of the printing press paved the way for "true" newspapers.

C. The technology which allowed it to be printed in multiple languages.

D. As the Governments started playing a larger role in people's lives.

E. None of these.

4. Which of the following statement is true regarding newspapers?

A. The first weekly newspaper was published in Germany by Johann Carolus in 1904.

B. The Relation qualifies as the world's first newspaper since it was printed in folio, not quarto.

C. The first English newspaper was published in 1695 in Oxford, England known as the Oxford Gazette.

D. The world's first broadsheet newspaper printed in quarto size was published in Amsterdam, called Courante uyt Italien, Duytslandt, &c.

E. The first English newspaper known as the Oxford Gazette, was renamed the London Gazette later.

5. Choose the word which is most nearly the SIMILAR in meaning to the word 'disseminating' printed in bold as used in the passage.

A. Agree B. Taunt
C. Barb D. Sneer
E. Spread

6. In ancient time what was the biggest challenge that the people had to face while circulating the news?

A. The biggest challenge was of printing the news on a paper.

B. Earlier each copy had to be handwritten; mass distribution was next to impossible.

C. It was a herculean task for the editors to get an affirmation by government for printing the news.

D. Both A and C

E. All are incorrect

Directions (Qs. No. 7-10): *In each of the questions given below a part of the sentence is given in bold. It is then followed by three options. Find the alternative that can replace the given bold part to make the sentence grammatically and contextually correct. If none of the alternatives is correct and the sentence is correct as it is then select option E as your choice.*

7. Economist Deena Khatkhate, **who will pass away** at the age of 92 on September 15 in Bethesda, Maryland, in the US, was an unusual man.

(*i*) who passed away
(*ii*) who shall passed away
(*iii*) who has passed away

A. Only (*ii*) B. Both (*i*) and (*iii*)
C. Both (*ii*) and (*iii*) D. Only (*iii*)
E. No correction required

8. A misogynist is a person **who is hating** women.

(*i*) Who are hating
(*ii*) Who have hate
(*iii*) Who hates

A. Both (*i*) and (*iii*) B. Only (*i*)
C. Both (*ii*) and (*iii*) D. Only (*iii*)
E. No correction required

9. Samira **is the better of the two girls** when it comes to solving hard mathematic problems.

(*i*) is the better of two girls
(*ii*) is better of the two girls
(*iii*) is better of two girls

A. Only (*i*) B. Only (*ii*)
C. Both (*ii*) and (*iii*) D. Both (*i*) and (*iii*)
E. No correction is required

10. There are two novels on the table which needs to be read before the exams, but **neither one are interesting.**

(*i*) neither one has interested
(*ii*) neither one is interesting
(*iii*) neither one were interesting

A. Only (*i*) B. Both (*i*) and (*ii*)
C. Only (*ii*) D. Both (*i*) and (*iii*)
E. No correction is required

Directions (Qs. No. 11-16): *Each question below has one blank, which is indicating that something has been omitted. Find out which option can be used to fill up the blank in the sentence in the same sequence to make it meaningfully complete.*

11. Homemade gifts can be completely ________ to what the recipient likes.

A. Alters B. Firmed
C. Tailored D. Polite
E. Liability

12. After much thought, Ted ________ not to travel abroad this summer.

A. Resolved B. Concludes
C. Resolves D. Commence
E. Passed

13. Bryan is ________ in his belief that the earth is flat.

A. Tentative B. Hasten
C. Unlikely D. Provided
E. Confident

14. The noodle maker was ________ in making his noodles and would never let another person take over the task.

A. Careless
B. Negligent
C. Cautious
D. Exciting
E. Inattentive

15. If it weren't for the ________ circumstances, he would have certainly lost his job.
A. Sharp
B. Intensify
C. Mitigating
D. Increase
E. Aggravate

16. When asked about her father, she lost her outward enthusiasm and became rather ________.
A. Reserved
B. Expansive
C. Talkative
D. Extrovert
E. Outgoing

Directions (Qs. No. 17-20): *In each of the questions given below four words are given in bold. These four words may or may not be in their correct position. The sentence is then followed by options with the correct combination of words that should replace each other in order to make the sentence grammatically and contextually correct. Find the correct combination of the words that replace each other. If the sentence is correct as it then select option E as your choice.*

17. Some American officials **lead** (A) to hope that **resumed** (B) sanctions on Iran will **appear** (C) to a popular **uprising** (D).
A. A-B
B. A-C
C. B-D and A-C
D. A-D
E. The sentence is correct

18. Tariffs (A) has **imported** (B) higher **China** (C) on 603 items **imposed** (D) from the US.
A. Only A-B
B. Only B-C
C. Both A-B and B-D
D. Both A-C and B-D.
E. The sentence is correct.

19. NATO ally **world** (A) leads the **Turkey** (B) in the **journalists** (C) of **number** (D) jailed.
A. A-B and C-D
B. Only B-C
C. A-C and B-D
D. A-D
E. The sentence is correct.

20. In 2016, **rising** (A) violence in **Pathankot** (B) by Islamic militants **culminated** (C) in attacks on Indian forces at Uri and **Kashmir** (D).
A. Both A-C and B-D
B. Both A-D and B-C
C. Only B-D
D. C-D
E. The sentence is correct.

Directions (Qs. No. 21-24): *Read each sentence to find out whether there is any grammatical or idiomatic error in it. The error, if any, will be in one part of the sentence. The number of that part is the answer. If there is 'No error', the answer is (E). (Ignore errors of punctuation, if any.)*

21. She held something (A)/ at her side which (B)/ was totally hiding (C)/ by the folds of her sari. (D)/ No error. (E)

22. The father forbade his son (A)/ to walk in the sun (B)/and play with (C)/ his friends on the road (D) / No error. (E)

23. The movement, which aims to (A)/ raise awareness about climate change, hopes (B)/ to bring people together to think about (C)/ what they can do for reduce harmful pollution. (D)/ No error (E)

24. I declined the invitation (A)/ not because I did not (B)/ want to go but (C)/ because I have no time.(D)/ No error (E)

Directions (Qs. No. 25-30): *In the following passage, some of the words have been left out, each of which is indicated by a number. Find the suitable word from the options given against each number and fill up the blanks with appropriate words to make the paragraph meaningfully complete.*

Stanford economist Nicholas Bloom is a true believer, and like many true believers, he lets his message __**(25)**__ his evidence. Based on a single study of a Chinese travel agency, he __**(26)**__ declares working from home a "future-looking technology" with "enormous potential." Not so fast. Bloom's study comes with serious limitations and is contradicted by a later Gallup report. However, while it is far too soon to draw broad __**(27)**__ from his findings, savvy business leaders can read between the lines and extract some valuable lessons for working __**(28)**__ with all employees.

Bloom __**(29)**__ on China's biggest travel agency, Ctrip, which wanted to expand while controlling office space costs. They __**(30)**__ a remote work trial, expecting that productivity would slip a little, but not enough to cancel out the savings. Instead, productivity shot up 13%, and attrition dropped 50%. When the work from home option was rolled out to the entire company and employees were given a choice, the productivity gains were 22%.

25. A. cut
B. outrun
C. exceeded
D. begin
E. choose

26. A. fast
B. enthusiastically
C. slowly
D. eager
E. appropriately

27. A. resulting
B. disappointments
C. conclusions
D. exercises
E. guarantees

28. A. optimally B. extremely
C. competitively D. abroad
E. everywhere

29. A. emphasising B. concentrates
C. learned D. matched
E. focused

30. A. establishes B. appointed
C. brought D. instituted
E. sold

Directions (Qs. No. 31-35) : *Rearrange the following six sentences/group of sentences (a), (b), (c), (d), (e) & (f) in proper sequence as to form a meaningful paragraph and then answer the given questions.*

(*a*) Apart from these, the care provided in these facilities is also not up to the mark.

(*b*) For instance, in 2015, there was one government hospital bed for every 1,833 people compared with 2,336 persons in decade earlier which is a good sign.

(*c*) India has made strides in the expansion of public services.

(*d*) For example, six out of every ten hospitals in the less developed States did not provide intensive care and a quarter of them struggled with issues like sanitation and drainage.

(*e*) For instance, there is one government hospital bed for every 614 people in Goa compared with one every 8,789 people in Bihar.

(*f*) However, as Lancet points out, this availability of beds has been inequitably distributed within the country.

31. Which of the following should be the **FIRST** sentence after the rearrangement?
A. (*a*) B. (*c*)
C. (*b*) D. (*f*)
E. (*e*)

32. Which of the following should be the **FIFTH** sentence after the rearrangement?
A. (*a*) B. (*d*)
C. (*e*) D. (*f*)
E. (*c*)

33. Which of the following should be the **SECOND** sentence after the rearrangement?
A. (*a*) B. (*b*)
C. (*f*) D. (*d*)
E. (*e*)

34. Which of the following should be the **FOURTH** sentence after the rearrangement?
A. (*e*) B. (*b*)
C. (*c*) D. (*f*)
E. (*d*)

35. Which of the following should be the **SIXTH (LAST)** sentence after the rearrangement?
A. (*c*) B. (*b*)
C. (*a*) D. (*d*)
E. (*f*)

Directions (Qs. 36 to 40): *In the following questions, each sentence has two blanks, each blank indicating that something has been omitted. Choose the set of words for the blanks which best fits the meaning of the sentence as a whole.*

36. There is no clear ____ as to why so many companies start at the same time with broadly the ____ ideas.
A. signal, aloof B. indication, same
C. explanation, related D. clues, equal
E. prove, like

37. Everything from our plastic water bottles and cosmetics to our non-stick frying pans, ________ chemicals that ________ in our bodies.
A. has, stays B. contains, accumulate
C. produces, dissolves D. have, dilute
E. comprises, harm

38. Doctors-in training ________ a lot about the workings of the human body ________ medical school and residency.
A. acquire, while B. receives, throughout
C. study, for D. trained, from
E. learn, during

39. There is a common ______ that runs _____ many of these ventures.
A. fibre, on B. cord, by
C. wired, between D. strand, next
E. thread, through

40. World economic growth, which was anyway ______, will be further dampened ______ to Brexit.
A. stumbling, thank B. gloomy, owing
C. low, as D. sputtering, due
E. slowed, now

Directions (Qs. Nos. 41 to 45): *Read each sentence to find out whether there is any grammatical error in it. The error, if any, will be in one part of the sentence. Select the part with the error as your answer. If there is no error, select 'No error' as your answer. (Ignore the errors of punctuation, if any).*

41. (A) The progress of the southwest monsoon/(B) is relatively slow as it is/(C) not getting a favourable system/(D) for move forward./(E) No error.

42. (A) Authorities have/(B) derived requests/(C) for private hospital care/(D) to the accused./(E) No error.

43. (A) The drive intended to creating/(B) an awareness of/(C) the perks of riding two wheelers/(D) without a helmet./(E) No error.

44. (A) Gold continued its rising streak/(B) for the fourth straight session/(C) to reclaim the/(D) psychologically significant thirty thousand mark./(E) No error.

45. (A) The system, which keeps/ (B) a record for personal and professional details/(C) of all community members,/ (D) was hacked./(E) No error.

Directions (Qs. Nos. 46 to 50): *In the following passage some of the words have been left out. Read the passage carefully and choose the correct answer to each question out of the five alternatives and fill in the blanks.*

Technology is the technical __(46)__ people use to __(47)__ their surroundings. It also means knowledge of using tools and machines to do tasks __(48)__. We use technology to control the world in which we live. Technology is people using knowledge, tools, and systems to make their lives easier and better. People use technology to refine their ability to do work. __(49)__ technology, people communicate better. Technology allows them to make more and better products. Our buildings are better through the use of technology. We travel in more comfort and speed as a __(50)__ of technology. Yes, technology is everywhere and can make life better.

46. A. data B. manpower C. sound D. humans E. means

47. A. relate B. capture C. improve D. grow E. built

48. A. locally B. centrally C. efficiently D. deeply E. vaguely

49. A. Through B. Without C. Since D. Help E. Although

50. A. source B. result C. matter D. precursor E. fortune

REASONING

Directions (Qs. 51 to 55): *In these questions, relationship between different elements is shown in the statements. The statements are followed by conclusions. Study the conclusions based on the given statements and select the appropriate answer.*

Give answer—

A. If only conclusion II is true
B. If only conclusion I is true
C. If both conclusions I and II are true
D. If either conclusion I or II is true
E. If neither conclusion I nor II is true.

51. **Statements:** $S \le L \le I = P \ge E > R$; $L > Q$
Conclusions: I. $P \ge S$
II. $I > R$

52. **Statements:** $G > R \le E = A \le T \le S$; $D \le A \le J$
Conclusions: I. $T \ge D$
II. $R > S$

53. **Statements:** $A \ge B > C \le D \le E < F$
Conclusions: I. $A \ge E$
II. $C < F$

54. **Statements:** $G > R \ge E = A \le T \le S$; $D \le A \le J$
Conclusions: I. $J > G$
II. $J = G$

55. **Statements:** $S \le L \le I = P \ge E > R$; $L > Q$
Conclusions: I. $L < R$
II. $E \ge Q$

Directions (Qs. 56 to 60): *Read the following information carefully and answer the given questions.*

Eight persons A, B, C, D, W, X, Y and Z belongs to eight different places in Delhi *i.e.,* Chanakyapuri, Dwarka, Karol Bagh, Lajpat Nagar, Mehrauli, Okhla, Rohini and Saket are placed in a circle not in a order as mentions above. W is sitting third to the left of Y. The person who is from Dwarka is to the immediate right of W and W is not from Okhla. B is sitting fourth to the right of Z. Z is not the neighbour of Y. Neither B nor Z is an immediate neighbour of W. X is from Chanakyapuri and is sitting third to the right of the person from Dwarka. The person from Mehrauli is sitting second to the left of person from Chanakyapuri. The person from Rohini is sitting second to the left of W. A who is from Lajpat Nagar is sitting exactly between X and Z. The person from Saket is sitting second to the right of the person from Lajpat Nagar. C is sitting third to the left of X.

56. Who amongst the following persons belongs to Okhla?
A. Y B. D
C. C D. B
E. None

57. What is A's position with respect to B?
A. Third to the right
B. Second to the right
C. Third to the left
D. Second to the left
E. Fourth to the right

58. How many people are sitting between Z and C when counted in an anticlockwise direction from C?

A. One B. Two
C. Three D. Four
E. None

59. Four of the following five pairs are alike in a certain way based on their positions in the above arrangement and so form a group. Which of the following does not belong to the group?

A. B-Rohini B. Z-Mehrauli
C. D-Okhla D. Y-Saket
E. X-Dwarka

60. Which of the following statements is false according to the above mentioned arrangement?

A. C is to the immediate right of the person from Karol Bagh.
B. The person from Lajpat Nagar is third to the right of the person from Mehrauli.
C. The person from Dwarka is sitting exactly between the persons from Karol Bagh and the Saket.
D. D is neither from Chanakyapuri nor from Karol Bagh.
E. There are only three people between A and C.

Directions (Qs. 61 to 65): *In each question below are given two/three statements followed by two conclusions numbered I and II. You have to take the given statements to be true even if they seem to be at variance with commonly known facts. Read all the conclusions and then decide which of the given conclusions logically follows from the given statements, disregarding commonly known facts.*

Give answer—

A. if only conclusion I follows.
B. if only conclusion II follows.
C. if either conclusion I or II follows.
D. if neither conclusion I nor II follows.
E. if both conclusions I and II follow.

61. Statements : All circles are a triangle.
Some triangle is rectangle.
All rectangles are square.

Conclusions:
I. All rectangles being triangles is a possibility.
II. All circles being square is a possibility.

62. Statements : Some chair is table.
Some bed is table.
No furniture is bed.

Conclusions:
I. All chairs being furniture is a possibility.
II. Some table is not bed is a possibility.

63. Statements : All circles are a triangle.
Some triangle is rectangle.
All rectangles are square.

Conclusions:
I. Some triangles are not rectangle.
II. No square is a circle.

64. Statements : All art are theater.
Some art are drama.

Conclusions:
I. All dramas being theater is a possiblity.
II. Some dramas are theater.

65. Statements : Some chair is table.
Some bed is table.
No furniture is bed.

Conclusions:
I. Some table is not furniture.
II. All tables being furniture is a possibility.

Directions (Qs. 66 to 68): *Read the given information carefully and answer the given question.*

B is 25 m south of A. C is 10 m east of B. D is 30 m north of C. E is 7 m east of D. X is 18 m south of E. M is 12 m south of X. C is 7 m west of M.

66. B is in which direction from Point D?

A. South B. South-West
C. North-East D. South-East
E. North

67. If Point W is 3 m to the north of A, then what is the distance between B and W?

A. 28 m B. 15 m
C. 21 m D. 24 m
E. 17 m

68. What is distance between B and M?

A. 17 m B. 15 m
C. 21 m D. 19 m
E. 13 m

Directions (Qs. 69 to 73): *Study the following information to answer the given questions.*

S, T, U, V, W, X, Y and Z are sitting in a straight line equidistant from each other (but not necessarily in the same order). Some of them are facing south while some are facing north.

(**Note:** Facing the same direction means, if one is facing north then the other also faces north and vice-versa. Facing the opposite directions means, if one is facing north then the other faces south and vice-versa).

S faces north. Only two people sit to the right of S. T sits third to the left of S. Only one person sits between T and X. X sits to the immediate right of W. Only one person sits between W and Z. Both the immediate neighbours of T face the same direction. U sits third to the left of X. T faces the opposite direction as S. Y does not sit at any of the extremes ends of the line. V faces the same direction as W. Both Y and U face the opposite direction of Z.

69. How many persons in the given arrangement are facing North?

A. More than four
B. Four
C. One
D. Three
E. Two

70. Four of the following five are alike in a certain way, and so form a group. Which of the following does not belong to the group?

A. W, X
B. Z, Y
C. T, S
D. T, Y
E. V, U

71. What is the position of X with respect to Z?

A. Second to the left
B. Third to the right
C. Third to the left
D. Fifth to the right
E. Second to the right

72. Who amongst the following sits exactly between Z and W?

A. T
B. Y
C. X
D. W
E. U

73. Who is sitting 2nd to the right of T?

A. Z
B. V
C. X
D. W
E. None of these

Directions (Qs. 74 to 76): *Study the following information and answer the given questions.*

- D is daughter of N. E is wife of N.
- G is sister of D. C is married to G.
- N has no son. K is mother of E.
- Q is only daughter of C.

74. How Q is related to D?

A. Daughter
B. Cousin
C. Niece
D. Sister-in-law
E. Cannot be determined

75. How N is related to K?

A. Brother-in-law
B. Cousin
C. Son-in-law
D. Sister
E. Brother

76. How many daughters N have?

A. One
B. Three
C. Two
D. Cannot be determined
E. None of these

Directions (Qs. 77 to 79): *There are six wires in a table (a), (b), (c), (d), (e) and (f). They have different length but not necessarily in the same order. (e) is greater than (c) but less than (d) and (b). (a) is greater than (d) and (b). (a) is not the longest wire. (f) is 13 cm long and (e) is 4 cm long.*

77. If *(d)* is 5 cm less than *(f)* what would be the length of *(d)*?

A. 7
B. 8
C. 9
D. Can't be determined
E. None of these

78. Which wire has least length?

A. *(b)*
B. *(a)*
C. *(c)*
D. *(e)*
E. None of these

79. If *(a)* is 10 cm length and *(b)* carry 5 cm length then what would be the length of *(c)*?

A. 6
B. 2
C. 7
D. 9
E. None of these

Directions (Qs. 80 to 85): *Study the given information carefully to answer the given question.*

M, N, O, P, Q, R and S are seven people live on seven different floors of a building but not necessarily in the same order. The lower most floor of the building is numbered 1, the one above that is numbered 2 and so on till the topmost floor is numbered 7. Each one of them have different income *i.e.*, 3500, 15000, 7500, 9000, 11000, 13500 and 5000. (But not necessarily in the same order.) M lives on an odd numbered floor but not on the floor numbered 3. The one who has income of 11000 lives immediately above M. Only two people live between M and the one who has income of 7500. The one who has income of 15000 lives on one of the odd numbered floors above P. Only three people live between O and the one who has income of 15000. The one who has income of 7500 lives immediately above O. The one who has income of 3500 lives immediately above the one who has income of 5000. S lives on an odd numbered floor. Only one person lives between N and Q. N lives on one of the floors above Q. Neither O nor M has income of 9000. Q does not has income of 7500.

80. How much income M has?

A. 13500
B. 5000
C. 7500
D. 15000
E. 3500

81. Which of the following combinations is true with respect to the given arrangement?

A. 13500-O
B. 15000-R
C. 5000-S
D. 11000-P
E. 9000-N

². If all the people are made to sit in alphabatical order from top to bottom, the positions of how many people will remain unchanged?

A. Four
B. None
C. Two
D. One
E. Three

³. Which of the following statements is true with respect to the given arrangement?

A. The one who has income of 5000 lives immediately below M.
B. R has income of 15000.
C. None of the given options is true.
D. Only four people live between P and S.
E. S lives immediately below Q.

. Who amongst the following lives on the floor numbered 2?

A. N
B. The one who has income of 3500
C. The one who has income of 5000
D. P
E. R

. How much income R has?

A. 13500
B. 5000
C. 7500
D. 15000
E. 3500

ections (Qs. 86 to 90): *In the following questions, each stion has a statement followed by two conclusions. Taking statement to be true, decide which of the given conclusions nitely follows from the given statement.*

cate your answer as—

A. if only I follows;
B. if only II follows;
C. either I or II follows;
D. if neither I nor II follows; and
E. if both I and II follow.

. **Statement :** Workers feel highly motivated when they get sense of involvement by participating in the management of companies.

Conclusions :

I. Workers should be motivated to produce more.
II. Workers should be allowed to participate in the management of companies.

Statement : Industrial revolution which first of all started in Europe has brought about modern age.

Conclusions :

I. Disparity between rich and poor results in revolution.
II. Revolution overhauls society.

Statement : America's defence secretary reiterated that they would continue to supply arms to Pakistan.

Conclusions :

I. Pakistan is incapable of manufacturing arms.
II. It would ensure peace in the region.

89. Statement : Poor people are more trustworthy as compared to the rich. They can do wonders if they are taken into confidence.

Conclusions :

I. Poor people are wonderful people.
II. By and large rich people are not trustworthy.

90. Statement : Government has spoiled many top ranking financial institutions by appointing bureaucrats as Directors of these institutions.

Conclusions :

I. Government should appoint Directors of the financial institutes taking into consideration the expertise of the person in the area of finance.
II. The Director of the financial institute should have expertise commensurate with the financial work carried out by the institute.

Directions (Qs. 91 to 95) : *Read the following information to answer the given questions :*

Following are the conditions for selecting candidates for Research Fellowship :

The candidate must—

(*i*) be a post-graduate with minimum of 60% marks.
(*ii*) not be more than 30 years as on 1. 9. 1993.
(*iii*) have at least 3 years' research experience.
(*iv*) have diploma in statistics.
(*v*) have secured at least 55% marks in the entrance test.
(*iv*) have finalised the topic for research.

However, in the case of a candidate who fulfills all other criteria except—

A. (*iii*) above but has M. Phil degree, should be given fellowship.
B. (*iv*) above should be referred to Dean.
C. (*i*) above but has atleast 55% marks in post-graduation, should be wait-listed.
D. (*v*) above but has atleast 50% marks, should be referred to Chairman.

Based on these criteria and information provided below, decide the course of action in each case. You are not to assume anything. If the data provided is not adequate to decide the given course of action, your answer will be "data inadequate". These cases are given to you as on 1. 9. 1993.

91. Vijay Gupta is 24 years old and has got 58% marks in the entrance examination. He has secured 63% marks in his post-graduation and 55% marks in M. Phil. He has got diploma in Statistics and has also finalised the topic for research.

A. Grant Fellowship
B. Refer to Dean
C. Refer to Chairman
D. Wait-list
E. Data inadequate

92. Ajoy Dwivedi has secured 65% marks in the post-graduation and has secured 5 years research experience. He has secured 65% marks in the entrance test and has finalised the research topic. His date of birth is 11. 8. 1965.

A. Grant Fellowship
B. Wait-list
C. Refer to Dean
D. Data inadequate
E. None of these

93. Madan Soren has got diploma in Statistics with 60% marks and post-graduation with 56% marks. His date of birth is 12. 12. 1968. He has got 1 year research experience and is still doing his M. Phil. He has secured 60% marks in the entrance exam and has also finalised the research topic.

A. Grant fellowship
B. Fellowship not to be granted
C. Refer to Dean
D. Data inadequate
E. Wait-list

94. 26 years old Mamta Kulkarni is M. Phil with 60% marks. She has secured 70% marks in the entrance examination and has finalised the topic for research. She has also got diploma in Statistics.

A. Grant Fellowship
B. Fellowship not to be granted
C. Refer to Chairman
D. Refer to Dean
E. Data inadequate

95. Chander Manoj has got 5 years' research experience and has finalised the research topic. He has got 56% marks in post-graduation and 60% marks in the entrance test. His date of birth is 15. 2. 1966. He has also got diploma in Statistics.

A. Grant Fellowship
B. Fellowship not to be granted
C. Refer to Dean
D. Data inadequate
E. None of these

Directions (Qs. 96 to 100) : *Study the following information carefullly and answer the questions given below :*

The admission ticket for an exhibition bears a password which is changed after every clock hour based on set of words chosen for each day.

The following is an illustration of the code and steps of rearrangement for subsequent clock hours. The time is 9 a.m. to 3 p.m.

Day's first password :

First Batch : 9 a.m. to 10 a.m.

is not ready cloth simple harmony burning.

Second Batch : 10 a.m. to 11 a.m.

ready not is cloth burning harmony simple.

Third Batch : 11 a.m. to 12 noon

cloth is not ready simple harmony burning.

Fourth Batch : 12 noon to 1 p.m.

not is cloth ready burning harmony simple.

Fifth Batch : 1 p.m. to 2 p.m.

ready cloth is not simple harmony burning.

96. If the password for 11 a.m. to 12 noon was—"soap shy miss pen yet the she", what was the password for the first batch?

A. shy miss pen soap yet the she
B. pen miss shy soap she the yet
C. miss soap pen shy she the yet
D. soap pen miss shy she the yet
E. None of these

97. If the password for 6th batch, *i.e.,* 2 p.m. to 3 p.m. is—"are trap cut he but say lap", what will be the password for 2nd batch, *i.e.,*10–11 a.m.?

A. are he cut trap lap say but
B. cut he are trap but say lap
C. he cut trap are lap say but
D. trap are he cut lap say but
E. None of these

98. If the password for the first batch was—"rate go long top we let have", which batch will have the password—"go rate top long have let we?"

A. Second
B. Third
C. Fourth
D. Fifth
E. None of these

99. Day's first password—"camel road no toy say me not", what will be the password for fourth batch, *i.e.,* 12 noon to 1 p.m.?

A. toy camel road no say me not
B. toy no road camel not me say
C. no road camel toy not me say
D. road camel toy no not me say
E. None of these

100. If the batch 2 of the day has following password—"came along net or else eky lot", what would be the password for batch 4, (*i.e.,* 12 noon to 1 p.m.)?

A. along net or came else key lot
B. or net along came lot key else
C. came or net along lot key else
D. net or came along else key lot
E. None of these

QUANTITATIVE APTITUDE

101. At present, Pia is 6 years older to Ray. The respective ratio between the present ages of Pia and Mini is 3 : 4. At present Ray is 14 years younger to Mini. What is Ray's present age?

A. 16 years
B. 20 years
C. 14 years
D. 18 years
E. 24 years

Directions (Qs. No. 102-106): *In these questions two equations numbered I and II are given. You have to solve both the equations and mark the appropriate answer.*

102. I. $4x^2 + 17x + 15 = 0$
II. $3y^2 + 19y + 28 = 0$
A. $x > y$
B. $x < y$
C. $x > y$
D. $x < y$
E. relationship between x and y cannot be established

103. I. $3x^2 - 17x + 22 = 0$
II. $5y^2 - 21y + 22 = 0$
A. $x > y$
B. $x < y$
C. $x > y$
D. $x < y$
E. relationship between x and y cannot be established

104. I. $3x^2 + 11x + 10 = 0$
II. $2y^2 + 13y + 21 = 0$
A. $x > y$
B. $x < y$
C. $x > y$
D. $x < y$
E. relationship between x and y cannot be established

105. I. $3x^2 + 13x + 14 = 0$
II. $8y^2 + 26y + 21 = 0$
A. $x > y$
B. $x < y$
C. $x > y$
D. $x < y$
E. relationship between x and y cannot be established

106. I. $3x^2 - 14x + 15 = 0$
II. $15y^2 - 34y + 15 = 0$
A. $x > y$
B. $x < y$
C. $x > y$
D. $x < y$
E. relationship between x and y cannot be established

Directions (Qs. No. 107-111): *Study the table to answer the given questions.*

Data related to expenses by companies A, B, C, D and E in the April 2012

Companies	Total Expenses (in Lakh rupees)	Expenses (in Percentage)	
		Marketing	Legal
A	90	24	18
B	80	23	8
C	74	30	25
D	65	20	10
E	70	15	9

(Note: Other than the mentioned expenses under the given heads, there may also be some other expenses. For calculation purposes, please consider the given expense heads only.)

107. What is the respective ratio between the marketing expenses of company A and the marketing expenses of company C?

A. 34 : 35
B. 32 : 33
C. 35 : 36
D. 36 : 37
E. 37 : 38

108. Total expenses of Company E in October 2012 was 20% more than the total given expenses of the same company in April 2012. How much was the Marketing expenses of the same Company in October 2012, if it was 25% of the total expenses of the same month? (in ₹ Lakhs)

A. 27
B. 24
C. 26
D. 21
E. 18

109. Marketing expenses of company D is less than marketing expenses of Company B, by approximately what per cent?

A. 20
B. 40
C. 39
D. 59
E. 29

110. What is the average total expenses of all the companies? (in ₹ Lakhs)

A. 75.25
B. 75.8
C. 75
D. 72.8
E. 72.25

111. What is the difference between the total expenses made by company C in legal and marketing together and the total expenses made by company E in legal and marketing together? (in ₹ Lakhs)

A. 24.5
B. 23.5
C. 22.9
D. 23
E. 23.9

Directions (Qs. No. 112-121): *What approximate value will come in place of the question mark (?) in the given questions? (You are not expected to calculate the exact value)*

112. $6399 \times 1\frac{5}{8} + 353 \div ? = 10444$

A. 14　　B. 22
C. 2　　D. 16
E. 8

113. $\sqrt{(624)} \times 14.02 + \sqrt{(404)} \times 15.97 = ?$

A. 670　　B. 570
C. 710　　D. 510
E. 610

114. 8461 ÷ 11.99 – 24.01 ÷ 5/100 = ?

A. 625　　B. 400
C. 25　　D. 900
E. 225

115. 14.85% of 679 + 19.9% of 219.89 = ?

A. 115　　B. 145
C. 65　　D. 105
E. 85

116. 1441 ÷ ? + 149.98 × 14.99 = 3006 – 254.91

A. 35　　B. 15
C. 25　　D. 45
E. 3

117. 19 30 44 67 117 ?

A. 236　　B. 272
C. 264　　D. 248
E. 254

118. 7 9 18 46 111 ?

A. 245　　B. 229
C. 233　　D. 248
E. 237

119. 7 24 58 109 ? 262

A. 183　　B. 189
C. 171　　D. 163
E. 177

120. 19 20 16 25 9 ?

A. 32　　B. 38
C. 34　　D. 42
E. 48

121. 7.4 9.2 11.4 14 17 ?

A. 19.8　　B. 22.6
C. 23　　D. 21
E. 20.4

122. A bag contains 5 red balls, 6 yellow balls and 3 green balls. If two balls are picked at random, what is the probability that either both are red or both are green in colour?

A. 3/7　　B. 5/14
C. 1/7　　D. 2/7
E. 3/14

123. In a 140 litres of mixture of milk and water, percentage of water is only 30%. The milkman gave 20 litres of this mixture to a customer. Then he added equal quantities of pure milk and water to the remaining mixture. As a result the respective ratio of milk and water in the mixture became 2 : 1. What was the quantity of milk added? (in litres)

A. 12　　B. 16
C. 18　　D. 8
E. 10

124. A boat can travel 4.2 km upstream in 14 minutes. If the respective ratio of speed of the boat in still water and speed of the stream is 7 : 1. How much time will the boat take to cover 17.6 km downstream? (in minutes)

A. 52　　B. 44
C. 48　　D. 36
E. 54

125. A starts a business with a capital of ₹ 1500. B joins the business 6 months later from the start of the business and C joins the business 8 months later from the start of the business. End of the year their respective share in profit was in ratio of 5 : 3 : 3. What is the sum of amount put in the business by B and C together?

A. ₹ 3300　　B. ₹ 3500
C. ₹ 4200　　D. ₹ 4800
E. ₹ 4500

126. The length of a rectangle is 4 m more than the side of a square and the breadth of the rectangle is 4 m less than side of the same square. The area of the square is 567 sq. m., what is the area of the rectangle? (in sq.m)

A. 549　　B. 545
C. 557　　D. 559
E. 551

127. A sells an item at 20% profit to B. B sells it to C at 10% profit. C sells it to D at ₹ 116 profit. Difference between the cost price of D and Cost price of A was ₹ 500. How much did B pay to A for the item?

A. ₹ 1,240　　B. ₹ 1,250
C. ₹ 1,440　　D. ₹ 1,450
E. ₹ 1,400

128. 10 men can finish a piece of work in 15 days. 8 women can finish the same piece of work in 25 days. Only 10 women started working and in few days completed certain amount of work. After that 3 men joined them. The remaining work was completed by 10 women and 3 men together in 5 days. After how many days 3 men joined 10 women?

A. 11
B. 13
C. 15
D. 10
E. 12

129. ₹ 16,000 was invested for three years, partly in Scheme A at the rate of 5% Simple Interest per annum and partly in scheme B at the rate of 8% Simple Interest per annum. Total interest received at the end was ₹ 3480. How much sum of money was invested in Scheme A?

A. ₹ 6,000
B. ₹ 6,500
C. ₹ 4,500
D. ₹ 4,000
E. ₹ 8,000

Directions (Qs. No. 130-134): *Refer to the graph and answer the given questions.*

Data related to number of hats sold by two stores (M and N) during six given months:

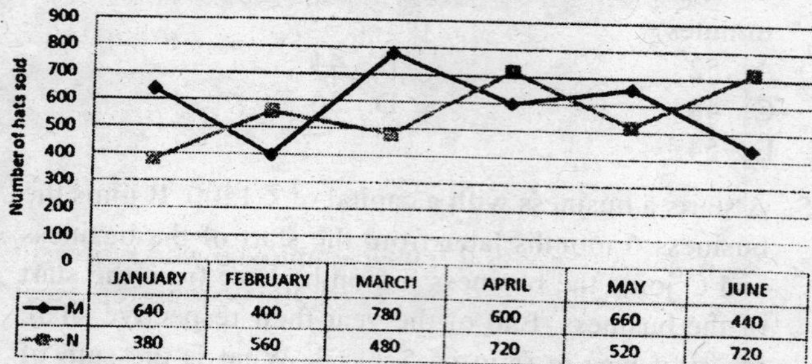

	JANUARY	FEBRUARY	MARCH	APRIL	MAY	JUNE
M	640	400	780	600	660	440
N	380	560	480	720	520	720

130. Number of hats sold by store M during January is what per cent of the total number of hats sold by the store N during March and April together?

A. $51\frac{1}{3}$
B. $55\frac{2}{3}$
C. $47\frac{1}{3}$
D. $53\frac{1}{3}$
E. $57\frac{2}{3}$

131. What is the average number of hats sold by store N during January, March, May and June?

A. 535
B. 525
C. 515
D. 500
E. 530

132. Stores M and N sells only two types of hats: Fedora Hats and Trilby Hats. If the respective ratio of total number of Fedora hats to total number of Trilby hats sold by stores M and N together during March is 9 : 5, what is the total number of Fedora hats sold by stores M and N together during March?

A. 990
B. 900
C. 720
D. 630
E. 810

133. If the total number of hats sold by stores M and N together in July is 15% more than the total number of hats sold by the same stores together during June, what is the total number of hats sold by the same stores together during July?

A. 1298
B. 1316
C. 1356
D. 1284
E. 1334

134. Number of hats sold by store M increased by what per cent from February to May?

A. 75
B. 55
C. 65
D. 70
E. 60

135. Monthly salary of Dex is 1/4th of his father's monthly salary. Dex's sister's monthly salary is 2/5th of their father's monthly salary. Dex's sister pays ₹ 12,800, which is 1/4th of her monthly salary as study loan. Savings and expenses made out of the monthly salary, by Dex is in the respective ratio 3 : 5. How much does Dex save each month?

A. ₹ 12,000/-
B. ₹ 10,600/-
C. ₹ 10,400/-
D. ₹ 12,600/-
E. ₹ 12,400/-

136. In a mixture of milk and water, the proportion of milk by weight is 60%. If from the 80 gm mixture, 20 gm of mixture is taken out and 6 gm of pure water is added to the mixture then find the ratio of milk and water in the new mixture.

A. 5 : 6
B. 6 : 5
C. 4 : 3
D. 3 : 2
E. 7 : 6

137. A sphere is melted and molded into solid cylinder. If radius of both solids is equal, then find the ratio of total surface area of sphere to the total surface area of cylinder.

A. 2 : 3
B. 4 : 3
C. 3 : 7
D. 6 : 7
E. 7 : 6

138. Three partners P, Q and R invested their amounts in ratio of 2 : 5 : 7. At the end of 6 months, 'P' added some more amount such that his investment become equals to half of sum of 'Q' and 'R' initial investment. If at the end of the year, Q's share in profit is Rs 425, then find the total profit.

A. ₹ 1250
B. ₹ 1360
C. ₹ 1840
D. ₹ 1050
E. ₹ 1450

139. A shopkeeper marks up price of LED 60% above its cost price and gives three successive discounts of $12\frac{1}{2}\%$, d% and 25%. If shopkeeper made a loss 16% on LED. Find the second discount allowed by shop?

A. 15%
B. 20%
C. 25%
D. $16\frac{2}{3}\%$
E. 17.5%

140. Speed of a boat in still water is 12 kmph and speed of stream is '*x*' kmph. If in travelling 270 km upstream boat takes $66\frac{2}{3}\%$ more time than travelling 270 km downstream, then find the value of '*x*'.
A. 2 kmph
B. 4 kmph
C. 1 kmph
D. 3 kmph
E. 6 kmph

Directions (Qs. No. 141-145): *Given below table shows total three types of items (A, B & C) sold by a store on five days of a week. Table also shows total type A items sold by store and percentage of items B and items C sold by store. Read the data carefully and answer following questions:*

Note: only three types of items sold by the store.

Days	Items A	% of items B	% of items C
Monday	240	32%	20%
Tuesday	320	48%	12%
Wednesday	420	45%	20%
Thursday	360	56%	20%
Friday	340	22%	10%

141. Total items B sold by store on Monday & Friday together are what percent less than total items C sold by store on Wednesday & Thursday together?
A. 60%
B. 50%
C. 20%
D. 30%
E. 10%

142. Find the difference between average number of items B sold by store on Tuesday & Thursday and average number of items A sold by store on Thursday & Friday?
A. 260
B. 264
C. 262
D. 272
E. 268

143. If total items B sold by store on Sunday is 25% more than that sold on Thursday and total items C sold on Sunday is 300% more than that sold on Friday, then find total number of items B & items C sold by store on Sunday?
A. 1250
B. 1150
C. 1050
D. 950
E. 1350

144. Total items C sold by store on Wednesday is what percent more than total items C sold by store on Monday and Tuesday together?
A. $26\frac{22}{49}\%$
B. $24\frac{22}{49}\%$
C. $22\frac{22}{49}\%$
D. $21\frac{22}{49}\%$
E. $18\frac{22}{49}\%$

145. Find the ratio between total items sold by store on Monday to total items sold by store on Thursday?
A. 1 : 5
B. 1 : 3
C. 1 : 7
D. 1 : 4
E. 1 : 2

Directions (Qs. No. 146-150): *Given data shows total male and female employee in three companies in a seminar. Read data carefully and answer the questions:*

In annual seminar of three companies, A, B and C some male and female employees represent their companies. Average number of female employees who represent A and B is 420. Total male employee in A and B is 1620. Number of female employees is $\frac{2}{3}$*rd* and $\frac{2}{5}$*th* of male employee in A and B respectively. Total female employee who represent C are 25% more than total female employee who represent A and total male employee who represent C are $33\frac{1}{3}\%$ more than total female employee who represent B.

146. Total employees who represent A is what percent more than total male employee who represent B?
A. $33\frac{1}{3}\%$
B. $30\frac{1}{3}\%$
C. $27\frac{1}{3}\%$
D. $29\frac{1}{3}\%$
E. $39\frac{1}{3}\%$

147. 25% of total female employee and 20% of total male employee who represent B & C together have MBA degree, then find total employee who do not have MBA degree?
A. 1624
B. 1424
C. 1824
D. 1648
E. 1244

148. Find the ratio between total male employee who represent B & C together to total female employee who represent A & C together?
A. 23 : 13
B. 23 : 14
C. 23 : 18
D. 23 : 12
E. 23 : 20

149. Find difference between Total male employees who represent C and total female employee who represent B?

A. 120 B. 140
C. 100 D. 160
E. 180

150. Find average number female in B & C?

A. 480
B. 420
C. 520
D. 540
E. 600

ANSWERS

1. (B) **2. (E)** **3. (B)**
4. (B) **5. (E)** **6. (B)**
7. (B) **8. (D)** **9. (E)**
10. (C) **11. (C)** **12. (A)**
13. (E) **14. (C)** **15. (C)**
16. (A) **17. (B)** **18. (D)**
19. (A) **20. (C)** **21. (C)**
22. (E) **23. (D)** **24. (D)**
25. (B) **26. (B)** **27. (C)**
28. (A) **29. (E)** **30. (D)**
31. (B) **32. (A)** **33. (B)**
34. (A) **35. (D)** **36. (B)**
37. (B) **38. (E)** **39. (E)**
40. (B) **41. (D)** **42. (D)**
43. (A) **44. (E)** **45. (B)**
46. (E) **47. (C)** **48. (C)**
49. (A) **50. (B)**

51. (C): $S \le L \le I = P \ge E > R; L > Q$

Conclusion-I : $S \le L \le I = P \Rightarrow P \ge S$ {True}

Conclusion-II : $I = P \ge E > R \Rightarrow I > R$ {True}.

52. (B): $G > R \le E = A \le T \le S; D \le A \le J$

Conclusion-I : $D \le A \le T \Rightarrow T \ge D$ {True}

Conclusion-II : $R \le E = A \le T \le S$

$\Rightarrow R > S$ {False}.

53. (A): $A \ge B > C \le D \le E < F$

Conclusion-I : $A \ge B > C \le D \le E$

$\Rightarrow$ No relation between A and E

$\therefore A \ge E$ {False}

Conclusion-II : $C \le D \le E < F \Rightarrow C < F$ {True}.

54. (E): $G > R \ge E = A \le T \le S, D \le A \le J$

Conclusion-I : $J \ge A = E \le R < G$

$\Rightarrow$ No relation between J and G

$\Rightarrow J > G$ {False}

Conclusion-II : $J = G$ {False}.

55. (E): $S \le L \le I = P \ge E > R; L > Q$

Conclusion-I : $L \le I = P \ge E > R$

$\Rightarrow$ No relation between L and R

$\Rightarrow$ $L < R$ {False}

Conclusion-II : $Q < L \le I = P \ge E$

$\Rightarrow$ No relation between Q & E

$\Rightarrow$ $Q \le E$ {False}.

For Qs. No. 56-60:

Circular sitting arrangement of Eight persons are like this.

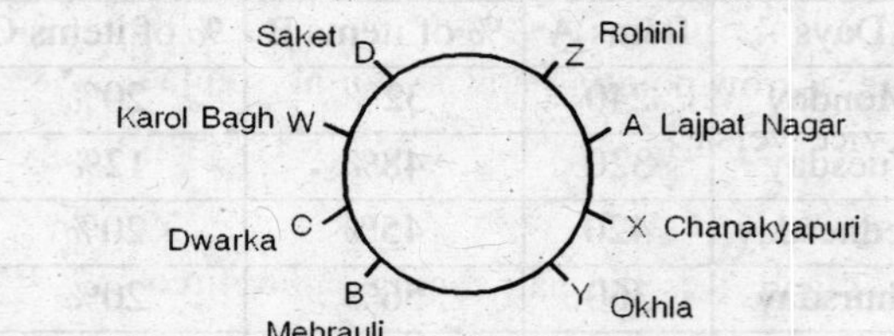

56. (A) **57. (A)** **58. (D)**
59. (E) **60. (C)**

61. (E):

Circle
Rectangle
Square
Triangle

62. (E):

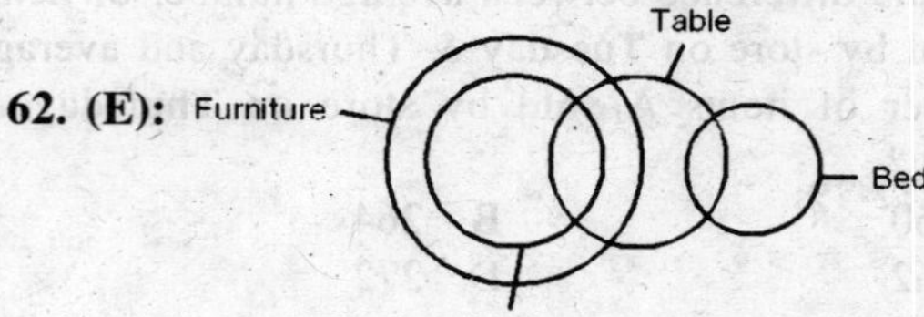

63. (A):

64. (C):

Or

Art
Drama
Theater
Theater
Drama
Art

65. (A):

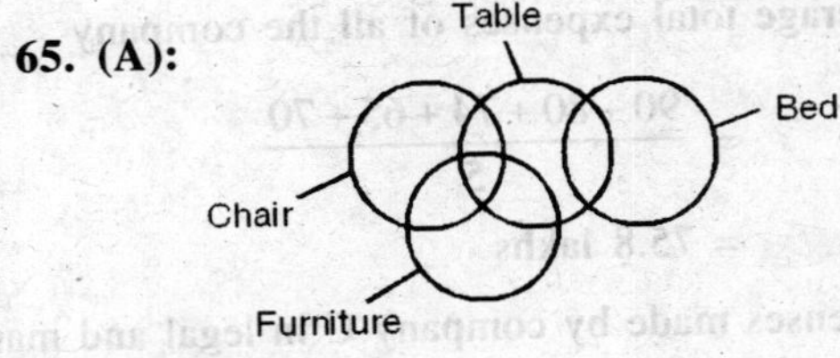

For Qs. No. 66-68

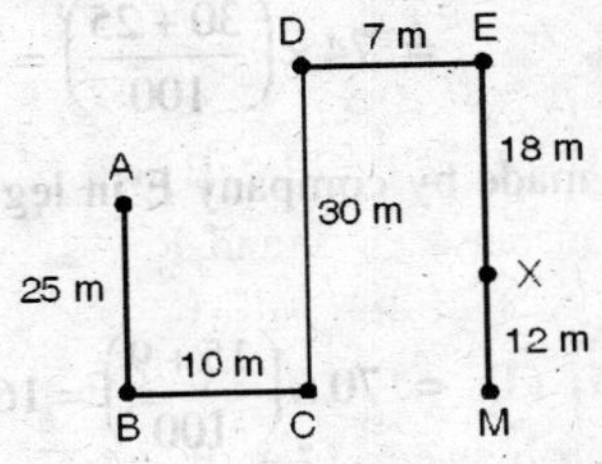

66. (B) **67. (A)** **68. (A)**

For Qs. No. 69-73:

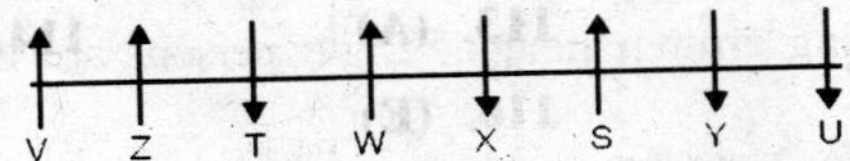

{Note : Arrow pointing upward for person facing North and vice versa.}

69. (B)

70. (D): T and Y is the pair facing same direction.

71. (B) **72. (A)** **73. (B)**

For Qs. No. 74-76:

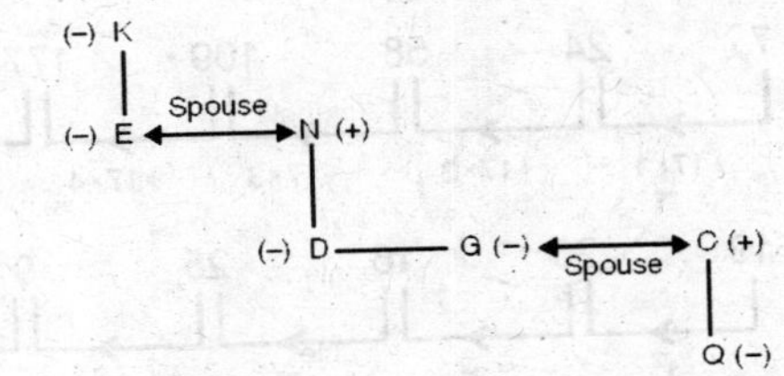

74. (C) **75. (C)** **76. (C)**

For Qs. No. 77-79:

F > A > D or B > E > C

13 cm 4 cm

77. (B): Wire (D)'s length = 13 – 5 = 8 cm.

78. (C): Wire (C)'s length is least.

79. (B): Length of C < 4 (= Length of wire E)

$\therefore$ Length of (C) = 2 cm.

80. (D) **81. (A)** **82. (C)**

83. (C) **84. (E)** **85. (C)**

86. (E) **87. (B)** **88. (D)**

89. (B) **90. (E)** **91. (A)**

92. (C) **93. (B)** **94. (E)**

95. (E) **96. (A)** **97. (A)**

98. (C) **99. (D)** **100. (A)**

101. (D): Let Ray's present age is x years.

Then Pia's present age is $(x + 6)$ years.

$$\frac{\text{Pia's age}}{\text{Mini's age}} = \frac{3}{4}$$

$$\frac{x+6}{\text{Mini's age}} = \frac{3}{4}$$

$$\text{Mini's age} = \frac{4}{3}(x+6)$$

Again, from question,

$$\frac{4}{3}(x+6) - 14 = x$$

$$4x - 3x = 42 - 24$$

$$x = 18$$

Ray's present age = 18 years.

102. (E): I. $4x^2 + 17x + 15 = 0$

$4x^2 + 12x + 5x + 15 = 0$

$(4x + 5)(x + 3) = 0$

$\Rightarrow$ $x = -3$ and $-5/4$

II. $3y^2 + 19y + 28 = 0$

$3y^2 + 12y + 7y + 28 = 0$

$(3y + 7)(y + 4) = 0$

$\Rightarrow$ $y = -4$ and $-7/3$

103. (A): I. $3x^2 - 17x + 22 = 0$

$3x^2 - 11x - 6x + 22 = 0$

$(3x - 11)(x - 2) = 0$

$\Rightarrow$ $x = 2$ and $11/3$

II. $5y^2 - 21y + 22 = 0$

$5y^2 - 11y - 10y + 22 = 0$

$(5y - 11)(y - 2) = 0$

$\Rightarrow$ $y = 2$ and $11/5$

i.e., $x > y$.

104. (C): I. $3x^2 + 11x + 10 = 0$

$3x^2 + 6x + 5x + 10 = 0$

$(3x + 5)(x + 2) = 0$

$\Rightarrow$ $x = -2$ and $-5/3$

II. $2y^2 + 13y + 21 = 0$

$2y^2 + 7y + 6y + 21 = 0$

$(2y + 7)(y + 3) = 0$

$\Rightarrow$ $y = -3$ and $-7/2$

i.e. $x > y$

105. (C): I. $3x^2 + 13x + 14 = 0$

$3x^2 + 7x + 6x + 14 = 0$

$(3x + 7)(x + 2) = 0$

$\Rightarrow \quad x = -2 \text{ and } -7/3$

II. $8y^2 + 26y + 21 = 0$

$8y^2 + 14y + 12y + 21 = 0$

$(4y + 7)(2y + 3) = 0$

$\Rightarrow \quad y = -3/2 \text{ and } -7/4$

i.e. $y > x$.

106. (A): I. $3x^2 - 14x + 15 = 0$

$3x^2 - 5x - 9x + 15 = 0$

$(3x - 5)(x - 3) = 0$

$\Rightarrow \quad x = 3 \text{ and } 5/3$

II. $15y^2 - 34y + 15 = 0$

$15y^2 - 25y - 9y + 15 = 0$

$(5y - 3)(3y - 5) = 0$

$\Rightarrow \quad y = 5/3 \text{ and } 3/5$

i.e. $x > y$.

107. (D): Marketing expenses of company A

$$= \frac{90 \times 24}{100} = 21.6 \text{ lakhs}$$

Marketing expenses of company C

$$= \frac{74 \times 30}{100} = 22.2 \text{ lakhs}$$

$$\text{Respective ratio} = \frac{21.6}{22.2} = \frac{36}{37}$$

108. (D): Total expenses of company E in Oct 2012

$$= \frac{70 \times 120}{100} = 84 \text{ lakhs}$$

Marketing expenses of company E in Oct 2012

$$= \frac{84 \times 25}{100} = 21 \text{ lakhs}$$

109. (E): Marketing expenses of company D

$$= \frac{65 \times 20}{100} = 13 \text{ lakhs}$$

Marketing expenses of company B

$$= \frac{80 \times 23}{100}$$

$= 18.4$ lakhs

$$\text{Percentage difference} = \left(\frac{18.4 - 13}{18.4}\right) \times 100$$

$= 29\%$

110. (B): Average total expenses of all the company

$$= \frac{90 + 80 + 74 + 65 + 70}{5}$$

$= 75.8$ lakhs

111. (E): Expenses made by company C in legal and marketing together

$$= 74 \times \left(\frac{30 + 25}{100}\right) = 40.7 \text{ lakhs}$$

Expenses made by company E in legal and marketing together

$$= 70 \times \left(\frac{15 + 9}{100}\right) = 16.8 \text{ lakhs}$$

Difference $= 40.7 - 16.8$

$= 23.9$ lakhs.

112. (E) **113. (A)** **114. (E)**

115. (B) **116. (E)**

117. (D):

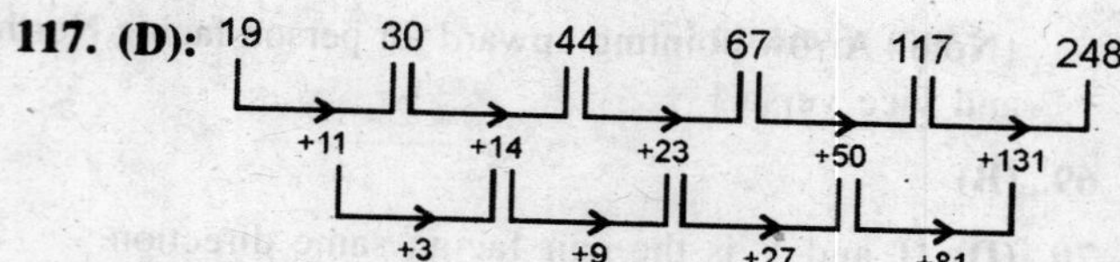

118. (E): 7 9 18 46 111 237

$1^3+1 \quad 2^3+1 \quad 3^3+1 \quad 4^3+1 \quad 5^3+1$

119. (E): 7 24 58 109 177 262

$+17\times1 \quad +17\times2 \quad +17\times3 \quad +17\times4 \quad +17\times5$

120. (C): 19 20 16 25 9 34

$+1^2 \quad -2^2 \quad +3^2 \quad -4^2 \quad +5^2$

121. (E): 7.4 9.2 11.4 14 17 20.4

+1.8 +2.2 +2.6 +3.0 +3.4

+0.4 +0.4 +0.4 +0.4

122. (C): Number of ways of selecting two red balls

$= {}^5C_2$

Number of ways of selecting two green balls

$= {}^3C_2$

Number of ways of selecting two balls out of total 14 (= 5 + 6 + 3) balls $= {}^{14}C_2$

Hence, required probability

$$= \frac{{}^5C_2 + {}^3C_2}{{}^{14}C_2} = \frac{5 \times 2 + 3}{7 \times 13} = \frac{13}{7 \times 13} = \frac{1}{7}$$

123. (A): After giving 20 ltrs to a customer

resulting mixture = 140 – 20 = 120 ltrs.

$$\text{milk contains} = 120 \times \frac{70}{100} = 84 \text{ ltrs.}$$

$$\text{water contains} = 120 \times \frac{30}{100} = 36 \text{ ltrs.}$$

Let x ltrs of milk and x ltrs of water is added to the mixture so that ratio of milk containts to water containts = 2 : 1.

$$\frac{84 + x}{36 + x} = \frac{2}{1}$$

$84 + x = 72 + 2x \Rightarrow x = 12$ ltrs.

Hence, milk added to the mixture = 12 ltrs.

124. (B): Let speed (meter/minute) of boat in still water = $7x$, then speed of stream = x.

upstream speed = $7x - x = 6x$

downstream speed = $7x + x = 8x$

From question,

$$6x = \frac{4.2 \times 1000}{14}$$

$$x = \frac{42 \times 1000}{14 \times 6} = 50 \text{ m/min.}$$

Time taken to cover 17.6 km downstream

$$= \frac{17.6 \times 1000}{50} = 44 \text{ min.}$$

125. (E): Let investment by B and C are ₹ x and ₹ y respectively.

From question,

Ratio of their profit = 5 : 3 : 3

$1500 \times 12 : x \times 6 : y \times 4 = 5 : 3 : 3$

or $\frac{1500 \times 12}{x \times 6} = \frac{5}{3} \Rightarrow x = 1800$

$\frac{1500 \times 12}{y \times 4} = \frac{5}{3} \Rightarrow y = 2700$

$\therefore x + y = 4500$

126. (E): Let side of square is x m

then length of rectangle = $(x + 4)$ m

breadth of the rectangle = $(x - 4)$ m

from question, area of square = 567

i.e. $x^2 = 567$

Area of rectangle = $(x + 4)(x - 4)$

$= x^2 - 16$

$= 567 - 16$

$= 551$ sq. m.

127. (C): Let cost price of A = x.

then, $$\text{S.P. of A} = x \times \frac{120}{100} = \frac{6x}{5} = \text{C.P. of B.}$$

$$\text{S.P. of B} = \frac{6x}{5} \times \frac{110}{100}$$

$$= \frac{33x}{25} = \text{C.P. of C.}$$

$$\text{S.P. of C} = \frac{33x}{25} + 116 = \text{C.P. of D.}$$

From question,

Cost Price of D – Cost Price of A = 500

C.P. of D = 500 + x

$$\frac{33x}{25} + 116 = 500 + x$$

$$\frac{33x}{25} - x = 500 - 116$$

$$\frac{8x}{25} = 384$$

$$x = \frac{384 \times 25}{8} = 1200$$

$$\therefore \text{ Cost Price of B} = \frac{1200 \times 120}{100} = 1440$$

128. (B): 1 man can finish same work in 10 × 15 = 150 days

1 woman can finish same work in 8 × 25 = 200 days.

Let 10 women work together for n days, then work finished in n days

$$= \frac{10n}{200} = \frac{n}{20} \text{ works}$$

$$\text{Remaining work} = \left(1 - \frac{n}{20}\right)$$

Work done by 10 women and 3 men in 5 days

$$= 5\left(\frac{10}{200} + \frac{3}{150}\right) = \frac{7}{20}$$

From question,

$$1 - \frac{n}{20} = \frac{7}{20}$$

$$\Rightarrow \frac{n}{20} = 1 - \frac{7}{20}$$

$n = 13$ days.

129. (D): Let sum invested in scheme A is x, then sum invested in scheme B is $(16000 - x)$

Interest = 3480

$$3480 = \frac{x \times 5 \times 3}{100} + \frac{(16000 - x) \times 8 \times 3}{100}$$

$$348000 = 15x + 16000 \times 24 - 24x$$

$$9x = 384000 - 348000$$

$$9x = 36000$$

$$x = 4000$$

Hence, Amount invested in scheme A = ₹ 4000

130. (D): Number of hats sold by M in January = 640

Number of hats sold by N in March and April together = 480 + 720 = 1200

Required per cent = $\frac{640}{1200} \times 100 = 53\frac{1}{3}\%$

131. (B): Average number of hats sold by N during January, March, May and June

$$= \frac{380 + 480 + 520 + 720}{4}$$

$$= 525$$

132. (E): Total number of hats sold by M and N together in March = 780 + 480 = 1260

Let number of Fedora hat = x

then number of Trilby hat = $1260 - x$

Required ratio = $\frac{x}{1260 - x} = \frac{9}{5}$

$$5x = 1260 \times 9 - 9x$$

$$14x = 1260 \times 9$$

$$x = \frac{1260 \times 9}{14} = 810$$

Hence, number of Fedora hat = 810.

133. (E): Total number of hats sold by M and N together in June

$$= 440 + 720 = 1160.$$

∴ Number of hat sold by M and N together in July

$$= 1160 \times \frac{115}{100} = 1334$$

134. (C): Percentage increase in hat selling from February to May

$$= \frac{660 - 400}{400} \times 100$$

$$= \frac{260}{400} \times 100 = 65\%$$

135. (A): Monthly salary of Dex's sister

$$= 4 \times 12800 = 51200$$

∴ Monthly salary of Dex

$$= \frac{51200 \times 5}{2} \times \frac{1}{4} = 32000$$

$$\frac{\text{saving}}{\text{expenses}} = \frac{3}{5} \Rightarrow \frac{\text{saving}}{\text{saving + expenses}} = \frac{3}{3+5} = \frac{3}{8}$$

$$\frac{\text{saving}}{\text{salary}} = \frac{3}{8} \Rightarrow \text{saving} = \frac{3}{8} \times \text{salary} = \frac{3}{8} \times 32000 = 12000$$

136. (B): Ratio of Milk and water in mixture = 60 : 40 = 3 : 2

Quantity of Milk left in mixture after 20 gm of mixture is taken out

$$= 60 \times \frac{3}{5} = 36 \text{ gm}$$

Quantity of water left = $60 \times \frac{2}{5}$ = 24 gm

∴ Required ratio = $\frac{36}{24 + 6}$ = 6 : 5.

137. (D): Let radius of sphere and cylinder is 'r'

So, volume of sphere = $\frac{4}{3}\pi r^3$

Volume of cylinder = Volume of sphere

$$\frac{4}{3}\pi r^3 = \pi r^2 h$$

$$h = \frac{4}{3}r$$

Total surface area of sphere = $4\pi r^2$

Total surface area of cylinder = $2\pi r(r + h)$

$$= 2\pi r\left(r + \frac{4}{3}r\right) = \frac{14}{3}\pi r^2$$

Required ratio = $\frac{4\pi r^2}{\frac{14}{3}\pi r^2} = \frac{6}{7} = 6 : 7.$

138. (B): Let investment of P, Q, R be $2x$, $5x$ and $7x$ respectively.

Let extra amount added by 'P' after six months be ₹ y

According to question

$$2x + y = \frac{1}{2}[5x + 7x]$$

$$2x + y = 6x$$
$$y = 4x$$

Ratio of profit share

$$P : Q : R = 2x \times 6 + (4x + 2x) \times 6 : 5x \times 12 : 7x \times 12$$
$$= 12x + 36x : 60x : 84x$$
$$= 48 : 60 : 84 = 4 : 5 : 7$$

Let the total profit = A

Then, Q's share in profit = 425

$$\Rightarrow \quad A \times \frac{5}{4+5+7} = 425$$

$$\Rightarrow \quad A = \frac{425 \times 16}{5}$$

$$\Rightarrow \quad A = 85 \times 16 = 1360$$

Hence, the total profit = ₹ 1360.

139. **(B):** Let C.P. of LED = ₹ $100x$

M.P. of LED = ₹ $160x$

$$\therefore \ 160x \times \frac{100 - 12\frac{1}{2}}{100} \times \frac{100-d}{100} \times \frac{100-25}{100} = 100x \times \frac{100-16}{100}$$

$$\Rightarrow 160x \times \frac{875}{1000} \times \frac{100-d}{100} \times \frac{75}{100} = 84x$$

$$\Rightarrow 160 \times \frac{35}{40} \times \frac{100-d}{100} \times \frac{3}{4} = 84$$

$$\Rightarrow 4 \times 35 \times \frac{100-d}{100} \times \frac{3}{4} = 84$$

$$\Rightarrow \quad 100 - d = 84 \times \frac{1}{35} \times \frac{1}{3} \times 100$$

$$\Rightarrow \quad 100 - d = 12 \times \frac{1}{5} \times \frac{1}{3} \times 100$$

$$\Rightarrow \quad 100 - d = 4 \times 20$$

$$\Rightarrow \quad 100 - d = 80$$

$$\Rightarrow \quad d = 100 - 80 = 20$$

Hence, $d = 20\%$.

140. **(D):** Speed of boat in still water = 12 kmph

Speed of Stream = x kmph

According to question

$$\frac{270}{(12-x)} = \left(100 + 66\frac{2}{3}\right)\% \text{ of } \frac{270}{12+x}$$

$$\Rightarrow \quad \frac{270}{12-x} = \left(1 + \frac{2}{3}\right) \times \frac{270}{12+x}$$

$$\Rightarrow \quad \frac{270}{12-x} = \frac{5}{3} \times \frac{270}{12+x}$$

$$\Rightarrow \quad (12 + x) \times 3 = 5 \times (12 \times x)$$

$$\Rightarrow \quad x = 3$$

So, speed of stream = x = 3 kmph.

141. **(B):** Total items B sold by store on Monday and Friday together

$$= \frac{240}{48} \times 32 + \frac{340}{68} \times 22$$
$$= 160 + 110 = 270$$

Total items C sold by store in Wednesday & Thursday together

$$= \frac{420}{35} \times 20 + \frac{360}{24} \times 20$$
$$= 240 + 300 = 540$$

$$\text{Required percentage} = \frac{540 - 270}{540} \times 100$$
$$= \frac{270}{540} \times 100 = 50\%.$$

142. **(C):** Average number of items B sold by store on Tuesday & Thursday

$$= \frac{\frac{320}{40} \times 48 + \frac{360}{24} \times 56}{2}$$

$$= \frac{384 + 840}{2} = 612$$

Average number of items A sold by store on Thursday & Friday

$$= \frac{360 + 340}{2} = \frac{720}{2} = 350$$

Required difference = 612 – 350 = 262.

143. **(A):** Total items B sold by store on Sunday

$$= \frac{360}{24} \times 56 \times \frac{125}{100} = 1050$$

Total items C sold by store on Sunday

$$= \frac{340}{68} \times 10 \times \frac{400}{100} = 200$$

Total items B & items C sold by store on Sunday = 1050 + 200 = 1250.

144. **(C):** Total items C sold on Wednesday

$$= \frac{420}{35} \times 20 = 240$$

Total items C sold on Monday & Tuesday together

$$= \frac{240}{48} \times 20 + \frac{320}{40} \times 12$$

$$= 100 + 96 = 196$$

$$\text{Required percentage} = \frac{240-196}{196} \times 100$$

$$= \frac{44}{196} \times 100$$

$$= 22\frac{22}{49}\% .$$

145. **(B):** $\text{Required ratio} = \dfrac{\dfrac{240}{48} \times 100}{\dfrac{360}{24} \times 100} = \dfrac{500}{1500} = 1 : 3.$

For Qs. No. 146 – 150.

According to given data:

Total number of female employee who represent A and B = 420 × 2 = 840

Let, Number of male employee who represent A = a

And, Number of male employee who represent B = b

According to question

$$a + b = 1620 \quad ...(i)$$

$$\frac{2}{3}a + \frac{2}{5}b = 840 \quad ...(ii)$$

On solving (i) & (ii)

$$a = 720, b = 900$$

Number of female employees who represent A

$$= \frac{2}{3} \times 720 = 480$$

Number of female employees who represent B

$$= \frac{2}{5} \times 900 = 360$$

Total Female employee who represent C

$$= 480 \times \frac{125}{100} = 600$$

Total male employee who represent C

$$= 360 \times \frac{4}{3} = 480$$

Companies	Male	Female
A	720	480
B	900	360
C	480	600

146. **(A):** Total employee who represent A

$$= 720 + 480 = 1200$$

$$\text{Required percentage} = \frac{1200-900}{900} \times 100 = 33\frac{1}{3}\% .$$

147. **(C):** Total employee who represent B & C who do not have MBA degree

$$= (900+480) \times \frac{80}{100} + (360+600) \times \frac{75}{100}$$

$$= 1104 + 720$$

$$= 1824.$$

148. **(C):** $\text{Required ratio} = \dfrac{(900+480)}{(480+600)} = 23 : 18.$

149. **(A):** Required difference = 480 – 360 = 120.

150. **(A):** $\text{Required average} = \dfrac{360+600}{2} = 480.$

MAIN EXAMINATION

PROFESSIONAL KNOWLEDGE (COMPUTER)

1. What is the full form of 'The EDVAC', the first generation computer?
A. The electronic discrete variable automatic computer
B. The electronic discrete variable automatic calculator
C. The electronic digital variable automatic computer
D. The electronic digital variable automatic calculator

2. What is the output of the code written in C?

```
void main()
{
int  k,   val=1;
k=  ++val*++val;
printf("%d",k);
}
```

A. 4 B. 1
C. 9 D. 16

3. Which one is the reserved word in C language?
A. Integer B. Volatile
C. Constant D. Automatic

4. The height of a tree is the length of the longest path from root to leaf. What is the maximum and minimum number of nodes in a binary tree of height 'n'?
A. $2^{n+1} - 1, n + 1$ B. $2^{n-1} - 1$
C. $2^{n-1}, n - 1$ D. $2^n, n + 1$

5. 2 Dimensional array (Matrices) with relatively high proportion of zero entries are called ______ while with low proportion of zero entries are called ______.
A. Regular Matrix; Non-Regular Matrix
B. Square Matrix; Dense Matrix
C. Transpose Matrix; Inverse Matrix
D. Sparse Matrix; Dense Matrix

6. How many interchanges will happen when the sequence of letters of "SORTED" is sorted using bubble sort?
A. 6 B. 36
C. 18 D. 11

7. Perverse Software is also known as ______.
A. application software
B. utility software
C. malicious software
D. diagnostic software

8. Which of the following is the feature(s) of High level programming languages?
I. Portability
II. Easy debugging
A. Only II B. Both I and II
C. Only I D. Neither I nor II

9. Which of the following are the key feature(s) of cloud computing?
I. Scalability
II. Self service
III. Pay-per-use
A. I and II B. I, II and III
C. I and III D. II and III

10. Which of the following is a non-positional number system?
A. Decimal B. Octal
C. Binary D. Roman

11. What is the function of Ctrl + T in MS Word?
A. Justify paragraph alignment
B. Hanging indent
C. Redo the last action
D. Undo last action

12. ______ mode allows transmission in both directions simultaneously.
A. Duplex B. Half simplex
C. Half duplex D. Simplex

13. Which of the following statement(s) is/are true about control unit?
I. It manages and coordinate the entire computer system.
II. It does not perform any actual processing on data.
A. Only I
B. Only II
C. Both I and II
D. Neither I nor II

14. Which of the following is a shortcut key to justify paragraph alignment in MS-Word?
A. Ctrl + S B. Ctrl + Y
C. Ctrl + I D. Ctrl + J

15. What will be the quotient when $(100001)_2$ is divided by $(110)_2$?
A. $(001)_2$ B. $(110)_2$
C. $(100)_2$ D. $(101)_2$

16. How many bits are required to represent $(1000)_{10}$ in BCD code?
A. 10 bits B. 16 bits
C. 32 bits D. 4 bits

17. Which of the following is/are the open-source software(s)?

I. PHP

II. Apache

A. Only II B. Only I

C. Both I and II D. Neither I nor II

18. Which of the following is/are true about little oh(o) asymptotic notation?

I. $f(x) = o(g(x))$ iff $f(x) = O(g(x))$

II. $f(x) = o(g(x))$ iff $f(x) \neq W(g(x))$

A. Only II B. Both I and II

C. Only I D. Neither I nor II

19. Which generation of computer used transistor?

A. Fourth B. Second

C. Third D. First

20. Which of the following statement(s) is/are true about binary search algorithm?

I. It is implemented on sorted array.

II. One must have direct access to the middle element in any sub-list.

III. It is implemented on sorted linked list.

A. I, II and III B. I and III

C. II and III D. I and II

21. Which of the following pair is correct?

I. RTL - Saturated bipolar logic family

II. ECL - Non-Saturated bipolar logic family

A. Only II B. Neither I nor II

C. Both I and II D. Only I

22. How many NOR gates are used to get AND gate from them?

A. 4 B. 3

C. 1 D. 2

23. ______ describes the process of deciding about putting data to different sites in distributed database system.

A. Data allocation B. Data mining

C. Data sharing D. Data storing

24. Which of the following is a Comparison operator in Structured Query Language?

A. + B. >=

C. / D. *

25. Which of the following is an alternative to the log-based recovery schemes in database recovery system?

A. Demand paging B. Prepaging

C. Shadow paging D. Defragmentation

26. ______ is a unique identifier created by database management system to identify the relative starting time of a transaction.

A. Shadow paging B. Spoofing

C. Deadlock D. Timestamp

27. In a JK flip flop, if J = K, then resulting flip flop is ______.

A. D B. SR

C. Clocked SR D. T

28. Which of the following is NOT a variant of time stamp-based method of concurrency control in database management system?

A. Multilevel time stamp ordering

B. Multi version time stamp ordering

C. Partial time stamp ordering

D. Total time stamp ordering

29. What is the meaning of this arithmetic micro-operation?

A. Content of R1 plus the 2's complement of R2 transferred to R3

B. Content of R1 plus R2 after increments transferred to R3

C. Content of R1 plus the 1's complement of R2 transferred to R3

D. Content of R1 plus R2 transferred to R3

30. ______ is a technique of breaking up database into logical units, which may be assigned for storage at the various sites in distributed database system.

A. Data fragmentation B. Data mining

C. Data normalization D. Data binding

31. In a stack, if a user tries to remove an element from an empty stack, it is called:

A. Underflow B. Empty collection

C. Overflow D. Garbage collection

32. Inheritance allows the following in C++ program:

A. Class Re-usability

B. Creating a hierarchy of classes

C. Extendibility

D. All options are correct

33. Which is the step in waterfall model that involves a meeting with the customer to understand the requirements?

A. Requirement Gathering

B. SRS

C. Implementation

D. Customer review

34. The PowerPoint view that displays only text-title and bullets is:

A. Outline view B. Notes page view

C. Slide sorter D. Slide show

35. Which is *not* the right approach of incremental testing approach?

A. Big bang approach

B. Top-down approach

C. Functional incrimination

D. Bottom-up approach

Institute of Banking Personnel Selection

IBPS–Specialist (IT) Officer Scale-I

Preliminary & Main Exam 2019-20*

Preliminary Exam held on - 29-12-2019

Main Exam held on - 25-01-2020

PRELIMINARY EXAMINATION

REASONING

Directions (Qs. 1 to 5): *Read the following information carefully and answer the questions given below.*

L, M, N, O, P, Q and R are seven employees who are working in the same company. They attend meeting in different department viz; Administrative, Security, Finance and HR department on different days from Monday to Sunday but not necessarily in the same order. One employee attends only one meeting and only one meeting is held on each day. There are two employees who attend meeting in administrative, security, HR department and only one employee attends meeting in Finance department.

L attends meeting on Thursday. There are two persons who attend meeting between L and the person who attends meeting in HR department. There are three persons who attend meeting between the persons who attend meeting in Administrative department and the one who attends meeting in Finance department. The one who attends meeting in administrative department attends before the one who attends in finance department. The one who attends meeting in finance department does not attend on Saturday. The number of persons who attend meeting between L and the one who attend meeting in finance department is same as the number of persons who attend meeting between O and the one who attends meeting in security department. The one who attends meeting in security department attend before O. O does not attend meeting in HR department. Q attends meeting on the day immediately before the day on which L attends meeting. O does not attend meeting on the day just after the day on which L attends meeting. The number of persons who attend meeting between L and P is same as the number of persons who attend meeting between L and R. P attends meeting in one of the day before the day on which R attends meeting. N attends meeting in administrative department. R does not attend meeting in security department.

1. Who among the following person attend meeting on Friday?

A. O　　B. M
C. P　　D. N
E. R

2. Which of the following combinations of "Person – Day"is true with respect to the given arrangement?

A. R – Friday　　B. M – Saturday
C. Q – Thursday　　D. P – Friday
E. P – Tuesday

3. L attends meeting in which of the following department?

A. Security　　B. HR
C. Administrative　　D. Finance
E. Either (A) or (B)

4. In this arrangement, Q is related to Monday, L is related to Security then N is related to?

A. Thursday
B. Wednesday
C. None of the given options is true
D. HR
E. Sunday

5. How`many persons attend meeting between P and O?

A. 3　　B. 4
C. 2　　D. 1
E. None of these

Directions (Qs. 6 to 10): *In these questions, a relationship between different elements is shown in the statements. The statements are followed by two conclusions. Give answer:*

A. If only conclusion I is true
B. If only conclusion II is true
C. If either conclusion I or II is true
D. If neither conclusion I nor II is true
E. If both conclusions I and II are true

6. Statements: $L > I = N > P$;
$I \geq R > K$; $N \leq E < Z$

Conclusions: I. $E > P$　II. $R < L$

7. Statements: $L > I = N > P$;
$I \geq R > K$; $N \leq E < Z$

Conclusions: I. $K > N$　II. $I < Z$

* *Based on Memory*

8. Statements: $S > A = N \geq D$; $A \geq L > E$; $M \leq L \leq D$

Conclusions: I. $S > E$ II. $L < S$

9. Statements: $S > A = N \geq D$; $A \geq L > E$; $M \leq L \leq D$

Conclusions: I. $A > M$ II. $A = M$

10. Statements: $P \geq V \geq R \leq E < Y$; $G \geq E > N$

Conclusions: I. $P > N$ II. $G \geq Y$

Directions (Qs. 11 to 15): *Study the following information and answer the given questions:*

A, B, C, D, E, F, G & H are eight friends and sitting around a circular table but not necessarily in same order. Some of them are facing inside and some of them are facing outside. A sits third to right of H. There is two people sits between H and B. C sits second to left of B. There is three people sits between B and E. D is second to left of F, who is not immediate neighbour of A. Immediate neighbours of H faces same direction as H. F sits third to left of A, who faces centre. The immediate neighbours of A face opposite to the direction of A.

11. Who is sitting third to right of F?
A. C B. B
C. A D. E
E. D

12. Who is facing inside?
A. AD B. AGH
C. AB D. ADC
E. None of these

13. Who sits opposite to H?
A. A B. D
C. F D. E
E. G

14. How many people are sitting between C and B, when counted from left of C?
A. Two B. Three
C. One D. Four
E. Five

15. Who is sitting exactly between D and C when counted from right of D?
A. HE B. CE
C. FH D. BF
E. DF

Directions (Qs. 16 to 20): *Study the following information carefully and answer the questions:*

Ten persons are sitting in 2 parallel rows containing 5 persons in each row. In 1st row M, N, O, P and Q are seated and are facing south. In 2nd row, U, V, X, Y and Z are seated and are facing north. Therefore in the given seating arrangement, each member seated in a row faces another member of the other row. They like different colours Red, Orange, Blue, Brown, Black, White, Yellow, Pink, Peach, and Grey (not necessarily in same order).

M doesn't like brown and P likes black. Y sits third to the left of U, who likes yellow. M faces immediate neighbour of Y, who likes orange. The one who likes peach sits at extreme end. O sits second to the right of M. The one who likes red faces the one who likes pink but M doesn't like pink. Only one person sits between N and P. V and Z are immediate neighbours. Z does not face M and N, who doesn't like grey. The one who faces U likes white. The one who faces an immediate neighbour of Y likes brown.

16. How many persons are seated between N and the one who likes white?
A. None B. One
C. Two D. Three
E. None of these

17. Who amongst the following faces P?
A. U
B. The one who likes pink
C. X
D. N
E. The one who likes grey

18. Which of the following is true regarding M?
A. N and X are immediate neighbours of M
B. M sits at one of the extreme ends of the line
C. M likes black
D. P sits immediate left of M
E. None of these

19. Who amongst the following pair sits exactly in the middle of the rows?
A. M, Z B. P, Y
C. None of these D. U, N
E. M, V

20. V likes which of the following colour?
A. Brown B. Pink
C. Black D. White
E. None of these

Directions (Qs. 21 to 25): *In each of the questions below are given three statements followed by two conclusions numbered I & II. You have to take the given statements to be true even if they seem to be at variance with commonly known facts. Read all the conclusions and then decide which of the given conclusions logically follows from the given statements disregarding commonly known facts.*

Give answer:
A. If only conclusion I is true
B. If only conclusion II is true
C. If either conclusion I or II is true
D. If neither conclusion I nor II is true
E. If both conclusions I and II are true

21. Statements : All remarks are feedbacks.
Some feedbacks are words.
No word is a digit.

Conclusions:
I. Some feedbacks are definitely not digits.
II. All digits being feedbacks is a possibility.

22. Statements : All remarks are feedbacks.
Some feedbacks are words.
No word is a digit.

Conclusions:
I. All remarks being words is a possibility.
II. At least some remarks are digits.

23. Statements : Some files are boxes.
All boxes are cartons.
No carton is a/plastic.

Conclusions:
I. No file is a plastic.
II. Some files are plastics.

24. Statements : Some desks are chairs.
Some chairs are seats.
No seat is a table.

Conclusions:
I. All desks can never be tables.
II. Some chairs are definitely not tables.

25. Statements : All routes are ways.
All ways are paths.
Some ways are bridges.

Conclusions:
I. At least some bridges are routes.
II. All routes being bridges is a possibility.

26. How Many such pairs of letters are there in the word **'TRANSFER'**, each of which has as many letters between them in the word as they have between them in the English alphabet?
A. None
B. One
C. Three
D. More than three
E. Two

27. What should come in place of question mark (?) in the following series based on the above arrangement?
BED EIG HMJ KQM ?
A. PUN B. OUQ
C. NUQ D. NUP
E. NUR

Directions (Qs. 28 and 29): *Read the following information carefully to answer the given questions.*

R is the sister of Q. M is the father of R. V is the son of Q. C is the maternal grandfather of V. M does not have married daughter.

28. How is R related to V?
A. Uncle
B. Aunt
C. Mother
D. Can't be determined
E. Nephew

29. If B is married to Q, then how is B related to M?
A. Grandson B. Son-in-law
C. Son D. Daughter-in-law
E. Can't be determined

Directions (Qs. 30 to 32): *Read the following information carefully to answer the given questions.*

A certain number of persons are seated in a row. The Row is arranged in a vertical manner and all are facing to north direction. Ranjan sits fourth from the left end of the row. There are two persons sit between Ranjan and Seema. Puja sits immediate right of Seema. There are as many persons sit between Puja and Seema as sit between Dinesh and Pooja. Dinesh does not sit to the left of Ranjan.

30. How many persons sit between Ranjan and Dinesh?
A. 3 B. None
C. 5 D. 4
E. 1

31. What is the position of Puja with respect to Ranjan?
A. Immediate right B. Third to the left
C. None of these D. Second to the left
E. Fourth to the right

32. How many persons sit in a row?
A. 4 B. 6
C. 0 D. 11
E. 9

Directions (Qs. 33 to 35): *Read the following information carefully to answer the given questions.*

There are six persons S, T, U, V, W and X, who got different marks in the examination. S got more marks than only U and X. T got less marks than W, who did not get the highest marks in the examination. The Second highest person got 92 marks.

33. How many persons got more marks than U?
A. Four
B. Two
C. Five
D. Can't be determined
E. One

34. If S got 69 marks and U got 68 marks, then which of the following statement is true?
A. X got the lower marks
B. U got the fifth highest marks
C. Five persons got more marks than X
D. All are true
E. X got 66 marks is a possibility

35. V got which of the following possible score?
A. 85 B. 66
C. 92 D. 89
E. 94

Directions (Qs. 36-40): *Study the following information carefully and answer the questions given below:*

In a certain code language,
'festival for woman only' is written as 'pa ge bo xu'
'provide peace to women' is written as 'wr dl nj ge'
'women like to celebrate' is written as 'ge ct fx wr'
'celebrate peace in festival' is written as 'dl bo sv ct'
(All codes are two letter codes only)

36. What may be the possible code for 'provide idea' in the given code language?
A. fx hy B. xu bo
C. hy nj D. nj xu
E. wr fx

37. What is the code for 'celebrate' in the given code language?
A. ct B. wr
C. sv D. dl
E. fx

38. In the given code language what does the code 'pa' stand for?
A. peace
B. either 'for' or 'only'
C. either 'women' or 'to'
D. celebrate
E. festival

39. What is the code for 'women' in the given code language?
A. bo
B. xu
C. ct
D. Other than those given as options
E. ge

40. If 'peace to mind' is coded as 'zg wr dl' in the given code language, then what is the code for 'mind in festival'?
A. zg bo dl B. dl zg sv
C. zg nj wr D. bo sv zg
E. sv wr bo

Directions (Qs. 41-45): *In each of the following questions relationship between different elements is shown in the statements. The statements are followed by two Conclusions numbered I and II. Study the Conclusions based on the given statements and select the appropriate answer.*

Give answer—
A. if only Conclusion II is true
B. if only Conclusion I is true
C. if both the Conclusion I and Conclusion II are true
D. if either Conclusion I or Conclusion II is true
E. if neither Conclusion I nor Conclusion II is true

(41-42): Statements: $S \leq L \leq I = P \geq E > R; L > Q$

41. Conclusions: I. $P \geq S$ II. $I > R$

42. Conclusions: I. $L < R$ II. $E \geq Q$

(43-44): Statements: $G > R \geq E = A \leq T \leq S$; $D \leq A \leq J$

43. Conclusions: I. $T \geq D$ II. $R > S$

44. Conclusions: I. $J > E$ II. $J = E$

45. Statements: $A \geq B > C \leq D \leq E < F$

Conclusions: I. $A \geq E$ II. $C < F$

Directions (Qs. 46-50): *Study the following information carefully and answer the questions given below:*

Ten person — J, K, L, M, N, O, P, Q, R and S — are sitting around a circular table facing the centre with equal distances between each other (but not necessarily in the same order). Each one of them is also related to M in some way or the other.

Only two persons sit between Q and L. M sits second to the left of Q. Only three persons sit between L and M's sister. M's son sits second to the right of M's sister. Only one person sits between M's son and S. J sits to the immediate right of R. R is neither the son nor the mother of M. S is an immediate neighbour of M's mother. Only three persons sit between M's mother and M's brother. M's daughter sits second to the left of M's brother.

M's father is not an immediate neighbour of M. M's wife sites third to the right of K. L is to the right of Q. Only four persons sits between M and M's father.

46. Who sits second to the right of R?
A. M's brother
B. M
C. R
D. N
E. M's daughter

47. How many persons sit between K and L, when counted from the left of K?
A. Six B. One
C. None D. Two
E. Four

48. Which of the following statements is true with respect to the given information?
A. R sits second to the right of M's wife.
B. K is an immediate neighbour of R.
C. M sits second to the left of L.
D. All the given options are true.
E. S is the daughter of L.

49. How is K related to R?
A. Son-in-law B. Uncle
C. Brother D. Niece
E. Daughter

50. Who amongst the following is the wife of M?
A. J B. L
C. O D. Q
E. N

QUANTITATIVE APTITUDE

Directions (Qs. No. 51-55): *Line chart given below shows number of labours (men and women) working in six different years. Study the data carefully and answer the following questions.*

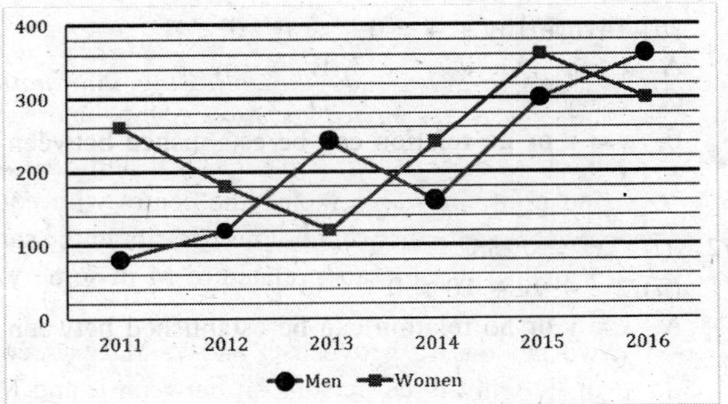

51. Total number of Men working in 2012 and 2013 together is what per cent of the total number of labours (Men + Women) working in 2014?
A. 60% B. 70%
C. 80% D. 90%
E. 40%

52. Average number of Women working in 2014, 2015 and 2016 together is how much more/less than average number of Men working in 2011, 2014 and 2016 together?
A. 100 B. 80
C. 90 D. 70
E. None of the given options

53. Number of Men working in 2017 is 15% more than that of 2015 while number of Women working in 2017 is 40% less than that of 2014. Find total number of labours (Men + Women) working in 2017?
A. 561 B. 456
C. 489 D. 594
E. 630

54. Find the ratio between total number of Labours working in 2012 and 2013 together to total number of labours working in 2015 and 2016 together?
A. 2 : 1 B. 1 : 2
C. 35 : 66 D. 11 : 10
E. None of the given options

55. Total number of Men working in all six years is how much more/less than total number of Women working in all six years together?
A. None of the given options
B. 140
C. 160
D. 180
E. 200

Directions (Qs. No. 56-61): *Find the wrong number in the following number series:*

56. 4, 5.1, 7.3, 10.6, 15, 20, 27.1
A. 5.1 B. 4
C. 7.3 D. 20
E. 27.1

57. 2, 3, 8, 31, 154, 924, 6460
A. 924 B. 6460
C. 154 D. 8
E. 31

58. 251, 252, 254, 227, 243, 118, 154
A. 251 B. 252
C. 227 D. 243
E. 154

59. 141, 156, 147, 162, 153, 165, 159
A. 156 B. 153
C. 147 D. 165
E. 159

60. 2, 6, 10, 19, 36, 69, 134
A. 134 B. 69
C. 6 D. 2
E. 10

61. 0.5, 2, 1, 4, 32, 512, 16384
A. 1 B. 2
C. 4 D. 32
E. 512

62. Ratio of present ages of A and B is 16 : 7. After 12 years, A's age is twice of B's age, then find present ages of A and B?
A. 64 year; 28 year B. 80 year; 35 year
C. None of these D. 96 year; 42 year
E. 102 year; 49 year

63. A man invested a certain sum in scheme A at 15% p.a. for 2 years and earned ₹ 1950 as simple interest. He increased his sum by ₹ 'x' and invested in another scheme B at 10% p.a. C.I. for 2 years and received ₹ 1680 as compound interest. Find the value of 'x'?
A. ₹ 1750 B. ₹ 1500
C. ₹ 1250 D. None of these
E. ₹ 1850

64. In a class there are 30 girls and 15 boys and total average weight of class is $47\frac{7}{15}$ kg. Total average weight of boys is 58 kg. Find the approximate average weight of girls?
A. 32 kg B. 42 kg
C. 52 kg D. 35 kg
E. 50 kg

65. Ram bought a bike at 20% discount on MRP. After 1 year Ram sell the bike to Ramesh at 10% loss. After 1 year more Ramesh sell the bike at 20% profit to Ranjan. If Ranjan paid ₹ 1,29,600, then find the M.R.P. of the bike?

A. ₹ 1,50,000
B. ₹ 2,25,000
C. ₹ 1,40,000
D. ₹ 2,00,000
E. ₹ 1,80,000

Directions (Qs. No. 66-70): *There are 450 coupons which can be used in Pedicure and Hair cutting. Ratio between Males to Females who use their coupons in Hair cutting is 13 : 7. Number of males who use their coupons in Pedicure is 72 more than number of females who use their coupon in Hair cutting. Total number of males who use their coupon in Pedicure and Hair cutting together is 174 more than total number of females who use their coupon in Pedicure and Hair cutting together.*

66. Males who use their coupon in Pedicure is what per cent of the Males who use their coupons in Hair cutting?

A. 200%
B. 100%
C. None of the given options
D. 0%
E. 150%

67. Find the ratio between total number persons who use their coupons in Pedicure to total number of persons who use their coupons in Hair cutting?

A. 52 : 23
B. None of the given options
C. 8 : 9
D. 8 : 7
E. 7 : 8

68. Females who use their coupon in Hair cutting is how much more than Females who use their coupon in Pedicure?

A. 15
B. 45
C. 30
D. None of the given options
E. 60

69. Out of males who use their coupons in Hair cutting, 25% belongs to city A, then find number of males who use their coupons in Hair cutting which doesn't belongs to city A?

A. None of the given options
B. 108
C. 126
D. 117
E. 135

70. Ratio between Males who use their coupon in Pedicure to that of in Spa is 4 : 5, while ratio between Females who use their coupon in Hair cutting to that of in Spa is 6 : 11. Find total number of people who use their coupons in Spa?

A. 349
B. 481
C. 300
D. 440
E. None of the given options

Directions (Qs. No. 71-76): *In each of these questions, two equations (i) and (ii) are given, you have to solve both the equations and give answer accordingly.*

71. (*i*) $2x^2 + 9x + 9 = 0$
(*ii*) $15y^2 + 16y + 4 = 0$

A. $x > y$
B. $x < y$
C. $x \geq y$
D. $x \leq y$
E. $x = y$ or no relation can be established between x & y.

72. (*i*) $2x^3 = \sqrt{256}$
(*ii*) $2y^2 - 9y + 10 = 0$

A. $x = y$ or no relation can be established between x & y.
B. $x < y$
C. $x \leq y$
D. $x \geq y$
E. $x > y$

73. (*i*) $6x^2 - 11x + 4 = 0$
(*ii*) $3y^2 - 5y + 2 = 0$

A. $x \leq y$
B. $x < y$
C. $x \geq y$
D. $x > y$
E. $x = y$ or no relation can be established between x & y.

74. (*i*) $3x^2 + 11x + 10 = 0$
(*ii*) $2y^2 + 11y + 14 = 0$

A. $x \geq y$
B. $x \leq y$
C. $x > y$
D. $x < y$
E. $x = y$ or no relation can be established between x & y.

75. (*i*) $12x^2 + 11x + 2 = 0$
(*ii*) $12y^2 + 7y + 1 = 0$

A. $x \geq y$
B. $x = y$ or no relation can be established between x & y.
C. $x < y$
D. $x \leq y$
E. $x > y$

76. (*i*) $21x^2 + 10x + 1 = 0$
(*ii*) $24y^2 + 26y + 5 = 0$

A. $x \leq y$
B. $x = y$ or no relation can be established between x & y.
C. $x \geq y$
D. $x > y$
E. $x < y$

77. 'A' can complete a work in 20 days while B is 25% more efficient than 'A'. B worked for 6 days and left, remaining work is completed by 'C' in 15 days. Find in how many days 'C' can complete the whole work alone?

A. 27 days
B. 21 days
C. 18 days
D. 24 days
E. 30 days

78. A man travels from Point P to Q with 90 km/hr and from Q to R with 60 km/hr. Total distance between P to R is 200 km. If his average speed is 75 km/hr then find the distance between P and Q?

A. 80 km
B. 120 km
C. 100 km
D. 150 km
E. None of the given options

79. A mixture contains wine and water in the ratio 5 : 1. On adding 5 litre of water, the ratio of wine to water becomes 5 : 2. The quantity of wine in the mixture is?

A. 20 *l*
B. 22 *l*
C. 24 *l*
D. 26 *l*
E. None of these

80. The average salary of the entire staff in an office is ₹ 3200 per month. The average salary of officers is ₹ 6800 and that of non-officers is ₹ 2000. If the number of officers is 5, then find the number of non-officers in the office?

A. 8
B. 12
C. 15
D. 5
E. None of these

Directions (Qs. No. 81-85): *Given bar graph shows the number of plain books and lined books (in hundreds) available at three different stores and the table shows the percentage of total books (Plain + lined) that was sold by different stores.*

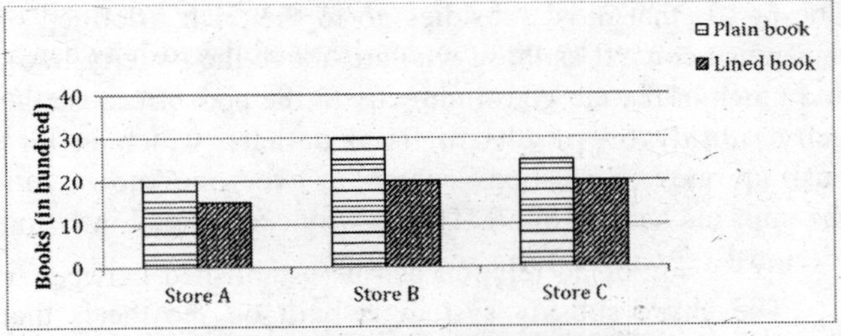

Stores	% of sold books
A	20%
B	40%
C	30%

81. The number of plain books sold by store A and store B was 30% and 40% respectively then find number of lined books sold by store A and store B together is what per cent of total books available at store A?

A. $22\frac{6}{7}\%$
B. $23\frac{4}{7}\%$
C. $25\frac{5}{7}\%$
D. 25%
E. None of these

82. Average of total books sold by stores B and C together is how much more than total unsold books of store A?

A. 1125
B. 1075
C. 1055
D. 1175
E. 1225

83. Ratio of sold plain and lined books for store C is 5 : 4 and for store B is 3 : 2. Then find the total plain books sold by these two stores together?

A. 1750
B. 1825
C. 1850
D. 1950
E. 1975

84. Unsold books of store A is approximately is what per cent more or less than total unsold books of store B and C together?

A. 48%
B. 54%
C. 59%
D. 52%
E. 57%

85. Selling price of each plain books and lined books sold by store B is ₹ 250 and ₹ 175 respectively. Then, find the total amount earned by store B on selling these books if 60% of lined books are sold by the store?

A. ₹ 2.5 lac
B. ₹ 3.6 lac
C. ₹ 3.5 lac
D. ₹ 3.8 lac
E. ₹ 4.1 lac

86. Find the probability that a number from 1 to 300 is divisible by 3 or 7?

A. $\frac{37}{75}$
B. $\frac{32}{75}$
C. $\frac{36}{75}$
D. $\frac{28}{75}$
E. $\frac{26}{75}$

87. 14 men can do a work in 18 days, 15 women can do a work in 24 days. If 14 men work for first three days and 10 women work after that for three days find the part of work left after that?

A. 3/4
B. 1/4
C. 1/2
D. 1/6
E. 1/5

88. Perimeter of a rectangle is x and circumference of a circle is 8 more than the perimeter of the rectangle. Ratio of radius of circle and length of the rectangle is 1 : 2 and ratio of length and breadth of rectangle is 7 : 3. Find the length of the rectangle?

A. 14
B. 21
C. 28
D. 35
E. 7

89. A invest on some scheme at 5% and B at 3% for two year. If the total sum invested by A and B is 4000 and the simple interest received by both is same then find the amount invested by A?

A. 1300
B. 1500
C. 2500
D. 2700
E. 2100

90. Two trains crosses each other in 14 sec when they are moving in opposite direction, and when they are moving in same direction they crosses each other in 3 minute 2 sec. Find the speed of the faster train by what per cent more than the speed of the slower train?

A. 16.67% B. 17.33%
C. 16.33% D. 17.67%
E. 18.33%

Directions (Qs. 91 to 95): *What will come in place of the question mark (?) in the following number series?*

91. 11 20 38 74 ?

A. 146 B. 154
C. 128 D. 132
E. 136

92. 15 21 38 65 101 ?

A. 124 B. 145
C. 136 D. 158
E. 162

93. 24 28 19 35 10 ?

A. 26 B. 36
C. 16 D. 46
E. 15

94. 7 16 45 184 915 ?

A. 2092 B. 5496
C. 1048 D. 4038
E. 3268

95. 12 19 35 59 90 ?

A. 134 B. 127
C. 132 D. 98
E. 114

Directions (Qs. 96 to 100): *In each of these questions, two equations (I) and (II) are given. You have to solve both the equations and give answer.*

A. if $x > y$
B. if $x \geq y$
C. if $x < y$
D. if $x \leq y$
E. if $x = y$ or relationship between x and y cannot be established.

96. I. $3x^2 - 22x + 7 = 0$
II. $y^2 - 15y + 56 = 0$

97. I. $2x^2 - 17x + 36 = 0$
II. $2y^2 - 19y + 44 = 0$

98. I. $x - \sqrt{169} = 0$
II. $y^2 - 169 = 0$

99. I. $3x^2 + 20x + 25 = 0$
II. $3y^2 + 14y + 8 = 0$

100. I. $3x^2 + 5x + 2 = 0$
II. $3y^2 + 18y + 24 = 0$

GENERAL ENGLISH

Directions (Qs. 101-107): *Read the following passage carefully and answer the questions given below it.*

Governments looking for easy popularity have frequently been tempted into announcing give-a-ways of all sorts; free electricity, virtually free water, subsidized food, cloth at half price, and so on. The subsidy culture has gone to extremes. The richest farmers in the country get subsidized fertilizers. University education, typically accessed by the wealthier sections, is charged at a fraction of cost. Postal services are subsidized, and so are railway services. Bus fares cannot be raised to economical levels because there will be violent protest, so bus travel is subsidized too. In the past, price control on a variety of items, from steel to cement, meant that industrial consumer of these items got them at less than actual cost, while the losses of the public sector companies that produced them were borne by the taxpayer! A study done a few years ago, came to the conclusion that subsidies in the Indian economy total as much as 14.5 per cent of gross domestic product. At today's level, that would work out to about ₹ 1,50,000 crore.

And who pay the bill? The theory—and the political fiction on the basis of which it is sold to unsuspecting voters is that subsidies go to the poor, and are paid for by the rich. The fact is that most subsidies go to the 'rich' (defined in the Indian context as those who are above the poverty line), and much of the tab goes indirectly to the poor. Because the lefty subsidy bill results in fiscal deficits, which in turn push up rates of inflation—which, as everyone knows, hits the poor the hardest of all. That is why taxmen call inflation the most regressive form of taxation.

The entire subsidy system is built on the thesis that people cannot help themselves, therefore governments must do so. That people cannot afford to pay for variety of goods and services, and therefore the government must step in. This thesis has been applied not just in the poor countries but in the rich ones as well; hence the birth of the welfare state in the west, and an almost Utopian social security system; free medical care, food aid, old age security, et.al. But with the passage of time, most of the wealthy nations have discovered that their economies cannot sustain this social safety net, which in fact reduces the desire among people to pay their own way, and takes away some of the incentive to work, in short, the bill was unaffordable, and their societies were simply not willing to pay. To the regret of many, but because of the laws of economies are harsh, most Western societies have been busy pruning the welfare bill.

In India, the lessons of this experience over several decades, and in many countries—do not seem to have been learnt or they are simply ignored in the pursuit of immediate votes. People who are promised cheap food or clothing do not in most cases look beyond the gift horses—to the question of who picks up the tab. The uproar over higher petrol, diesel and cooking gas prices ignored this basic question; if the user of cooking gas does not want to pay for its cost, who should pay? Diesel in the country is subsidised, and if the user of diesel does not want to pay for its full cost, who does he or she think should pay the balance of the cost? It is a simple question, nevertheless if remains unasked.

The Deva Gowda government has shown some courage in biting the bullet when it comes to the price of petroleum products. But it has been bitten by much bigger subsidy bug. It wants to offer food at half its cost to everyone below the poverty line, supposedly estimated at some 380 million people. What will be the cost? And of course, who will pick up the tab? The Andhra Pradesh Government has been bankrupted by selling rice at ₹ 2 per kg. Should the Central Government be bankrupted too, before facing up to the question of what is affordable and what is not? Already, India is perennially short of power because the subsidy on electricity has bankrupted most electricity boards, and made private investment wary unless it gets all manner of state guarantees. Delhi's subsidised bus fares have bankrupted the Delhi Transport Corporation, whose buses have slowly disappeared from the capital's streets. It is easy to be soft and sentimental, by looking at programmes that will be popular. After all, who does not like a free lunch? But the evidence is surely mounting that the lunch isn't free at all. Somebody is paying the bill. And if you want to know who, take at the country's poor economic performance over the years.

101. Which of the following should not be subsidised over the years?

A. University education
B. Postal services
C. Steel
D. Other than those given as options
E. All of the above options

102. The statement that 'subsidies are paid by the rich and go to the poor' is:

A. fiction
B. fact
C. fact, according to the author
D. fiction, according to the author
E. Other than those given as options

103. Why do you think that the author calls the Western social security system Utopian?

A. The countries belief in the efficacy of the system was bound to turn out to be false.
B. The system followed by these countries is the best available in the present context.
C. Everything under this system was supposed to be free but people were charging money for them.
D. The theory of system followed by these countries was devised by Dr. Utopia.
E. All the options are responsible

104. It can be inferred from the passage that the author

A. believes that people can help themselves and do not need the government.
B. believes that the theory of helping with subsidy is very destructive.
C. believes in democracy and free speech.
D. is not a successful politician.
E. believes that subsidies are the best way to help poor.

105. Which of the following is not a victim of extreme subsidies?

A. The poor
B. The Delhi Transport Corporation
C. The Andhra Pradesh Government
D. Other than those given as options
E. The rich

106. Which of the following is not true in the context of the passage?

A. Where subsidies are concerned, the poor ultimately pay the tab.
B. Inflation is caused by too much subsidies.
C. Experts call subsidies the most regressive form of taxation.
D. Fiscal deficits are caused due to heavy subsidy bills.
E. None of the following is true in the context of the passage.

107. A suitable title to the passage would be:

A. There's no such thing as a free lunch
B. The Economic Overview
C. Deva Gowda's Government and its Follies
D. It takes Two to Tango
E. The Rich and the Poor: Extreme Partiality

Directions (Qs. 108 to 112): *Rearrange the following Six sentences (a), (b), (c), (d), (e) and (f) in the proper sequence to form a meaningful paragraph and then answer the questions given below.*

(*a*) It is the only country in the world that is carbon negative, which means it produces more oxygen than it consumes.
(*b*) Bhutan, sandwiched between the two most populous nations on Earth, suffers for their sins.
(*c*) So far, so good. But then, two things happened.
(*d*) Carbon sinks, 70% forest cover, powered almost entirely by mountain streams—Bhutan is a poster child for green living.
(*e*) Glaciers are beginning to melt, flash floods and heavy rains—and even droughts—are common, and temperatures are climbing.
(*f*) One, India and China got richer.

108. Which of the following should be the First sentence of the given paragraph?

A. (*e*) B. (*d*)
C. (*c*) D. (*b*)
E. (*a*)

109. Which of the following should be the Third sentence of the given paragraph?

A. (*a*) B. (*b*)
C. (*c*) D. (*d*)
E. (*e*)

110. Which of the following should be the Last sentence of the given paragraph?

A. (*a*) B. (*d*)
C. (*c*) D. (*b*)
E. (*e*)

111. Which of the following should be the Fourth sentence of the given paragraph?

A. (*f*) B. (*c*)
C. (*b*) D. (*e*)
E. (*d*)

112. Which of the following should be the Second sentence of the given paragraph?

A. (*b*) B. (*d*)
C. (*a*) D. (*c*)
E. (*e*)

Directions (Qs. 113 to 120): *In the following brief passage, some of the words have been left out. First read the passage over and try to understand what it is about. Then fill in the blanks with the help of the alternatives given.*

Big ideas come from tackling __(113)__ problems. When one is confronted with an overwhelming task, it's pieces. Business jargon is full of phrases about that, like "pilot projects" and "low-hanging fruit." They have their place, but in the repertory of management __(114)__, they should share their place with bold approaches to big challenges. Much of today's most valuable management knowledge came from wrestling with such issues. The most complicated workplace in the middle of the last century was the automobile assembly plant. Drawn to its complexity where Peter F. Drucker, W. Edwards Deming, and Taiichi Ohno, among others. The work they and their disciples did, applied in industry after industry, is the basis of the best that we know about operations, managing people, innovation, organizational design, and much more.

The most complex workplaces are tertiary care hospitals. These vast__(115)__employ tens of thousands of people who, under one roof, do everything from neurosurgery to laundry. Each patient – that is to say, each "job" — calls on a different set of people with a different constellation of__(116)__; even when the two patients have the same diagnosis, success may be__(117)__ differently. This is complexity of an order of magnitude greater than automobile assembly, and anyone who__(118)__hospitalized knows that management has thus far been unequl to the scope of task. The workers, managers, consultants, and scholars __(119)__ crack this nut will reshape industries and institutions just as__(120)__as Drucker, Deming, and Ohno did.

113. A. small B. big
C. irrelevant D. buildings
E. minor

114. A. weakness B. strength
C. power D. practice
E. symptom

115. A. houses B. institute
C. demagogue D. forts
E. enterprises

116. A. barbarity B. talent
C. skills D. unskilled
E. barbaric

117. A. managed B. officious
C. delivered D. measured
E. postponed

118. A. are been B. have being
C. have been D. has been
E. is be

119. A. who B. whom
C. whose D. which
E. whomsoever

120. A. profoundly B. gradually
C. superficially D. speciously
E. earnest

Directions (Qs. 121 to 130): *Identify the error in the sentences given below, if there is no error, click option (E).*

121. A. The need to set up
B. a good library in the locality
C. has been in the minds of people
D. for some time now.
E. No error

122. A. Most people would have
B. attended the union meeting
C. if they had
D. had longer notice of it.
E. No error

123. A. He took to
B. reading Times
C. for better knowledge
D. of the facts.
E. No error

124. A. When children have difficulty understanding
B. a certain mathematical process, it is often because
C. their teachers do not understand it conceptually
D. themselves and do not present it in a way that children can understand.
E. No error

125. A. Studies show that the lives of millions of mothers
B. and their children could be saved if countries would
C. invest in programs that ensures a healthy pregnancy,
D. and safe childbirth.
E. No error

126. A. Film viewers claim that
B. the number of scenes depicting alcohol consumption
C. have increased dramatically over
D. the last decade.
E. No error

127. A. Forty per cent of the people alive today have
B. never made a phone call, but
C. thirty per cent still have no electricity connections
D. to their homes.
E. No error

128. A. Workers with less
B. personal problems are
C. likely to be
D. more productive in their work.
E. No error

129. A. Everyone who visits Singapore
B. is impressed by its cleanliness,
C. which is mainly a result of rigorous implementation
D. of their strict laws.
E. No error

130. A. The bridal dress was
B. most unique: the prince
C. designed it and his
D. mother provided the lace fabric.
E. No error

Directions (Qs. 131 to 135): *Each sentence below has two blanks, each blank indicating that something has been omitted. Choose the words that best fit the meaning of the sentence as a whole.*

131. The proposal has been .... and will be sent to the cabinet for final ....
A. designed, process
B. drafted, approval
C. amend, sanction
D. said, objection
E. mentioned, figure

132. The fake diesel factory was being .... under the .... of a dairy.
A. operated, operation
B. captured, array
C. functioned, alias
D. run, garb
E. activated, control

133. The moment, the staff opened the office, unidentified ...., ... weapons entered and asked the cashier to hand over the keys to the vault.
A. miscreants, brandishing
B. object, carrying
C. persons, had
D. people, associating
E. man, lifting

134. The singer, who has been very .... about his faith in the party, also .... at the grand event.
A. vocal, performed
B. strong, sang
C. open, dance
D. loud, came
E. creative, present

135. Over the years, the town has .... popularity as the best .... for paragliding and pilot from across the world visit it.
A. acquired, spot
B. claim, one
C. gained, destination
D. sought, wonder
E. sent, place

Directions (Qs. 136-140): *In the following questions, read each sentence to find out whether there is any grammatical error in it. The error, if any, will be in one part of the sentence. Mark the part with the error as your answer. Ignore the errors of punctuation, if any.*

136. Many citizens are gravitating (A)/ towards the nation's (B)/ second-largest State because it offer (C)/ ample job opportunities. (D)/ No error (E)

137. Most African nations were largely (A)/ shielded from the 2008 financial crisis (B)/ by China's insatiable demand (C)/ for natural resources. (D)/ No error (E)

138. Skeptics worries that the devaluation (A)/ of the country's currency is (B)/ a desperate move to (C)/ bail out struggling exporters. (D) No error (E)

139. Consumers are constantly been (A)/ encouraged to take (B)/ advantage of the (C)/ lowered interest rates. (D)/ No error (E)

140. Emerging economies are (A)/ dominating the news (B)/ but for (C)/ all the wrong reasons. (D)/ No error (E)

Directions (Qs. 141-145): *Rearrange the given six sentences/ group of sentences 1, 2, 3, 4, 5 and 6 in a proper sequence as to form a meaningful paragraph and then answer the given questions.*

1. Global investors are quaking over the prospect of a devastating stump in the world's second biggest economy.
2. A possible answer could be that the country's troubles raise doubts about whether its policy-makers have the tools to keep their economy growing at a healthy place something that has been a constant reassurance for more than two decades.
3. And they are fast losing confidence that the country's policy-makers, seemingly so sure-footed in the past, know how to solve the problem.
4. However, such a domino effect is significant but hardly catastrophic, so why the hysteria?
5. China is exporting something new to the world economy fear.
6. Apart from the shrinking confidence, the biggest fear is that a collapsing Chinese economy would derail others around the world — from emerging markets in Chile and Indonesia to industrial powers such as the United States.

141. Which of the following should be the **SECOND** sentence after rearrangement?
A. 1 B. 2
C. 6 D. 4
E. 5

142. Which of the following should be the **FIRST** sentence after rearrangement?
A. 1 B. 3
C. 2 D. 6
E. 5

143. Which of the following should be the **SIXTH (last)** sentence after rearrangement?
A. 5 B. 4
C. 1 D. 2
E. 6

144. Which of the following should be the **FIFTH** sentence after rearrangement?
A. 1 B. 4
C. 5 D. 6
E. 3

145. Which of the following should be the **FOURTH** sentence after rearrangement?
A. 1 B. 2
C. 3 D. 6
E. 4

Directions (Qs. 146-150): *In the following passage, there are blanks, each of which has been numbered. Against each blank, five words are suggested, one of which fits the blank appropriately. Find out the appropriate word in each case.*

Primary school enrolment in India has been a success story. __(146)__ due to various programmes and drives to increase enrolment even in remote areas. With enrolment reaching at least 96 per cent since 2009, and girls __(147)__ up 56 per cent of new students between 2007 and 2013, it is clear that many __(148)__ of access to schooling have been __(149)__. Improvement in infrastructure has been the __(150)__ behind achieving this and now in India 98 per cent habitations have a primary school within one kilometre and 92 per cent have an upper primary school within a three kilometre walking distance.

146. A. most B. properly
C. totally D. optionally
E. largely

147. A. coming B. reaching
C. counting D. making
E. touching

148. A. issue B. opportunities
C. problems D. efforts
E. exertions

149. A. accustomed B. addressed
C. met D. forwarded
E. dissolved

150. A. main B. forced
C. force D. compulsion
E. awareness

ANSWERS

1 D	**2** E	**3** A	**4** B	**5** B	**6** E	**7** B	**8** E	**9** C	**10** D
11 D	**12** C	**13** B	**14** C	**15** D	**16** C	**17** E	**18** D	**19** E	**20** B
21 E	**22** A	**23** C	**24** B	**25** B	**26** C	**27** D	**28** B	**29** D	**30** D
31 E	**32** E	**33** D	**34** D	**35** C	**36** C	**37** A	**38** B	**39** E	**40** D
41 C	**42** E	**43** B	**44** D	**45** A	**46** B	**47** C	**48** E	**49** D	**50** A
51 D	**52** A	**53** C	**54** B	**55** E	**56** D	**57** A	**58** B	**59** D	**60** C
61 B	**62** D	**63** B	**64** B	**65** A	**66** B	**67** E	**68** C	**69** D	**70** A
71 B	**72** C	**73** E	**74** A	**75** B	**76** B	**77** D	**78** B	**79** E	**80** C
81 C	**82** A	**83** D	**84** B	**85** E	**86** B	**87** A	**88** C	**89** B	**90** A

91	92	93	94	95	96	97	98	99	100
A	B	D	B	B	D	E	E	E	E
101	**102**	**103**	**104**	**105**	**106**	**107**	**108**	**109**	**110**
E	D	B	B	E	C	A	B	C	E
111	**112**	**113**	**114**	**115**	**116**	**117**	**118**	**119**	**120**
A	C	B	D	E	C	D	D	A	A
121	**122**	**123**	**124**	**125**	**126**	**127**	**128**	**129**	**130**
C	A	D	D	C	A	B	E	C	B
131	**132**	**133**	**134**	**135**	**136**	**137**	**138**	**139**	**140**
B	D	A	A	C	C	B	A	A	E
141	**142**	**143**	**144**	**145**	**146**	**147**	**148**	**149**	**150**
A	E	D	B	D	E	D	C	B	C

EXPLANATORY ANSWERS

1-5.

Day	Employees	Department
Monday	M	HR
Tuesday	P	Security
Wednesday	Q	Administrative
Thursday	L	Security
Friday	N	Administrative
Saturday	R	HR
Sunday	O	Finance

11-15.

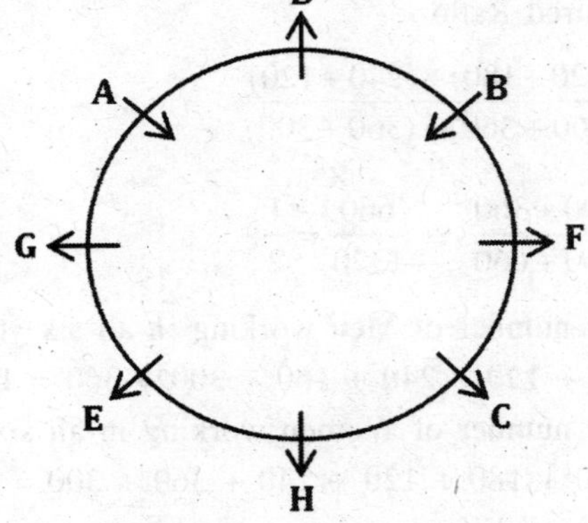

16-20.

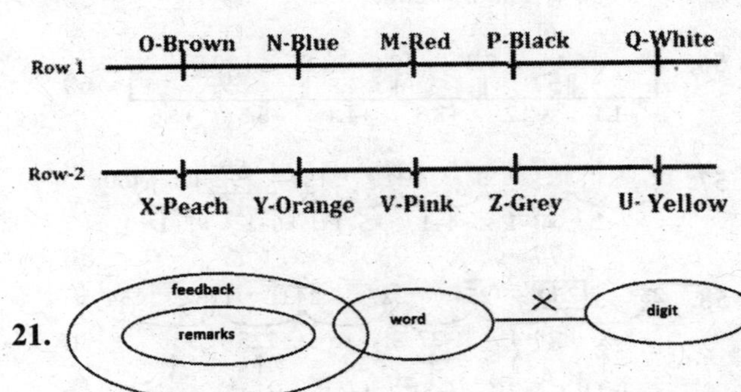

21.

22.

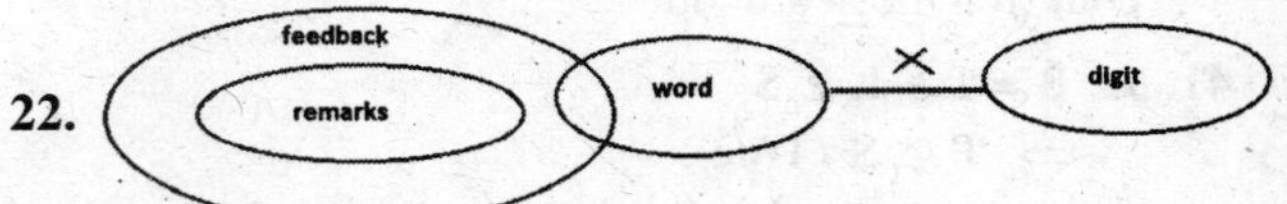

23.

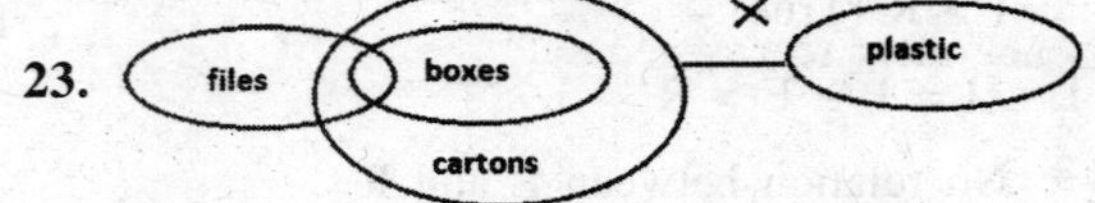

24.

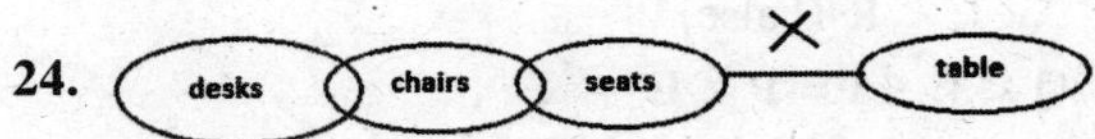

25.

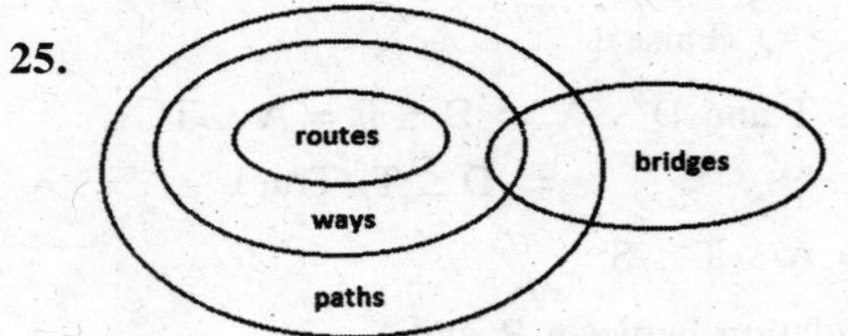

26. 'AE, EF, NR'

27. B E D (+1, +2) E I G (+2, +2) H M J (+3, +2) K Q M (+4, +2)

∴ N U P (+5, +2)

28-29.

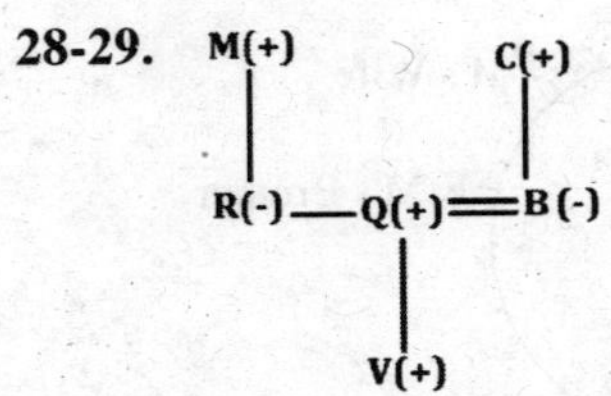

30-32.

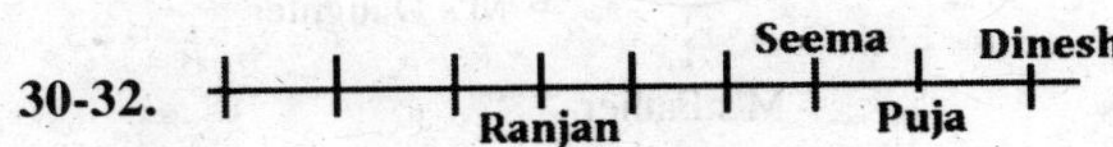

33. 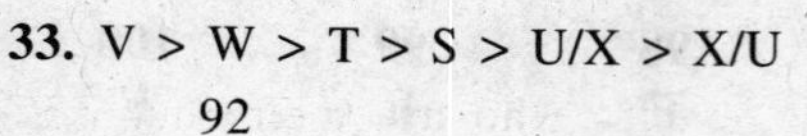
V > W > T > S > U/X > X/U
92

34. V > W > T > S > U > X
92 69 68

35. V > W > T > S > U/X > X/U
92

36-40.

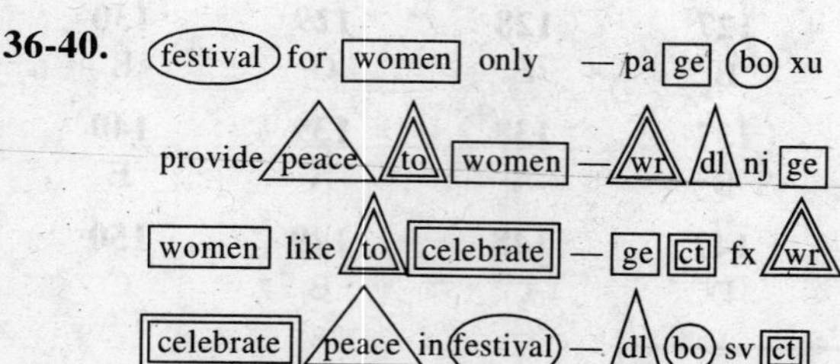

36. 'hy' code is not used in this question so, 'hy' is the code for the word 'idea'.

41. I. P = I ≥ L ≥ S
⇒ P ≥ S (True).
II. I = P ≥ E > R
⇒ I > R (True).

42. I. L ≤ I = P ≥ E > R
⇒ No relation between L and R.
∴ L < R (False)
II. Q < L ≤ I = P ≥ E
⇒ No relation between Q and E.
∴ E ≥ Q (False)

43. E = A ≤ T and D ≤ A ⇒ D ≤ E = A ≤ T
⇒ D ≤ T (True)
R ≥ E = A ≤ T ≤ S
⇒ No relation between R and S
∴ R > S (False)

44. I & II: E = A ≤ J
⇒ either J > E or J = E (True).

45. I. A ≥ B > C ≤ D ≤ E
⇒ No relation between A and E.
∴ A ≥ E (False)
II. C ≤ D ≤ E < F ⇒ F > C (True).

46-50.

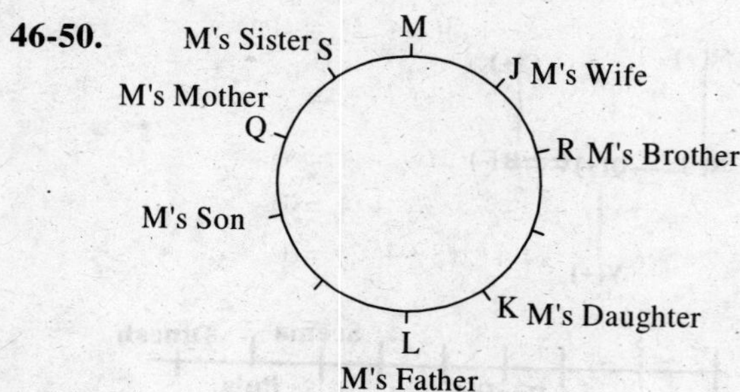

51. Required % = $\frac{120+240}{160+240} \times 100$

$= \frac{360}{400} \times 100 = 90\%.$

52. Average number of Women working in 2014, 2015 and 2016 together

$= \frac{1}{3}[240+360+300]$

$= \frac{900}{3} = 300$

Average number of Men working in 2011, 2014 and 2016 together

$= \frac{1}{3}[80+160+360]$

$= \frac{600}{3} = 200$

Required difference = 300 − 200 = 100.

53. Number of Men working in 2017

$= \frac{115}{100} \times 300 = 345$

Number of Women working in 2017

$= \frac{60}{100} \times 240 = 144$

Total number of labours working in 2017
= 345 + 144 = 489.

54. Required Ratio

$= \frac{(120+180)+(240+120)}{(300+360)+(360+300)}$

$= \frac{300+360}{660+660} = \frac{660}{1320} = \frac{1}{2}.$

55. Total number of Men working in all six years
= 80 + 120 + 240 + 160 + 300 + 360 = 1260
Total number of Women working in all six years
= 260 + 180 + 120 + 240 + 360 + 300 = 1460
Required difference
= 1460 − 1260 = 200.

56. 4 5.1 7.3 10.6 15 **[20.5]** 27.1
+1.1 +2.2 +3.3 +4.4 +5.5 +6.6

57. 2 3 8 31 154 **[923]** 6460
×2−1 ×3−1 ×4−1 ×5−1 ×6−1 ×7−1

58. 251 **[250]** 254 227 243 118 154
−1 +4 −27 +16 −125 +36
↑ ↑ ↑ ↑ ↑ ↑
$(-1)^3$ $(+2)^2$ $(-3)^3$ $(+4)^2$ $(-5)^3$ $(+6)^2$

59. 141 156 147 162 153 [168] 159

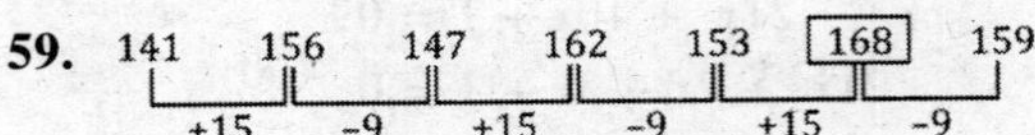

60. 2 [5] 10 19 36 69 134

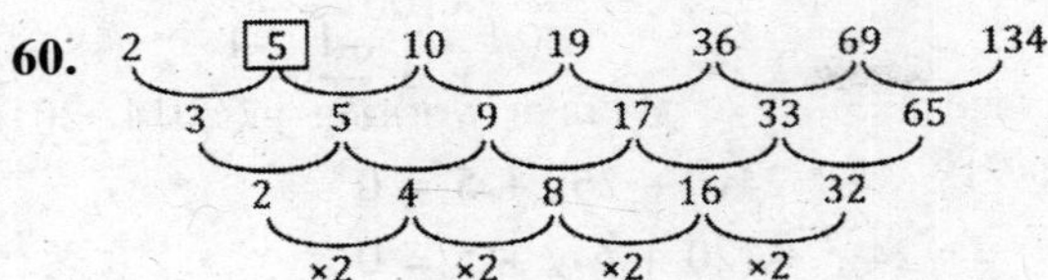

61. 0.5 [0.5] 1 4 32 512 16384

×1 ×2 ×4 ×8 ×16 ×32

62. Let present age of A and B be $16x$ year and $7x$ year respectively

According to question,

$$\frac{16x+12}{7x+12} = \frac{2}{1}$$

$\Rightarrow$ $2x = 12$

$\Rightarrow$ $x = 6$

Present age of A = 96 year

Present age of B = 42 year.

63. $$\text{Sum} = \frac{1950 \times 100}{2 \times 15}$$

$= ₹\ 6500$

CI in 2 years at 10% per annum

$$= 10 + 10 + \frac{10 \times 10}{100} = 21\%$$

According to question,

$$(6500 + x) \times \frac{21}{100} = 1680$$

$\Rightarrow$ $(6500 + x) = 8000$

$\Rightarrow$ $x = ₹\ 1500.$

64. Total weight of students $= 47\frac{7}{15}(15+30)$

$= 2136$ kg

Total weight of boys $= 15 \times 58 = 870$ kg

Average weight of girls $= \left(\frac{2136-870}{30}\right)$ kg

$= 42.2 \text{ kg} \simeq 42$ kg.

65. Ram's cost price= M.R.P. $\times \frac{80}{100}$

Ramesh C.P. = M.R.P. $\times \frac{80}{100} \times \frac{90}{100}$

Ranjan C.P. = M.R.P. $\times \frac{80}{100} \times \frac{90}{100} \times \frac{120}{100}$

$= ₹\ 1{,}29{,}600$

$\Rightarrow$ M.R.P. $= ₹\ 1{,}50{,}000.$

For Qs. 66-70.

Let, Males and females who use their coupons in Haircutting be $13x$ and $7x$ respectively.

$\Rightarrow$ Males who use their coupons in Pedicure

$= 7x + 72$

Then Females who use their coupons in Pedicure

$= 450 - 13x - 7x - 7x - 72$

$= 378 - 27x$

Pedicure		Hair cutting	
Males	**Females**	**Males**	**Females**
$7x + 72$	$378 - 27x$	$13x$	$7x$

According to question,

$7x + 72 + 13x - (7x + 378 - 27x) = 174$

$40x - 306 = 174$

$40x = 480$

$x = 12$

Pedicure		Hair cutting	
Males	**Females**	**Males**	**Females**
156	54	156	84

66. Required % $= \frac{156}{156} \times 100 = 100\%$.

67. Required ratio $= \frac{156+54}{156+84} = \frac{210}{240} = \frac{7}{8}$.

68. Required difference = 84 – 54 = 30.

69. Number of males who use their coupons in Hair cutting which doesn't belongs to city A

$= 156 \times \frac{75}{100} = 117.$

70. Males who use their coupons in Spa

$= 156 \times \frac{5}{4} = 195$

Females who use their coupons in Spa

$= 84 \times \frac{11}{6} = 154$

Total number of people who use their coupon in Spa

$= 195 + 154 = 349.$

71. (*i*) $2x^2 + 9x + 9 = 0$

$2x^2 + (6 + 3)x + 9 = 0$

$2x(x + 3) + 3(x + 3) = 0$

$x = \frac{-3}{2}, -3.$

(*ii*) $15y^2 + 16y + 4 = 0$

$15y^2 + 10y + 6y + 4 = 0$

$5y(3y + 2) + 2(3y + 2) = 0$

$y = \frac{-2}{5}, \frac{-2}{3}.$

$x < y.$

72. (*i*)
$$2x^3 = 16$$
$$x^3 = 8$$
$$x = 2$$

(*ii*)
$$2y^2 - 9y + 10 = 0$$
$$2y^2 - (5 + 4)y + 10 = 0$$
$$2y^2 - 5y - 4y + 10 = 0$$
$$y(2y - 5) - 2(2y - 5) = 0$$
$$y = 2, \frac{5}{2}$$
$$x \leq y.$$

73. (*i*)
$$6x^2 - 11x + 4 = 0$$
$$6x^2 - (8 + 3)x + 4 = 0$$
$$6x^2 - 8x - 3x + 4 = 0$$
$$2x(3x - 4) - 1(3x - 4) = 0$$
$$x = \frac{1}{2}, \frac{4}{3}$$

(*ii*)
$$3y^2 - 5y + 2 = 0$$
$$3y^2 - (3 + 2)y + 2 = 0$$
$$3y^2 - 3y - 2y + 2 = 0$$
$$3y(y - 1) - 2(y - 1) = 0$$
$$y = \frac{2}{3}, 1$$

No relation between x and y.

74. (*i*)
$$3x^2 + 11x + 10 = 0$$
$$3x^2 + 6x + 5x + 10 = 0$$
$$3x(x + 2) + 5(x + 2) = 0$$
$$x = -2, \frac{-5}{3}$$

(*ii*)
$$2y^2 + 11y + 14 = 0$$
$$2y^2 + 7y + 4y + 14 = 0$$
$$y(2y + 7) + 2(2y + 7) = 0$$
$$y = -2, \frac{-7}{2}$$
$$x \geq y.$$

75. (*i*)
$$12x^2 + 8x + 3x + 2 = 0$$
$$4x(3x + 2) + 1(3x + 2) = 0$$
$$x = \frac{-2}{3}, \frac{-1}{4}$$

(*ii*)
$$12y^2 + 7y + 1 = 0$$
$$12y^2 + 4y + 3y + 1 = 0$$
$$4y(3y + 1) + 1(3y + 1) = 0$$
$$y = \frac{-1}{3}, \frac{-1}{4}$$

No relation between x and y.

76. (*i*)
$$21x^2 + 10x + 1 = 0$$
$$21x^2 + 7x + 3x + 1 = 0$$
$$7x(3x + 1) + 1(3x + 1) = 0$$
$$x = \frac{-1}{3}, \frac{-1}{7}$$

(*ii*)
$$24y^2 + 26y + 5 = 0$$
$$24y^2 + (20 + 6)y + 5 = 0$$
$$24y^2 + 20y + 6y + 5 = 0$$
$$4y(6y + 5) + 1(6y + 5) = 0$$
$$y = \frac{-5}{6}, \frac{-1}{4}$$

No relation between x and y.

77. B can complete work alone in
$$20 \times \frac{4}{5} = 16 \text{ days}$$

Let C alone can complete work in 'x' days

According to question,
$$\frac{6}{16} + \frac{15}{x} = 1$$
$$\Rightarrow \quad \frac{15}{x} = \frac{10}{16}$$
$$\Rightarrow \quad x = \frac{15 \times 16}{10}$$
$$= 24 \text{ days.}$$

78. Let distance between P to Q and Q to R be 'x' and 'y' respectively.

According to question,
$$75 = \frac{200}{\frac{x}{90} + \frac{y}{60}}$$
$$60x + 90y = 200 \times 90 \times 60 \times \frac{1}{75}$$
$$2x + 3y = 480$$

and
$$x + y = 200$$
$$\Rightarrow \quad x = 120 \text{ km}$$

and
$$y = 80 \text{ km.}$$

79. Let wine and water are $= 5x : x$

Now,
$$\frac{5x}{x+5} = \frac{5}{2}$$
$$\Rightarrow \quad 10x = 5x + 25$$
$$x = 5$$
$$\Rightarrow \quad 25 : 5 \mid 25 : 10$$

Before mixture | After mixture

Quantity of wine = 25 l.

80. 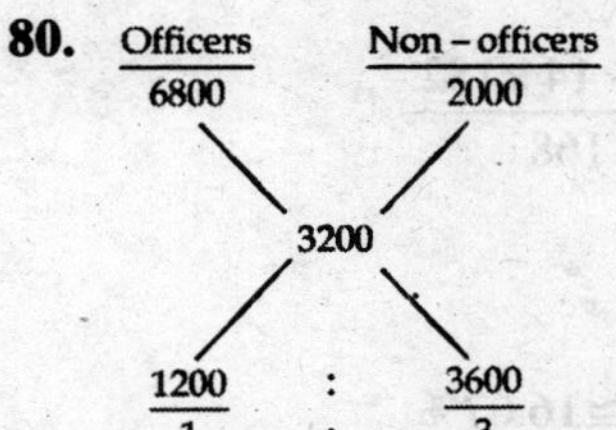

Number of non-officers = $\frac{3}{1} \times 5 = 15.$

81. Total books sold by store A

$= 3500 \times \frac{20}{100} = 700$

Total plain books sold by store A

$= 2000 \times \frac{30}{100} = 600$

Total lined books sold by store A

$= 700 - 600 = 100$

Total books sold by store B

$= 5000 \times \frac{40}{100} = 2000$

Plain books sold by store B

$= 3000 \times \frac{40}{100} = 1200$

Total lined books sold by store B

$= 2000 - 1200 = 800$

Required % $= \frac{900}{3500} \times 100 = \frac{180}{7}\% = 25\frac{5}{7}\%.$

82. Average of total books sold by stores B and C

$= \frac{1}{2}\left(50 \times \frac{40}{100} \times 100 + 45 \times \frac{30}{100} \times 100\right) = 1675$

Unsold books of store A

$= 3500 \times \frac{80}{100} = 2800$

Required difference = 2800 – 1675 = 1125.

83. Total books sold by store C

$= 45 \times 100 \times \frac{30}{100} = 1350$

Plain books sold by C

$= 1350 \times \frac{5}{9} = 750$

Plain books sold by store B

$= \frac{3}{5} \times 5000 \times \frac{40}{100} = 1200$

Required number of books

= 1200 + 750 = 1950.

84. Unsold books of store A

$= 3500 \times \frac{80}{100} = 2800$

Unsold books of store B and C together

$= 5000 \times \frac{60}{100} + 4500 \times \frac{70}{100} = 6150$

Required % $= \frac{6150 - 2800}{6150} \times 100 = 54\%.$

85. Number of total books sold by store B

$= 5000 \times \frac{40}{100} = 2000$

Number of lined books sold

$= 2000 \times \frac{60}{100} = 1200$

Total amount earned

= ₹ (800 × 250 + 1200 × 175)

= ₹ 4.1 lac.

86. Number of numbers between 1 to 300 divisible by 3 = 100

Number of numbers between 1 to 300 divisible by 7 = 42

Number of numbers between 1 to 300 divisible by both 3 and 7 *i.e.,* 21 = 14

Number of numbers between 1 to 300 divisible by 3 or 7 = 100 + 42 – 14 = 128

$\therefore$ Required probability $= \frac{128}{300} = \frac{32}{75}.$

87. Part of work done by 14 men in 3 days

$= \frac{3}{18} = \frac{1}{6}$

Part of work done by 1 women in 1 day

$= \frac{1}{15 \times 24}$

Part of work done by 10 women in 3 days

$= \frac{10 \times 3}{15 \times 24} = \frac{1}{12}$

Portion of the work finished

$= \frac{1}{6} + \frac{1}{12}$

$= \frac{2+1}{12} = \frac{3}{12} = \frac{1}{4}$

Remaining portion of the work

$= 1 - \frac{1}{4} = \frac{3}{4}$ work.

88. Let, length of rectangle = 7 m
and breadth of rectangle = 3 m

$$2(7\text{ m} + 3\text{ m}) = x$$
$$\Rightarrow \quad x = 20\text{ m}$$
$$\frac{r}{l} = \frac{1}{2}$$
$$\Rightarrow \quad 2r = l = 7\text{ m}$$
$$C = 2\pi r$$
$$x + 8 = 2\pi r$$
$$= (2r) \times \pi$$
$$\Rightarrow \quad 20\text{ m} + 8 = 7\text{ m} \times \frac{22}{7}$$
$$= 22\text{ m}$$
$$\Rightarrow \quad 2\text{ m} = 8$$
$$\Rightarrow \quad \text{m} = 4$$

$\therefore$ Length of rectangle = 7 × 4 = 28

89. Let, amount invested by A = ₹ x

$$\therefore \quad \frac{x \times 5 \times 2}{100} = \frac{(4000 - x) \times 3 \times 2}{100}$$
$$\Rightarrow \quad 10x = 24000 - 6x$$
$$\Rightarrow \quad 16x = 24000$$
$$\Rightarrow \quad x = \frac{24000}{16} = 1500$$

Hence, amount invested by A = ₹ 1500

90.
$$S_1 = \frac{t_1 + t_2}{t_1 \times t_2}$$
$$= \frac{14 + 182}{14 \times 182}$$
$$= \frac{196}{14 \times 182}\text{ m/s}$$
$$S_2 = \frac{t_2 - t_1}{t_1 \times t_2}$$
$$= \frac{182 - 14}{14 \times 182} = \frac{168}{14 \times 182}\text{ m/s}$$
$$\text{Difference} = \frac{196}{14 \times 182} - \frac{168}{14 \times 182}$$
$$= \frac{28}{14 \times 182} = \frac{1}{91}\text{ m/s}$$
$$\text{Required \%} = \frac{\frac{1}{91} \times 100}{\frac{168}{14 \times 182}}$$
$$= \frac{1}{91} \times \frac{100 \times 14 \times 182}{168}$$
$$= \frac{50}{3}\%$$
$$= 16.666\% \cong 16.67\%$$

91. 11 20 38 74 [146]
+ 9, + 18, + 36, + 72
× 2, × 2, × 2

Hence, 146 will come in place of the question mark.

92. 15 21 38 65 101 [145]
+ 6, + 17, + 27, + 36, + 44
+ 11, + 10, + 9, + 8

Hence, 145 will come in place of the question mark.

93. 24 28 19 35 10 [46]
$+ (2)^2$, $- (3)^2$, $+ (4)^2$, $- (5)^2$, $+ (6)^2$

Hence, 46 will come in place of the question mark.

94. 7 16 45 184 915 [5496]
× 2 + 2, × 3 − 3, × 4 + 4, × 5 − 5, × 6 + 6

Hence, 5496 will come in place of the question mark.

95. 12 19 35 59 90 [127]
+ 7, + 16, + 24, + 31, + 37
+ 9, + 8, + 7, + 6

Hence, 127 will come in place of the question mark.

96. I.
$$3x^2 - 22x + 7 = 0$$
$$3x^2 - 21x - x + 7 = 0$$
$$\Rightarrow \quad 3x(x - 7) - 1(x - 7) = 0$$
$$\Rightarrow \quad (x - 7)(3x - 1) = 0$$
$$\Rightarrow \quad x = 7 \text{ or } x = \frac{1}{3}$$

II.
$$y^2 - 15y + 56 = 0$$
$$y^2 - 8y - 7y + 56 = 0$$
$$\Rightarrow \quad y(y - 8) - 7(y - 8) = 0$$
$$\Rightarrow \quad (y - 8)(y - 7) = 0$$
$$\Rightarrow \quad y = 8 \text{ or } y = 7$$

Clearly, $x \le y$

97. I.
$$2x^2 - 17x + 36 = 0$$
$$2x^2 - 8x - 9x + 36 = 0$$
$$\Rightarrow \quad 2x(x - 4) - 9(x - 4) = 0$$

$\Rightarrow \quad (x - 4)(2x - 9) = 0$

$\Rightarrow \quad x = 4 \text{ or } x = \frac{9}{2}$

II. $\quad 2y^2 - 19y + 44 = 0$

$2y^2 - 11y - 8y + 44 = 0$

$\Rightarrow \quad y(2y - 11) - 4(2y - 11) = 0$

$\Rightarrow \quad (2y - 11)(y - 4) = 0$

$\Rightarrow \quad y = \frac{11}{2} \text{ or } y = 4$

Clearly, No relation between x and y.

98. I. $\quad x - \sqrt{169} = 0$

$\Rightarrow \quad x = \sqrt{169}$

$\Rightarrow \quad x = +13$

II. $\quad y^2 - 169 = 0$

$\Rightarrow \quad y^2 = 169$

$\Rightarrow \quad y = \sqrt{169} = \pm 13$

Clearly, $x = y$ or relationship between x and y can not be established.

99. I. $\quad 3x^2 + 20x + 25 = 0$

$3x^2 + 15x + 5x + 25 = 0$

$\Rightarrow \quad 3x(x + 5) + 5(x + 5) = 0$

$\Rightarrow \quad (x + 5)(3x + 5) = 0$

$\Rightarrow \quad x = -5 \text{ or } x = -\frac{5}{3}$

II. $\quad 3y^2 + 14y + 8 = 0$

$3y^2 + 12y + 2y + 8 = 0$

$\Rightarrow \quad 3y(y + 4) + 2(y + 4) = 0$

$\Rightarrow \quad (y + 4)(3y + 2) = 0$

$\Rightarrow \quad y = -4 \text{ or } y = -\frac{2}{3}$

Clearly, No relation can be establish between x and y.

100. I. $\quad 13x^2 + 5x + 2 = 0$

$\Rightarrow \quad D = b^2 - 4ac$

$= 25 - 4 \times 13 \times 2$

$= 25 - 104 = -79$

$D < 0$

$\therefore$ roots are not real.

II. $\quad 3y^2 + 18y + 24 = 0$

$\Rightarrow \quad 3y^2 + 6y + 12y + 24 = 0$

$\Rightarrow \quad 3y(y + 2) + 12(y + 2) = 0$

$\Rightarrow \quad (y + 2)(3y + 12) = 0$

$\Rightarrow \quad y = -2$

or $\quad y = -4$

Clearly, relation between x and y can not be established.

MAIN EXAMINATION

PROFESSIONAL KNOWLEDGE (COMPUTER)

1. What is the value of variable z after executing the following code in C++?

```
int x = 5;
int y = 5;
int z = 5;
if (x > 3)
if (y > 4)
if (z > 5)
z+= 1;
else
z+= 2;
else
{z+= 3; x+= 2;}
z+= 3;
```

A. 7 B. 10
C. 5 D. 9
E. 8

2. In Java, which of these data types is used to store command line arguments?
A. Integer B. Stack
C. String D. Array
E. None of these

3. Which of the following softwares are needed to satisfy a user's specific processing requirements?
A. DTP Software B. Application Software
C. Graphics Software D. Systems Software
E. None of these

4. The number of swapping needed to sort the numbers 8, 22, 7, 9, 31, 19, 5, 13 in ascending order using bubble sort is:
A. 11 B. 13
C. 14 D. 15
E. None of the above

5. Any given truth table can be represented by:
A. Sum of Products (SOP) of boolean expression
B. Karnaugh Map
C. Product of Sum (POS) of boolean expression
D. All of the above
E. None of these

6. Which of the following sorting procedure is the slowest?
A. Heap Sort B. Shell Short
C. Bubble sort D. Quick Tree
E. None of these

7. Which tag(s) can handle mouse events in Netscape?
A.
 B. <IMG>
C. <A> D. <GMI>
E. None of the above

8. Which of these interface is implemented by Thread class?
A. Connections
B. Set
C. Runnable
D. MapConnections
E. None of these

9. Predict the output of following C++ code segment:

```
#include<iostream.h>
void main()
{
int x[]={1,2,3,4};
int*p,**q,*t;
p=x;
cout<<*p;
t=x+1;
q=&t;
cout<<*++p<<**q<<*t++;}
```

A. 1233 B. 1232
C. 1223 D. 1245
E. 1254

10. Which of the following input combinations is not allowed in an SR flip-flop?
A. S = 0, R = 0
B. S = 0, R = 1
C. S = 1, R = 0
D. S = 1, R = 1
E. S = 3, R = 9

11. What does print(os.geteuid()) print in Python?
A. Both the group id and the user of the current process
B. The effected user id of the current process
C. The group id of the current process
D. Only current process
E. None of the above

12. Class derived: public base1, public base2 { } is an example of:
A. Hierarchical inheritance
B. Polymorphic inheritance
C. Multiple inheritance
D. Multilevel inheritance
E. None of the above

13. Which of the following sorting techniques will be the best if number of swapping done is the only measure of efficiency?

A. Selection sort
B. Bubble sort
C. Insertion sort
D. Copy sort
E. All of the above

14. ________ JavaScript statements embedded in an HTML page can respond to user events such as mouse-clicks, form input, and page navigation.

A. Local
B. Server-side
C. Client-side
D. Native
E. None of the above

15. How many flip-flop will be required to divide the input frequency by 64?

A. 4
B. 6
C. 8
D. 5
E. 7

16. In a linked list implementation of a queue with two pointers Front & Rear, the time needed to insert element in a queue of length 'n' is:

A. O(n)
B. O(1)
C. $O(n \log_2 n)$
D. $O(\log_2 n)$
E. None of the above

17. The maximum frequency at which digital data can be applied to gate is:

A. Binary level transaction period
B. Operational speed
C. Charging time
D. Propagation speed
E. None of the above

18. In Real Time Interactive Audio Video, Jitter is introduced in real-time data by the delay between:

A. Pixels
B. Layers
C. Frames
D. Packets
E. Images

19. In order to allow only one process to enter its critical section, binary semaphore are initialized to:

A. 0
B. 2
C. 1
D. 3
E. 5

20. A decimal number has 25 digits. The number of bits needed for its equivalent binary representation is, approximately:

A. 60
B. 75
C. 50
D. 80
E. 70

21. The first three bytes (parts) of a MAC address represents:

A. Card Number
B. Net ID
C. Manufacturer-id
D. Domain Name
E. None of the above

22. Which of the following is NOT a type of SQL constraint?

A. PRIMARY KEY
B. UNIQUE
C. JOIN KEY
D. FOREIGN KEY
E. None of the above

23. Given the following piece of code in Java:

```
public class MyThread extends Thread{
public String text;
public void run(){
System.out.print(text);
}
}
public class Test{
public static void main(String args[]){
MyThread t1 = new MyThread()}t1.text = "one";
MyThread t2 = new MyThread()}t2.text = "two";
t1.start();
t2.start()};
System.out.print("three");
}
}
```

A. If you execute this program, the result is always one two three.
B. If you execute this program, the result is always three one two.
C. Compilation will fail.
D. The result of this program is undetermined.
E. None of the above

24. In which of the storage placement strategies is a program placed in the largest available hole in the main memory?

A. Best fit
B. First fit
C. Buddy
D. Worst fit
E. None of the above

25. Which of the following register is loaded with the contents of the memory location pointed by the PC?

A. Program counter
B. Memory data register
C. Memory address register
D. Instruction register
E. None of the above

26. If the number of bits in a virtual address of a program is 12 and the page size is 0.5k bytes, then numbers of pages in the virtual address space is:

A. 32
B. 128
C. 64
D. 264
E. None of the above

27. Which of the following is true about HAVING clause?
A. Acts like a WHERE clause but is used for columns rather than groups.
B. Acts EXACTLY like a WHERE clause.
C. Acts like a WHERE clause but is used for rows rather than columns.
D. Acts like EXACTLY
E. None of the above

28. The flip-flops which operate in synchronism with external clock pulses are called:
A. Asynchronous flip-flops
B. Synchronous flip-flops
C. Either (A) or (B)
E. Both of the above
D. None of the above

29. In a relational Database, a table joined with itself is called:
A. Outer Join B. Self Join
C. Join D. Equi Join
E. None of the above

30. Given a function in Python that does not return any value, what value is thrown by it, by default, when executed in shell?
A. int B. void
C. bool D. kool
E. None

31. Give the output of the following program in C++.

```
#include<iostream.h>
class a
{int x;
public;
a(){cout<<"it is raining"; x=0;}};
class b: public a
  {
  int y;
  b(){cout<<"cats and dogs";}
  public;
  b(int) {cout<<"hi";}
  };
void main() {b ob(6);}
```

A. it is raining hi
B. hi it is raining
C. cats and dogs it is raining
D. it is raining cats and dogs hi
E. None of the above

32. Cartesian product in relational algebra is:
A. a Unary operator.
B. a Ternary operator.
C. not defined.
D. a Binary operator.
E. None of the above

33. How many Boolean functions of three variables f(x,y,z) have the property that f(x,y,z)=(f(x',y',z'))?
A. 64 B. 16
C. 256 D. 8
E. 180

34. The _____ operator is used to compare a value to a list of literals values that have been specified.
A. IN B. BETWEEN
C. ALL D. ANY
E. None of the above

35. Which of the following about XML not true?
A. XML is case sensitive
B. XML allows you to create your own tags
C. With XML, the white-space in a document is truncated
D. XML is designed to transport & store data, with focus on what data is
E. None of the above

36. Which of these package contains classes and interfaces for networking?
A. java.net B. java.network
C. java.util D. java.io
E. None of the above

37. A media file containing audio or video is downloaded and stored on the clients local file system in:
A. Regular download
B. Virtual time streaming
C. Real time streaming
D. Progressive download
E. None of the above

38. Lossy and lossless are classifications of:
A. files
B. multimedia storage systems
C. compression algorithms
D. All of the above
E. None of the above

39. A program to detect overall system malfunction:
A. System Analysis
B. Utilities
C. System Diagnostics
D. System Software
E. None of the above

40. What is the error in the following code?

```
class t
{
void print();
}
```

A. Class t should contain data members.
B. Function print() should be defined.
C. Function print() should be declared as static.
D. No error
E. None of the above

41. Whenever crawler crawls the website then any page not having link is called:

A. Home page
B. Doorway page
C. Dead end page
D. Absolute page
E. None of the above

42. Which of following is not true about Java Servlet?

A. allows developers to customize any java enabled server
B. is key component of server side java development
C. is a small pluggable extension to a server that enhances functionality
D. runs only in Windows Operating System
E. None of the above

43. Which of these is not a core datatype in Python?

A. Lists
B. Tuples
C. Dictionary
D. Class
E. None of the above

44. How many arguments can be passed to main()?

A. Only 1
B. Infinite
C. System Dependent
D. Only 2
E. None of the above

45. What will be the output of following C++ program?

```
#include<iostream.h>
void main()
{int y=9, z=2;
float x;
x=y/z;
cout<<x;}
```

A. 4
B. 5
C. 4.0
D. 4.5
E. 7.5

46. Which of the following picture format is not allowed to be imported in Windows Movie Maker?

A. .gif
B. .psd
C. .jpeg
D. .bmp
E. All the above

47. What is the worst case time complexity of straight insertion sort algorithm to sort 'n' elements?

A. $O(n^2)$
B. $O(n)$
C. $O(n^{1.2})$
D. $O(n \log_2 n)$
E. None of the above

48. A combination of an encryption algorithm and a decryption algorithm is called a:

A. plain text
B. original text
C. shift cipher
D. cipher
E. None of the above

49. Two's complement can be obtained from ones complement by:

A. putting 1 as the leading bit
B. subtracting 1
C. adding 1
D. adding 2
E. None of the above

50. Data management systems may be implemented as:

A. System software
B. Computer program
C. Application software
D. All of the above
E. None of the above

51. In which area of the primary storage section are the intermediate processing results held temporarily?

A. Input storage area
B. Program storage area
C. Working storage space
D. Output storage area
E. None of the above

52. Computer virus is a software program which has the essential ability to:

A. Damage programs
B. Damage data
C. Clone itself
D. Hide itself
E. None of the above

53. The entire Row in Excel can be selected by:

A. Ctrl + Spacebar
B. Ctrl + Spacebar + shift
C. Shift + Spacebar
D. All of the above
E. None of the above

54. What is the output of the following program in Java?

```
public class Test
{
public static void main(String[]args)
{
private static final int value = 5;
float total;
total = value + value/2;
System.out.println(total);
}
}
```

A. 7.5
B. 7.0
C. 5.0
D. 5.5
E. None of the above

55. The master slave JK flip-flop is effectively a combination of:

A. two T flip-flop
B. an SR flip-flop and a T flip-flop
C. an SR flip-flop and a D flip-flop
D. a T flip-flop and a D flip-flop
E. None of the above

56. Which of these keywords is used to prevent content of a variable from being modified in Java?

A. static
B. last
C. final
D. constant
E. None of the above

57. **What is the use of iframe in HTML?**

A. To display a web page without browser
B. To display a web page with animation effect
C. To display a web page within a web page
D. All of the above
E. None of the above

58. **A 17 bit binary number has an accuracy equivalent to the decimal fraction?**

A. $\frac{1}{6400}$ B. $\frac{1}{1024}$

C. $\frac{1}{2048}$ D. $\frac{1}{4096}$

E. None of the above

59. **Following sequence of operations is performed on a stack:**

push(1), push(2), pop(), push(1), push(2), pop(), pop(), pop(), push(2), pop()

A. 2, 1, 2, 2, 1 B. 2, 2, 1, 2, 2
C. 2, 2, 1, 1, 2 D. 2, 1, 2, 2, 2
E. None of the above

60. **For each program in program memory the CPU goes through a:**

A. execute-store-decode sequence
B. fetch-execute-decode sequence
C. fetch-decode-execute sequence
D. decode-fetch-execute sequence
E. None of the above

ANSWERS

1	2	3	4	5	6	7	8	9	10
B	C	B	C	D	C	C	C	B	D
11	**12**	**13**	**14**	**15**	**16**	**17**	**18**	**19**	**20**
B	C	A	C	B	B	B	D	C	B
21	**22**	**23**	**24**	**25**	**26**	**27**	**28**	**29**	**30**
C	C	D	D	D	B	E	B	B	E
31	**32**	**33**	**34**	**35**	**36**	**37**	**38**	**39**	**40**
A	D	B	A	C	A	D	C	C	D
41	**42**	**43**	**44**	**45**	**46**	**47**	**48**	**49**	**50**
C	D	D	B	A	B	A	D	C	D
51	**52**	**53**	**54**	**55**	**56**	**57**	**58**	**59**	**60**
C	C	C	E	B	C	C	D	C	C

Previous Paper (Solved)

Institute of Banking Personnel Selection

IBPS–Specialist (IT) Officer Scale-I

Preliminary & Main Exam 2018-19*

Preliminary Exam held on - 29-12-2018

Main Exam held on - 27-01-2019

PRELIMINARY EXAMINATION

REASONING

Directions (Qs. No. 1-5): *Read the following information carefully to answer the following questions.*

Twelve friends P, Q, R, S, T, U, A, B, C, D, E and F are sitting in a straight line facing north but not necessarily in the same order. F sits third to the right of S. B sits fourth to the right of P, who is not the immediate neighbour of U. C and D are not immediate neighbours of F, who sits second to the right of E. There are two persons between U and A. There are two persons between D and Q. S is not an immediate neighbour of A. E sits at the fifth position from the right end. F is sixth to the right of T. C is not an immediate neighbour of D and Q.

1. Who among the following sit at the extreme ends of the line?

A. B, C
B. P, D
C. T, C
D. R, F
E. None of these

2. Who among the following sits third to the right of the fourth to the left of Q?

A. R
B. C
C. A
D. E
E. None of these

3. How many persons are there between C and the one who sits on the immediate left of S?

A. Two
B. Three
C. Four
D. One
E. None of these

4. Who among the following are immediate neighbours of R?

A. F and D
B. E and T
C. A and C
D. F and Q
E. None of these

5. Which of the following statements is/are true?

A. There are three friends between F and R
B. T and B are immediate neighbours
C. C sits at one of the ends of the line
D. P is on the immediate left of D
E. None of these

Directions (Qs. No. 6-10): *Study the following information carefully and answer the given questions:*

Twelve persons are sitting in two parallel rows containing six persons each, in such a way that there is an equal distance between adjacent persons. In row-1, J, K, L, M, N and O are seated (but not necessarily in the same order) and all of them are facing south. In row-2, C, D, E, F, G and H are seated (but not necessarily in the same order) and all of them are facing north. Therefore, in the given seating arrangement each person seated in a row faces another person of the other row.

M sits third to the left of J. The person facing M sits second to the left of H. Two persons are sitting between H and E. L and K are immediate neighbours. L and K do not sit at any of the extreme ends of the line. Only one person sits between N and L. The person facing K is an immediate neighbour of C. G is not an immediate neighbour of E. D does not face M.

6. Who amongst the following sits seconds to the right of the person who faces F?

A. L
B. K
C. N
D. J
E. Cannot be determined

7. Which of the following statements regarding N is true?

A. N sits second to the left of L
B. M sits to immediate left of N
C. H faces N
D. K is an immediate neighbour of N
E. The person who faces N is an immediate neighbour of D

8. Who amongst the following faces E?

A. M
B. K
C. L
D. J
E. Cannot he determined

* *Based on Memory*

9. Who amongst the following sits exactly between H and F?

A. G B. C
C. D D. E
E. Cannot be determined

10. Four of the following live are alike in a certain way based on the given seating arrangement and thus form a group. Which is the one that does not belong to the group?

A. O B. C
C. H D. L
E. J

Directions (Qs. No. 11-15): *Study the information given below and answer the questions based on it.*

Some persons were born in the same year but in different months *i.e.* from January to December. Only two persons were born before A. R is the youngest person. The number of person born before Q is same as after R. Two months gap between R and C. P is the 2nd eldest person. S was born in May. M is elder to C but younger to S. K was born in a month which was having 31 days. The number of persons born before A is same as after C. The number of month gap between Q and S is same as M and R. P was not born in March and C was not born in July. R was not born in December. The number of month gap between A and M is same as M and K.

11. Who among the following was born in October?

A. No one B. R
C. K D. S
E. M

12. What is the total number of person?

A. 6 B. 7
C. 8 D. 9
E. 5

13. Who among the following is the eldest?

A. Q B. A
C. C D. R
E. K

14. Which of the following is TRUE?

A. Q was born in February
B. Only one person was born after R
C. M was born in March
D. A was born in a month which was having 30 days
E. C was born in October

15. Who among the following is the youngest?

A. Q B. A
C. C D. R
E. K

Directions (Qs. No. 16-20): *Study the information given below and answer the questions based on it.*

A, B, C, D, E, F, G and H are eight students of a school. They study in standards VI, VII, and VIII with not more than three in any standard. Each of them has a favorite subject from Physics, Geography, English, Marathi, Mathematics, Chemistry, Biology and Economics but not necessarily in the same order.

D likes Chemistry and studies in standard VIII with only H. B does not study in standard VII. E and A study in the same standard but not with B. C and F study in the same standard. Those who study in standard VI do not like Mathematics or Biology. F likes Physics. The one who studies in standard VIII likes English. C does not like Geography. A's favorite subject is Marathi and G does not like Biology.

16. Which of the following groups of students studied in VII standard?

A. DHA B. EAG
C. BCF D. ABC
E. Cannot be determined

17. Which of the following combinations of student-standard-subject is correct?

A. D-VIII-Biology B. A-VI-Marathi
C. G-VII-Math D. F-VIII-Economics
E. None of these

18. What is C's favorite subject?

A. Chemistry B. English
C. Biology D. Economics
E. Geography

19. In which standard does C study?

A. VI B. VII
C. VIII D. Either VI or VIII
E. None of these

20. Which subject does H like?

A. Marathi B. Physics
C. English D. Geography
E. None of these

Directions (Qs. No. 21-25): *Study the information given below and answer the questions based on it.*

Nine boys Vikash, Kamal, Sunil, Saurabh, Rohit, Sanjay, Amit, Anit and Sushil stays in a nine floor building and all of them stays on different floors. Each of them likes different girls namely—Sanjana, Surabhi, Amita, Anita, Komal, Suhana, Kumkum, Saroj and Susheela. Each boys belongs to different cities *i.e.* Patna, Lucknow, Chennai, Varanasi, Mirzapur, Allahabad, Mathura, Noida and Agra but necessarily in the same order. The topmost floor is numbered 9, the floor below it is numbered 8 and so on, and the ground floor is numbered 1.

The one who likes Surabhi stays on an even numbered floor. Sanjay does not belong to Allahabad. The one who belongs to Lucknow stays on the topmost floor. The one who likes Sanjana stays immediately below the one who likes Amita. Sanjay likes Anita and does not stay on the ground floor. Vikash belongs to Chennai and stays on an even numbered floor and he likes Sanjana. Saurabh stays on the second floor and belongs to Mirzapur. There are three boys between the one who likes Suhana and the one who likes Komal. The one who likes Suhana stays below the boy who likes Komal. The one who belongs to Allahabad stays on the third floor. The one who likes Saroj does not stay on sixth floor. There is one floor between the floors in which the one who likes Susheela and the one who likes Kumkum stay. Kamal stays on an even numbered floor below the floor on which Vikash stays. There are two floors between the floors on which the boys who are from Mathura and Chennai. The boy who likes Komal is from Mathura. Sushil belongs to Patna. The one who belongs to Noida stays on the fourth floor. Kamal does not belong to Varanasi and does not like Anita and Komal. There are three floors between the floors on which Sushil and Amit stay. Sunil stays on a floor immediately above the Anit's floor. The one who likes Kumkum stays immediately above Sushil. There is one floor between the floors on which Sanjay and Amit stay.

21. Which among the following boys likes Anita?
A. Sanjay B. Amit
C. Anit D. Rohit
E. Vikash

22. Who among the following stays between the floor of Sunil and Saurabh?
A. Anit B. Amit
C. Kamal D. Vikash
E. Rohit

23. Which of the following combinations is true?
A. Sanjay – Suhana – Varanasi
B. Amit – Amita – Allahabad
C. Rohit – Saroj – Varanasi
D. Sunil – Susheela – Noida
E. Kamal – Surabhi – Chennai

24. If 'Sanjay' is related to 'Mathura', 'Vikash' is related to 'Agra', in the same way 'Kamal' is related to?
A. Allahabad B. Patna
C. Chennai D. Noida
E. Varanasi

25. How many boys stay between the one who likes Amita and the one who likes Kumkum?
A. Five B. Two
C. One D. Six
E. Four

Directions (Qs. No. 26-30): *In these questions, a relationship between different elements is shown in the statements. The statements are followed by two conclusions.*

26. Statements : $A \geq P = S > T, V < B = T > X$
Conclusions : I. $A > X$ II. $P < B$
A. only conclusion I is true
B. only conclusion II is true
C. either conclusion I or II is true
D. neither conclusion I nor II is true
E. both conclusions I and II are true

27. Statements : $S > U > V, Y < U < Z, Z < X > W$
Conclusions : I. $S < Z$ II. $X > Y$
A. only conclusion I is true
B. only conclusion II is true
C. either conclusion I or II is true
D. neither conclusion I nor II is true
E. both conclusions I and II are true

28. Statements : $P < X < Y < Q, S > Y < T, P = V > R$
Conclusions : I. $V < S$ II. $T > R$
A. only conclusion I is true
B. only conclusion II is true
C. either conclusion I or II is true
D. neither conclusion I nor II is true
E. both conclusions I and II are true

29. Statements : $A \geq B > C, D \geq E = F \geq G, H \geq I = E$
Conclusions : I. $H < C$ II. $H > D$
A. only conclusion I is true
B. only conclusion II is true
C. either conclusion I or II is true
D. neither conclusion I nor II is true
E. both conclusions I and II are true

30. Statements : $A \geq B > C, D \geq E \geq F > B,$
$P \geq Q > E = S$
Conclusions : I. $P < B$ II. $S > A$
A. only conclusion I is true
B. only conclusion II is true
C. either conclusion I or II is true
D. neither conclusion I nor II is true
E. both conclusions I and II are true

Directions (Qs. No. 31-35): *In each of the questions below are given four statements followed by four conclusions numbered I, II, III and IV. You have to take the given statements to be true even if they seem to be at variance from commonly known facts. Read all the conclusions and then decide which of the given conclusions logically follows from the given statements disregarding commonly known facts.*

31. Statements : All lotus are beautiful.
All beautiful are Rose.
No Rose are stinky.
All sky are Rose.

Conclusions : I. All stinky are beautiful is a possibility.
II. Some stinky are lotus.
III. Some Rose are Stinky is a possibility.
IV. All beautiful can never be Sky.
A. None follows B. Only I and IV follow
C. Only II follows D. Only II and III follow
E. None of these

32. Statements : Some planes are waters.
Some waters are doors.
All doors are guitars.
No guitar is a flat.

Conclusion : I. At least some guitars are Planes.
II. All doors are flat is a possibility.
III. Some planes are both waters and doors.
IV. At least some flat is a door.

A. Only IV follows
B. Only either II or III follow
C. Only III follows
D. Only I follows
E. None follows

33. Statements : Some red are blue.
Some blue are grey.
All grey are white.
No white is black.

Conclusion : I. No black is grey.
II. Some blue are white.
III. Some black are red.
IV. No black is red.

A. Only I and II follow
B. Only either III or IV follows
C. Only I and either III or IV follow
D. Only I, II and either III or IV follow
E. None of these

34. Statements : All red are white.
Some white are pink.
Some pink are yellow.
No yellow is blue.

Conclusion : I. No blue is pink.
II. Some pink are red.
III. Some blue are red.
IV. Some blue are pink.

A. None follows
B. Only either I or IV follows
C. Only I follows
D. Only III & IV follow
E. All follow

35. Statements : All green are pink.
Some pink are black.
Some black are blue.
All blue are white.

Conclusions : I. Some black are white.
II. Some blue are pink.
III. Some pink are green.
IV. No green is white.

A. None follows
B. Only I and III follows
C. Only III follows
D. Only either I or II follows
E. None of these

Directions (Qs. No. 36-40): *In each question below is given a statement followed by two courses of action numbered I and II. You have to assume everything in the statement to be true and on the basis of the information given in the statement. Decide which of the suggested courses of action logically follow(s) for pursuing. Give answer:*

36. Statement : The government of India has launched a new scheme known as "Digital India" to help promote Digital Banking.

Course of action:
I. Traditional Banks should embrace the new scheme as it relates to the modern trend of digitalized banking.
II. Traditional Banks should do nothing as a bunch of money transaction apps cannot replace the traditional banking system, and hail it as a useless scheme.

A. If only course of action I follows
B. If only course of action II follows
C. If both I and II follow
D. If neither I nor II follows
E. If either I or II follows

37. Statement : A student was caught cheating in a class-test.

Course of action:
I. The teacher should report him to the principal.
II. Teacher should accept his test answer sheet and leave him with a final warning.

A. Only course of action I follows
B. Only course of action II follows
C. Both I and II follow
D. Neither I nor II follows
E. Either I or II follows

38. Statement : IT companies have stated that a large number of Engineers employed in their firms are not suitable for employment as they lack basic programming skills.

Course of action:
I. They should fire all unskilled and unproductive employees.
II. They should not fire the employees.

A. Only course of action I follows
B. Only course of action II follows
C. Both I and II follow
D. Neither I nor II follows
E. Either I or II follows

39. Statement : State police of Bihar came under the cloud with recent news that 9 lakh liters of liquor has been missing from the police station after the declaration of Bihar a dry state. The police department claimed that the whole of the liquor had been drunk by rats.

Course of Actions:
I. A thorough investigation should be ordered and those who are liable if any then they must have to be punished.

II. Suspension of those police officers who claim that rats drunk the liquor.
A. If only course of action I follow
B. If only course of action II follows
C. If both the course of action follows
D. If neither course of action fallows
E. Data inadequate

40. Statement : There has been an allegation on some of army officers that they had been involved in illegal arms trade with a few arms smuggler.

Course of Actions:

I. An investigation should be ordered by the Indian government to reveal the actual culprits.
II. They should be punished with court marshal.
A. Only course of action I follows
B. Only course of action II follows
C. Both I and II follow
D. Neither I nor II follows
E. Either I or II follows

Directions (Qs. No. 41-45): *The question below, there is a statement followed by two conclusions/assumptions numbered I and II. You have to assume everything in the statement to be true. Then consider the two conclusion/assumption together and decide which of them follows/implicit beyond a reasonable doubt from the information given in the statement.*

41. Statement : High pressure boilers are hazardous pieces of equipment, which are strictly regulated with special laws.

Conclusions:

I. If not regulated, high pressure boilers will be easily available in the market
II. High pressure boilers are rare.
A. Only conclusion I follows
B. Only conclusion II follows
C. Both conclusion I and II follows
D. Neither conclusion I nor II follows
E. Either conclusion I or II follows

42. Statement : The principal announced that students who score more than 95% will get special prize and medal. Kevin scored 96% but was found to have cheated in some of the exams.

Conclusions:

I. Kevin is going to get special prize and medal.
II. Kevin might not get any prize.
A. Only conclusion I follows
B. Only conclusion II follows
C. Both conclusion I and II follows
D. Neither conclusion I nor II follows
E. Either conclusion I or II follows.

43. Statement : Using calculator for simpler calculations adversely affects mathematical abilities of children.

Assumptions:

I. Using calculator for complex calculations may not affect mathematical abilities adversely.
II. Complex calculations cannot be done manually without the help of a calculator.
A. Only I is implicit
B. Only II is implicit
C. Either I or II is implicit
D. Neither I or II is implicit
E. Both I and II are implicit

44. Statement : An advertisement by Easy Air, a private airliner reads: 'Travel to Meerut by our airlines and get a chance to win an all-expenses-paid holiday to Bangkok'.

Assumptions:

I. Easy Air flights are available for Bangkok.
II. The city of Meerut has an airport.
A. Only I is implicit
B. Only II is implicit
C. Either I or II is implicit
D. Neither I or II is implicit
E. Both I and II are implicit

45. Statement : Ms. Suu Kyi, a recipient of the Nobel Peace Prize, has found it pragmatic not to challenge the official rhetoric in Myanmar, which suggests the military's actions were aimed at tackling "terror" in Rakhine.

Conclusions:

I. Ms. Suu Kyi does not want to upset the fragile balance of power.
II. Ms. Suu Kyi's action shows lack of empathy for the Rohingya in a country.
A. only conclusion I follows
B. only conclusion II follows
C. both conclusion I and II follow
D. neither conclusion I nor II follows
E. either conclusion I or II follows

Directions (Qs. No. 46-50): *Each of the question below consists of a question and three statements numbered I, II and III given below it. You have to decide whether the data provided in three statement are sufficient to answer the question.*

46. How many daughters does W have?
I. B and D are the sister of M.
II. M's father T is the husband of W.
III. Out of the three children which T has, only one is a boy.
A. I and III are sufficient to answer the question
B. All I, II and III are required to answer the question
C. I and II are sufficient to answer the question
D. Question cannot be answered even with all I, II and III
E. II and III are sufficient to answer the question

47. Among A, B, C, D, E, F and G, is B greater than F?

I. A is either greater or equal to B which is lesser than C which is equal to D which is greater than E which is either greater or equal to F which is equal to G.

II. A is lesser or equal to B which is equal to C which is greater to D which is greater to E which is lesser to F which is lesser to G.

III. A is greater to B which is greater to C which is equal to D which is greater or equal to E which is greater to F which is lesser to G.

A. I and II
B. II and III
C. III
D. Any Two
E. All of the above

48. In which direction is M with respect to N?

I. M is to the south of G, which is to the west of H. G is to the east of T.

II. N is between G and H.

III. N is to the north-west of T.

A. Only I and II
B. Only I
C. Only II and III
D. Only I and III
E. Only I and either II or III

49. Are writers not words?

I. Some writers are covers. No cover is a page.

II. All writers are books. Some books are covers.

III. No book is a word. Some words are pens.

A. Only I
B. Only II and III
C. Only I and III
D. I, II and III together are not sufficient
E. Only I and II

50. Who among Nitesh, Mahi, Rita, Priya, Neha and Rahul, each having different heights, is the tallest?

I. Mahi is taller than Nitesh but shorter than Neha.

II. Only two of them are shorter than Rita.

III. Priya is taller than only Rahul.

A. Only I and III
B. Only I and II
C. Only II and III
D. All I, II and III together
E. None of these

GENERAL ENGLISH

Directions (Qs. No. 51-55): *Read the following passage carefully and answer the questions that follow. Certain words/phrases are printed in bold to help you locate them while answering some of the questions.*

The Cabinet decision to allow spectrum trading will give a huge **impetus** to the on-going efforts for making broadband available in even the remotest parts of the country under the Digital India campaign. There are many compelling reasons why the time is ripe for the introduction of spectrum trading. One of the objectives of the new National Telecom Policy is to achieve a base of 600 million broadband users, with a minimum access speed of 2 Mbps by 2020. The Centre wants to create digital infrastructure to provide utility services like banking, education and healthcare to every Indian citizen. These ambitious targets can be achieved only if every operator in the country has access to adequate spectrum. The more spectrums an operator holds, the more data traffic it can carry over its network. Despite several rounds of auctions in the last two years, the quantum of airwaves with Indian telecom companies is less than that of their global counterparts. Mobile companies in the US and Japan, for instance, are able to offer high speed video services because they have 30-40 MHz of spectrum. In contrast, a 3G operator in India has only 5 MHz. Spectrum trading will allow the operators to get access to a larger pool of air waves, in turn ensuring that spectrum does not lie fallow. The option to trade spectrum also introduces an element of liquidity to its value. Interest in future auctions will increase because operators can bid with the knowledge that they can get returns by further leasing the airwaves. For smaller operators who are looking for an exit, trading gives them the opportunity to monetize their key asset without going through complex merger or acquisition deals.

However, the guidelines approved by the Cabinet have some concern areas which, if not addressed, could make it difficult for operators to trade spectrum. For example, the spectrum seller will have to pay 11 to 13 per cent of the proceeds to the government in the form of licence fee and spectrum usage charge. This could be a major **deterrent** if the operator is debt-laden or in an exit mode. The other big concern is the rule asking operators who bought spectrum in the 800 MHz band in the 2013 auctions, to first pay the price arrived at in the 2015 auction if they want to enter into a trading deal. Though the prices arrived at in the 2013 auctions were significantly lower than in 2015, both were market-driven processes. Thus the Centre's view that it did not receive the full price then is misplaced.

The benefits of sharing resources can be seen in the telecom tower business where operators were able to drive down costs and improve efficiencies by sharing space on towers. Similar sharing is now happening in the optical fibre cable infrastructure. Spectrum trading will benefit consumers, since at least those operators with adequate spectrum will be able to offer better quality of service. That said, quality improvement across the board will be achieved only when more spectrum is made available.

51. According to the given passage, which among the following is TRUE?
A. Mobile companies in the US and Japan are able to offer high speed video services.
B. Mobile companies in US and Japan have 30-40 MHz of spectrum.
C. A 3G operator in India has only 5 MHz Spectrum trading.
D. All are true
E. Only A and B are true.

52. According to the passage, how will Spectrum trading benefit the consumers in India?
A. Quality of services will improve.
B. Broad spectrum will be made available.
C. The cost of telecom companies will rise.
D. All the above
E. Only A and B

53. Which of the following concerns in the guidelines approved by the Cabinet needs to be addressed by the Government?
A. The spectrum seller will have to pay license fee and spectrum usage charge to the government.
B. The cost was higher for the bidders in the auction of 2013.
C. The rule asking operators who bought spectrum in the 2013 auctions, to first pay the price arrived at in the 2015 auction if they want to enter into a trading deal.
D. All of the above
E. Only A and C

54. Which of the following is the MOST SIMILAR in meaning to "impetus"?
A. Momentum B. Block
C. Check D. Hindrance
E. Incentive

55. Which of the following is the MOST OPPOSITE in meaning to "deterrent"?
A. Disincentive B. Encouragement
C. Damper D. Curb
E. Restraint

Directions (Qs. No. 56-65): *Read the following passage carefully and answer the questions that follow. Certain words are printed in bold to help you locate them while answering some of these.*

With half the fiscal year nearly complete, it is not surprising that the government is beginning to **fret** over the slow progress of the disinvestment programme. Of the budgeted ₹ 69,500 crore from PSU stake sales, only ₹ 12,700 crore has been raised so far. Reports that the Centre wants the EPFO to park part of the money that it has been allowed to invest in equity market in the CPSE ETF, highlights this desperation. Almost half the stocks in this ETF are companies that have been hard hit by the crash in commodity prices. This is not an asset the EPFO should be investing in now. The Centre, staring at yet another failure to meet its divestment target, appears ready to use any means to inch towards the target set for this year.

The urgency stems from the tight fiscal condition that the country is currently in. The fiscal deficit for the April to June period has already covered 69.3 per cent of the current year's target. This is despite a 36 per cent increase in indirect tax collection in the first five months of the current fiscal, thanks to the steep hike in excise duty on petrol and diesel, and the higher rate of service tax. A slowdown in income tax collection, along with a wide shortfall in the money raised through selling stakes in public sector companies, can make it a challenge for the Centre to meet this fiscal year's targeted deficit of 3.9 per cent of GDP. The increase in pension pay-outs for defence personnel is expected to add pressure on this goal. Inability to raise sufficient revenue can result in the government cutting back on investments, **pegging** back growth.

But the Centre has only itself to blame for this **predicament.** That the divestment department has gone about its task in a very **lackadaisical** manner in recent times is borne out by the fact that the gap between proceeds from stake sales and the budgeted target has been between 20 and 65 per cent since 2011-12. Given the decision to almost double its target for this fiscal, the Centre could have shown more **alacrity** in front-loading the sales this fiscal year, when the equity market was buoyant. The success of the REC's offer for sale in April highlights investor willingness to subscribe when the outlook for stocks is rosy. The divestment department needs to employ professionals to advise it on the timing of the sales better. Anyone who was tuned in to the stock market would have known that the second half of the year was expected to be rocky for stocks, given the impending monetary policy normalisation by the Fed. The offer for sale mechanism being employed for these stake sales also needs a rethink. With a retail discount of 5 per cent and the almost immediate availability of allotted shares, many investors have taken to short-term speculation through these offers.

56. What is the author of the above passage trying to suggest through it?
A. The tardiness in PSU stake sales will pressure the fiscal deficit.
B. The offer for sale mechanism for stake sales of companies must be remodelled.
C. The disinvestment programme is not furthering with a desired pace.
D. Only A and C
E. All of the above

57. Why the author believes that it is a challenge for the Centre to meet this fiscal year's targeted deficit of 3.9 per cent of GDP?
A. The fiscal deficit for the April to June period has already covered 69.3 per cent of the current year's target.

B. Slowdown in income tax collection.
C. Wide shortfall in the money collected through selling stakes in public sector companies.
D. All of the above
E. None of the above

58. Which among the following statements is **TRUE** according to the passage given above?
A. ₹ 12,500 crore has been raised so far through PSU stake sales.
B. In the first five months of the current fiscal there has been a 36 per cent increase in indirect tax collection.
C. The difference in proceeds from stake sales and the budgeted target is around 20 and 55 per cent since 2011-12.
D. Only A and C
E. Only B and C

59. What could be the results of the Centre's inability to raise sufficient revenues?
A. Government might cut back its investments.
B. The growth of the country could be pegged back.
C. Steep hike in excise duty on petrol and diesel may take place.
D. Only A and B
E. All A, B and C

60. Which among the following is **NOT TRUE** according to the passage given above?
A. A person who knows about stock market would have known that the second half of the year would be unhealthy for stock sales.
B. Many investors have bought the shares of the disinvestment portfolio just because of the 5% retail discount and immediate availability of stocks.
C. The targeted deficit of fiscal year 2011-12 is 3.9% of the GDP.
D. Only B and C
E. All are correct

61. Which among the following express the opposite meaning of the word "Fret" as given in the passage?
A. Affront
B. Calm
C. Anguish
D. Brood
E. Chafe

62. Which among the following express the opposite meaning of the word "Pegging" as given in the passage?
A. Clinch
B. Fasten
C. Remove
D. Tighten
E. Pin

63. Which among the following express the similar meaning of the word "Predicament" as given in the passage?
A. Fix
B. Fortune
C. Solution
D. Quandary
E. Ease

64. Which among the following express the SIMILAR meaning of the word "Lackadaisical" as given in the passage?
A. Abstracted
B. Careful
C. Active
D. Hard-working
E. Caring

65. Which among the following express the similar meaning of the word "Alacrity" as given in the passage?
A. Avidity
B. Cessation
C. Idleness
D. Repose
E. Inaction

Directions (Qs. No. 66-71): *In the following passage there are blanks each of which has been numbered. These numbers are printed below the passage and against each, five words/ phrases are suggested, one of which fits the blank appropriately.*

Citing intensifying regulatory uncertainty, Wells Fargo is __**66**__ roughly 200 agreements with builders, brokers and other real estate firms that the bank uses to bolster its mortgage business. One of the nation's largest mortgage lenders, Wells Fargo __**67**__ that it was ending all mortgage marketing services and desk rental agreements with builders and real estate brokers. These arrangements are widespread throughout the highly competitive mortgage industry, where lenders scrap to find __**68**__ borrowers. Such arrangements involve, for example, Wells renting desk space from a home builder in an effort to more easily sell mortgages to the home buyers passing through the sales office. "The decision was made as a result of increasing __**69**__ surrounding regulatory oversight of these types of arrangements," the bank said in a statement. A bank spokesman said the move was not related to a specific regulatory problem or investigation. Rather, he said, the bank was responding to broader regulatory scrutiny of such arrangements, which are __**70**__ by the Real Estate Settlement Procedures Act. The federal law is meant to __**71**__ mortgage lenders, real estate brokers, builders and any other party involved in the home buying process from handing out or receiving kickbacks in exchange for referrals.

66. Find out the appropriate word in each case.
A. serving
B. giving
C. signed
D. having
E. proclaiming

67. Find out the appropriate word in each case.
A. noticed
B. say
C. announced
D. given
E. established

68. Find out the appropriate word in each case.
A. good
B. eligible
C. sustainable
D. amiable
E. passable

69. Find out the appropriate word in each case.

A. confusion B. burden
C. pressures D. uncertainty
E. curiosity

70. Find out the appropriate word in each case.

A. held B. told
C. acclaimed D. given
E. governed

71. Find out the appropriate word in each case.

A. provide B. prevent
C. allow D. accept
E. pause

Directions (Qs. No. 72-77): *In the given question, select the sentence which should follow the given statement in a grammatically and conceptually appropriate manner.*

72. Even though the school premises had a lot of space __________.

A. there were plenty of play areas for the children
B. there was no playground for the children
C. yet it remain underutilized
D. there was no shortage of classrooms
E. none of the above

73. Political power is just as permanent as today's newspaper. Ten years down the line, ______ the most powerful man in any state today.

A. Political power shall have shifted weight into the hands of
B. New political parties shall have emerged
C. Few shall know, or care about
D. A new party may have absorbed into its ranks
E. None of these

74. Evolving in the mid-eighteenth century, from the pleasure houses of Japan where courtesans who would entertain the samurai, ________

A. would discuss the state matters secretly.
B. would hold plays which would entertain the crowd.
C. the first geisha was actually men.
D. the first geisha were actually men, who entertained the guests with drums and music.
E. the first geisha will be actually men, who entertained the guests with drums and music and were all warriors.

75. The media's relationship with democracy has allowed people ______.

A. As well as the conviction that media should be democratic itself and media ownership concentration is not democratic
B. The right to participate in media and share the information they found and want to contribute to the people through the media.
C. To be seen as a theater in modern societies in which political participation is enacted through a medium of talk and a realm of social life which public opinion can be formed
D. To communicate with one another through digital media and share the information they want to
E. None of the above

76. The influences in our lives—family, school, church, work environment, friends ______

A. all have made their silent unconscious impact on us and help shape our frame of reference, our paradigms, our maps.
B. try to change outward attitudes and behaviours which does very little good in the long run
C. shows how powerfully our paradigms affect the way we interact with other people.
D. begin to realize that others see them differently from their own apparently equally clear and objective point of view
E. None of the above

77. To enjoy good health, to bring true happiness to one's family, to bring peace to all, one must first discipline ________

A. to clear a good place for man's dwelling
B. and control one's own mind
C. to create a hindrance in the music that is in nature
D. to know the vast world outside
E. None of the above

Directions (Qs. No. 78-82): *Select the phrase/connector from the given three options which can be used to form a single sentence from the two sentences given below, implying the same meaning as expressed in the statement sentences. Pick out the option which when used to start a sentence combines both the above sentences in one.*

78. Flagging off partnerships in a host of economic and development projects through a Memorandum of Understanding has been done. The two Prime Ministers have set the stage for long-term collaboration in spheres ranging from energy and infrastructure to special economic zones.

I. Since
II. While
III. The reason behind the

A. Only I B. Only II
C. Only III D. All of the above
E. None of these

79. New Delhi's anxiety over Chinese presence might be justified. It should avoid using the China lens to view Sri Lanka, respecting the country's autonomy to engage with any willing partner.

I. While
II. Awhile
III. Among

A. Only I B. Only II
C. Only III D. Both I and III
E. None of these

80. The Modi government's fiscal deficit bumped to 3.5% of GDP in 2017-18, a slippage from the figure targeted in the budget. 3% of the GDP was envisaged in the fiscal consolidation unveiled earlier.

I. In the first place
II. Although
III. As a result

A. Only I
B. Only III
C. Only II
D. Both II and III
E. All of these

81. The partition was enforced by the ruling government. People started rushing towards their side of the town before the riots began.

I. Nevertheless
II. As soon as
III. In place of

A. Only I
B. Only III
C. Only I and III
D. Only II and III
E. None of these

82. The U.S. Administration announced its intent to withdraw from the Paris Agreement on climate change against a backdrop of rising carbon emissions, extreme weather events that devastated homes; and one of the top three hottest years on record. The momentum continued as other countries held firm in their determination to honour national and international commitments under Paris, in the face of the U.S. announcement.

I. Additionally
II. By comparison
III. Yet

A. Only I
B. Only II
C. Both I and III
D. Only III
E. All of these

Directions (Qs. No. 83-87): *In the given question, there are five sentences numbered 1,2,3,4 and 5. Read the sentences and find out which of the combinations is correct and mark the respective option.*

83. 1. Goa has so much for the fun-loving tourists.
2. Goa is always ready to welcome its guests.
3. No place can beat Goa in India.
4. Thus tourists receive a very warm treatment in Goa.
5. Whenever we think of a beach holiday,

A. 12453
B. 15324
C. 15432
D. 12543
E. 12345

84. 1. Safdar, Ajay and I dashed out of the classroom as the bell rang.
2. He was our leader.
3. It was the lunch break and we had a whole hour to play.
4. Safdar was the tallest, also the strongest amongst us.
5. Ajay and I followed him meekly like lambs.

A. 14523
B. 15423
C. 12345
D. 13524
E. 13425

85. 1. When you infuse creativity into your writing, you try to
2. You can paint it with your words thus selection of words is important
3. Stoke the emotions of your readers by narrating a story
4. In this way you can make a story that they can relate to easily
5. Thus creative writing classes are getting popular these days

A. 13425
B. 13245
C. 14523
D. 13254
E. 12543

86. 1. Online bingo or Internet bingo sites are virtual in nature.
2. It includes online blackjack, slots, roulette and poker.
3. The odds are undoubtedly better online.
4. These sites allow users to place bets on bingo games.
5. There are several benefits of playing online.

A. 14253
B. 12345
C. 12435
D. 14325
E. 15432

87. 1. Hospitals require one centralized software
2. Since all the functions and working of the hospital will depend on it
3. System which smartly manages a lot of functions
4. It should be able to manage a huge crowd and Should not crash easily
5. The entire hospital can then be easily managed by one software solution

A. 12345
B. 13245
C. 12354
D. 13425
E. 14325

Directions (Qs. No. 88-92): *In the following question, a part of the sentence is printed in bold. Below the sentence alternatives to the bold part are given at (A), (B), (C) and (D) which may help improve the sentence. Choose the correct alternative. In case the given sentence is correct, your answer is (E) i.e. No correction required.*

88. Many subsequent attempts at human **self-definition has faced similar problems** in relation to exceptionality.

A. self-defining has faced similar problems
B. self-definition have faced similar problems
C. self-definition has faced similar problem
D. self-definition has faced similarity problems
E. No correction required

89. They wanted to show how desire interacts with the material world, and to **examine how it were entwined with politics.**

A. examination how it were entwined with politics
B. examine how it were entwine with politically
C. examine how it was entwined with politics
D. examine why it were entwined at politics
E. No correction required

90. That all meaningful experience **requires tapping in to a divine realm** will trigger a severe frown in any non-believer.

A. required tapping in to a divine realm
B. requires tapping into a divine realm
C. requires tapping in to at divine realm
D. required tapped in to a divine realms
E. No correction required

91. Although China has recognized India's sovereignty over Sikkim and had initiated the trade at Nathu La pass, the Doklam fiasco **could mean trouble at all** ends.

A. could mean trouble by all
B. could mean trouble for all
C. could meant trouble at all
D. can mean trouble by all
E. No correction required

92. For centuries, caste dictated almost every aspect of Hindu religious and social life, **with every group occupying** a specific place in this complex hierarchy.

A. by every group occupying
B. with each group occupying
C. by each group occupying
D. through every group occupying
E. No correction required

Directions (Qs. No. 93-97): *Rearrange the following six sentences (a), (b), (c), (d), (e) and (f) in the proper sequence to form a meaningful paragraph: then answer the questions given below them.*

(*a*) Having a bank account for the purpose of savings and remittances has always been the central objective behind banking.

(*b*) Keeping in mind the goal of financial inclusion and extending finance to small businesses and low-income households, under-serviced by traditional commercial banks.

(*c*) The Reserve Bank of India's decision to allow 10 players to set up small finance banks out of the 72 applicants may seem conservative.

(*d*) The need for institutions with greater penetration and wide distribution models has, to some extent, been met with the issue of payments banks licences.

(*e*) With more than half the population in India still unable to access such basic services,

(*f*) But by permitting eight microfinance institutions (MFIs) to set up small banks, the RBI has chosen wisely.

93. Which of the following will be the **Fourth** sentence?

A. (*a*) B. (*b*)
C. (*f*) D. (*d*)
E. (*c*)

94. Which of the following will be the **First** sentence?

A. (*a*) B. (*f*)
C. (*c*) D. (*d*)
E. (*e*)

95. Which of the following will be the **Last** sentence?

A. (*f*) B. (*d*)
C. (*c*) D. (*e*)
E. (*a*)

96. Which of the following will be the **Third** sentence?

A. (*a*) B. (*b*)
C. (*c*) D. (*d*)
E. (*e*)

97. Which of the following will be the **Fifth** sentence?

A. (*a*) B. (*f*)
C. (*c*) D. (*d*)
E. (*e*)

Directions (Qs. No. 98-100): *In each question below, a sentence is broken into four parts which are marked as (A), (B), (C) and (D). One of them may be grammatically or structurally wrong in the context of the sentence. The letter of that word is the answer. If there is no wrong word or group of words, your answer will be (E), i.e., 'No error'. (Ignore the errors of punctuation, if any).*

98. (A) There is just not enough/(B) timing in my job to sit around/(C) talking about how we feel/(D) about each other./(E) No error.

99. (A) Reasonable ambition, if supported/(B) at persistent efforts,/(C) is likely to yield/(D) the desired results./(E) No error.

100. (A) Even after worked in the office/(B) for as many as fifteen years,/(C) he still does not understand/(D) the basic objectives of the work./(E) No error.

QUANTITATIVE APTITUDE

Directions (Qs. No. 101-105): *What will come in place of the question mark (?) in the following number series?*

101. 51, 60, 42, 78, ?, 150

A. 96
B. 108
C. 6
D. 144
E. None of these

102. 82, ?, 286, 373, 436, 451

A. 155 B. 175
C. 139 D. 145
E. 187

103. 20, 32, 30, ?, 105, 360, 577.5

A. 85 B. 90
C. 80 D. 75
E. 70

104. 49, 193, 766, 3055, 12208, ?
A. 47062
B. 49643
C. 48105
D. 48817
E. 46611

105. 21, 27, 64, 204, ?, 4150
A. 828
B. 700
C. 510
D. 705
E. 599

Directions (Qs. No. 106-110): *Given below is the table shows five types of mobile phones sold by two sellers (X and Y). Table shows cost price, profit percentage and market price of the phones.*

Table

Brand	X			Y		
	C.P.	Profit%	M.P.	C.P.	Profit%	M.P.
MI	-	-	-	-	25%	-
Lenovo	-	20%	25000	-	12%	-
Vivo	-	-	-	-	-	28000
Apple	-	20%	-	-	-	-
Oppo	-	35%	-	-	30%	-

106. How much percentage C.P. of Lenovo phones sold by seller X is less than M.P. of Oppo sold by seller Y. If X gave 10% discount on Lenovo phone while seller Y gave 20% discount on Oppo phone on M.P.?
A. 23.33%
B. 24.43%
C. 27.88%
D. 25.59%
E. 29%

107. What is the ratio between C.P. of Apple phone sold by seller X to C.P. of MI phone sold by seller Y, if M.P. of Lenovo sold by X and M.P. of MI sold by Y is 56.25% more than the M.P. of Oppo sold by Y. (take S.P. equals to M.P.)
A. 15/13
B. 12/11
C. 13/12
D. 10/13
E. 18/7

108. If seller Y sells Vivo phone at 20% discount, he got ₹ 2400 as profit and if he give 30% discount, he losses ₹ 400. Then what will be the profit percentage if a total 8 phones sold by seller Y, 2 phones at 20% discount and 6 phones at 30% discount.
A. 1.4%
B. 1.2%
C. 1.7%
D. 1.5%
E. 1.9%

109. If the ratio between S.P. of lenovo and M.P. of Vivo sold by Y is 3 : 4 then what is the average of cost price of 2 phones of lenovo bought by X and 6 phones of Lenovo bought by Y if X gave 10% discount of M.P.
A. 10000
B. 18750
C. 18710
D. 14750
E. 15000

110. If the average C.P. of Apple and Oppo bought by 'X' is 14000 and average S.P. of Apple and Oppo by 'X' is 18000 then what will be the difference between the C.P. of Apple and Oppo laptop bought by seller 'X'?
A. 4000
B. 5000
C. 6000
D. 7000
E. 9000

Directions (Qs. No. 111-115): *In the following questions two equations are given. You have to solve both the equations and give answers:*

111. $2x^2 - 31x + 84 = 0$
$3y^2 + y - 2 = 0$
A. If $x > y$
B. If $x \geq y$
C. If $x < y$
D. If $x \leq y$
E. If $x = y$ or no relation can be established between x and y.

112. $6x^2 + 14x - 12 = 0$
$6y^2 + 11y + 4 = 0$
A. If $x > y$
B. If $x \geq y$
C. If $x < y$
D. If $x \leq y$
E. If $x = y$ or no relation can be established between x and y.

113. $x^2 - 30x + 216 = 0$
$y^2 - 21x + 108 = 0$
A. If $x > y$
B. If $x \geq y$
C. If $x < y$
D. If $x \leq y$
E. If $x = y$ or no relation can be established between x and y.

114. $8x^2 + 21x - 9 = 0$
$3y^2 + 28y + 25 = 0$
A. If $x > y$
B. If $x \geq y$
C. If $x < y$
D. If $x \leq y$
E. If $x = y$ or no relation can be established between x and y.

115. $4x^2 - 15x + 14 = 0$
$3x^2 \quad 6x + 3 = 0$
A. If $x > y$
B. If $x \geq y$
C. If $x < y$
D. If $x \leq y$
E. If $x = y$ or no relation can be established between x and y.

116. A man invested certain sum on money of ₹ 10000 in three different schemes P, Q and R in such a way that he will get simple interest as 20%, 39% and 13%. If amount invested in scheme Q is 30% of amount invested in scheme R, he earned an interest of ₹ 4000 in 2 years. Find the amount invested in scheme P.
A. ₹ 5000
B. ₹ 4000
C. ₹ 3000
D. ₹ 1000
E. ₹ 6000

117. According to a new plan rolled out by bank, the rate of simple interest on a sum of money is 10% p.a. for the first 2 years, 12% p.a. for the next three years, and 4% p.a. for the period beyond the first five years. The simple interest accrued on a sum for a period of 9 years is ₹ 11,520. A person invested P amount of sum in this new plan and also invested same P amount of sum for 2 years on the other scheme which offers 10% compound interest. Find the compound interest he got on the sum after 2 years?

A. ₹ 3360
B. ₹ 3450
C. ₹ 3120
D. ₹ 3250
E. None of these

118. Three cooks have to make 80 cakes, they are known to make 20 cakes every minute working together. The first cook began working alone and made 20 cakes having worked for sometime more than 2 minutes. The remaining part of the work was done by the second and the third cook working together. It took a total of 8 minutes to complete 80 cakes. How many minutes would it take the first cook alone to bake 160 cakes for birthday party next day?

A. 30 minutes B. 32 minutes
C. 40 minutes D. 45 minutes
E. None of these

119. Two trains of lengths 200 m and 300 m pass each other with constant and same speeds on parallel tracks in opposite directions. The drivers and guards are at the extremities of the trains. The time gap between the drivers passing each other and first driver-guard pair passing each other is 30 s. How much later will the other driver-guard pair pass by?

A. 20 sec B. 30 sec
C. 15 sec D. 15 sec
E. Can't be determined

120. In a school, there are 76 students. In an examination, the difference between the highest and the least marks is 33. When the average of their marks was taken without considering the highest marks then the average was reduced by 2% but when the average of their marks was taken without considering the least marks then the average of the marks was increased by 3%. Find the original average of the marks of all the candidates?

A. 8.8 B. 9.8
C. 11 D. 19
E. Can't be determined

Directions (Qs. No. 121-125): *What approximate value will come in place of the question mark (?) in the following questions? (You are not expected to calculate the exact value).*

121. 62.5% of 18920 + ? % of 5325 = 16827

A. 86 B. 102
C. 77 D. 82
E. 94

122. $(14.989)^2 + (121.012)^3 + 2090 = ?$

A. 1239219 B. 1119391
C. 1669319 D. 1773876
E. None of these

123. 61.99% of 2004.85+ 69.99% of 1706.03 = ?

A. 2445 B. 2497
C. 2437 D. 2520
E. 2350

124. $(9000)^{1/3}$ * (10/9) / (40% of 120) = ? / 8% of 600 * $(100/81)^{1/2}$

A. 28 B. 21
C. 44 D. 57
E. 69

125. $(15.98)^2 + (19.09)^2$ – 29.92% of 799.87 = ?

A. 354 B. 377
C. 254 D. 294
E. 315

Directions (Qs. No. 126-130): *Study the following information carefully and answer the questions given below:*

The given information briefs about the percentage of work done by five sanitation workers in Municipal Corporation of Delhi and also the number of hours taken by sanitation workers to complete the respective percentage of same work.

Five workers Mahendra, Rampal, Vijay, Ramesh and Suresh do the sanitation work together. Mahendra did 37.5% of the work in 9 hours while Rampal does 20% of the work in 3.2 hours. Vijay took 35 hours to finish 125% of the work while Ramesh took 9 hours to complete 25% of the work. Suresh takes 27 hours to finish 150% of the work.

126. Out of the given five sanitation workers, who has the highest efficiency?

A. Mahendra B. Rampal
C. Vijay D. Ramesh
E. Suresh

127. Out of the given pairs, who will complete the work in the minimum time if they are working together?

A. Mahendra and Ramesh
B. Ramesh and Suresh
C. Rampal and Mahendra
D. Suresh and Mahendra
E. Rampal and Vijay

128. Find the number of hours taken by Mahendra, Ramesh and Suresh for the completion of work if they work together.

A. 6 hours B. 8 hours
C. 12 hours D. 16 hours
E. None of these

129. Mahendra, Rampal and some other sanitation worker named Ajay can complete the work in 8 hours. They are paid ₹ 12000 and the amount is divided between them on the basis of their work done. What is the share of Ajay?
A. ₹ 2000 B. ₹ 3000
C. ₹ 4000 D. ₹ 5000
E. ₹ 6000

130. If Rampal is $x\%$ more efficient than Vijay, then find the value of x.
A. 20 B. 25
C. 40 D. 50
E. 75

131. The distance between two stations A and B is 180 km. From a station C, which is between A and B, two cars x and y started simultaneously with speeds of 11 kmph and 13 kmph towards A and B respectively. After reaching their respective destinations, they reverse their direction and continue travelling. When X crosses C and travels an additional 5 km, it crosses y. What is the distance AC?
A. 120 km B. 150 km
C. 80 km D. 70 km
E. None of these

132. Menka, Nishu and Ojasvi entered into a partnership in a partnership company. Ojasvi got retired and her sons Dev and Eshan are taken as partners in the firm. The ratio of share in the profit of Dev and Eshan is 3: 5. Menka's share is double than Eshan's share and Nishu receives ₹ 10500 out of the total profit of ₹ 37500. In what ratio the profit will be shared among Menka, Nishu, Dev and Eshan?
A. 7 : 10 : 3 : 5 B. 10 : 3 : 7 : 5
C. 10 : 7 : 3 : 5 D. 5 : 3 : 7 : 10
E. None of the above

133. Pipes A, B and C are attached to a cuboidal pool which empty it at the rate of 12 litres/hour, 15 litres/hour and 25 litres/hour, respectively. The length, breadth and height of the pool are in the ratio of 7 : 2 : 1 respectively. The sum of the length, breadth and height is 40 m. If pipe A and B are open in the 1st hour and pipe B and C are open in the 2nd hour and this pattern continues, then how long will it take to completely empty (1/500)th of the pool? [Round off to the nearest decimal]
A. 55 hours B. 54 hours
C. 56 hours D. 50 hours
E. 53 hours

134. Three vessels contain alcoholic solutions with the concentrations of alcohol as 0.25, 0.5 and 0.75 respectively. 4 litres from the first, 6 litres from the second and 8 litres from the third are mixed. What is the ratio of alcohol and water in the resultant mixture?
A. 1 : 2 B. 1 : 3
C. 1 : 1 D. 5 : 9
E. 5 : 4

135. The speed of boat A in still water and speed of stream B are 40 km/hr and 20 km/hr respectively. The speed of boat B in still water and speed of stream A are 'x' km/hr and 'y' km/hr respectively. The sum of time taken by boat A to cover 450 km upstream and the same distance downstream in stream A is 24 hours and the sum of the time taken by boat B to cover 320 km upstream and 320 km downstream in stream B is 12 hours. Find $x + y$.
A. 90 km/hr B. 70 km/hr
C. 20 km/hr D. 15 km/hr
E. None of these

Directions (Qs. No. 136-140): *The question given is followed by the information in statements. You have to decide the information in which of the statements is necessary and sufficient to answer the question and mark answer accordingly.*

136. Every man in a certain class either belongs to group A, belongs to group B, or belongs to both groups. 20% of group A consists of men and 65% of group B consists of men. What percentage of the two groups together is made up of men?
(1) Group A contains 50 people.
(2) Group B contains 100 people.
A. Statement (1) ALONE is sufficient, but statement (2) alone is not sufficient to answer the question asked
B. Statement (2) ALONE is sufficient, but statement (1) alone is not sufficient to answer the question asked
C. BOTH statements (1) and (2) TOGETHER are sufficient to answer the question asked, but NEITHER statement ALONE is sufficient
D. EACH statement ALONE is sufficient to answer the question asked
E. Statements (1) and (2) TOGETHER are NOT sufficient to answer the question asked, and additional data are needed

137. A 40 m long wire is cut into three pieces. What is the length of the largest piece?
I. Two pieces are each 2 m shorter than the longest piece.
II. Two pieces of the wire are of the same length.
A. I alone
B. II alone
C. Either I alone or II alone
D. Both I and II
E. Both I and II are not sufficient

138. What is the weighted average of marks obtained by Ankur?
I. History, English and Hindi have weights 7, 10, 13 respectively
II. Simple arithmetic mean of History and English is 150, which is twice the average of English and Hindi

A. I alone
B. II alone
C. Either I alone or II alone
D. Both I and II
E. Both I and II are not sufficient

139. If each of the 20 bolts of fabric on a shelf is either 100 per cent cotton, 100 per cent wool, or a mixture of cotton and wool, how many bolts contain both cotton and wool?

(1) Of the 20 bolts, 18 contain some wool and 14 contain some cotton.
(2) Of the 20 bolts, 6 are 100 per cent wool

A. Statement (1) ALONE is sufficient, but statement (2) alone is not sufficient to answer the question asked
B. Statement (2) ALONE is sufficient, but statement (1) alone is not sufficient to answer the question asked
C. BOTH statements (1) and (2) TOGETHER are sufficient to answer the question asked, but NEITHER statement ALONE is sufficient
D. EACH statement ALONE is sufficient to answer the question asked
E. Statements (1) and (2) TOGETHER are NOT sufficient to answer the question asked, and additional data are needed

140. A farmer has a total of 60 pigs, cows, and horses on his farm. How many pigs does he have?

(1) The ratio of horses to cows is 2 : 9.
(2) He has more than 36 cows.

A. Statement (1) ALONE is sufficient, but statement (2) alone is not sufficient to answer the question asked
B. Statement (2) ALONE is sufficient, but statement (1) alone is not sufficient to answer the question asked
C. BOTH statements (1) and (2) TOGETHER are sufficient to answer the question asked, but NEITHER statement ALONE is sufficient
D. EACH statement ALONE is sufficient to answer the question asked
E. Statements (1) and (2) TOGETHER are NOT sufficient to answer the question asked, and additional data are needed

141. Piyush went to buy an article. The shopkeeper sold the article at the marked price but told him to pay 20% tax on the marked price if he asked for the bill. Piyush manages to get the discount of 5% on the actual marked price of the article. Besides he manages to avoid paying 20% tax on the already discounted price. He paid the shopkeeper ₹ 2280 without tax after the discount. What is the amount of discount he got?

A. 500 B. 550
C. 600 D. 650
E. 700

142. One container contains a mixture of spirit and water in the ratio 2 : 3 and another contains the mixture of spirit and water in the ratio 3 : 2. How much quantity from the second should be mixed with 10 litres of the first so that the resultant mixture has ratio of 4 : 5?

A. 2.86 litres B. 3.45 litres
C. 4.31 litres D. 5.67 litres
E. 8.94 litres

143. The average age of a class of 30 students and a teacher reduced by 0.5 years if we exclude the teacher. If the initial average age is 14 years and then the age of the teacher is

A. 29 years B. 30 years
C. 35 years D. 32 years
E. 33 years

144. 3 bell ring at an interval of 48, 72, 108 second. If they ring at 6 : 00 am then after this at what time they will ring together?

A. 6 : 07 : 12 B. 6 : 08
C. 6 : 05 : 13 D. 6 : 10
E. 6 : 12

145. When one-fifth of a number x, is added to 118, it becomes equal to y^2. If one-eighth of y is equal to 2.5, what is the value of x?

A. 1420 B. 1310
C. 1410 D. 1460
E. 1470

Directions (Qs. No. 146-148): *Study the following data carefully and answer the questions:*

Percentage of women opted different specialization

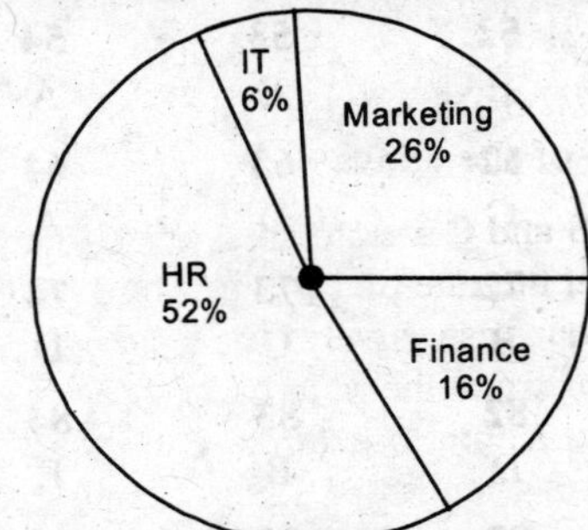

Number of men opted different specialization

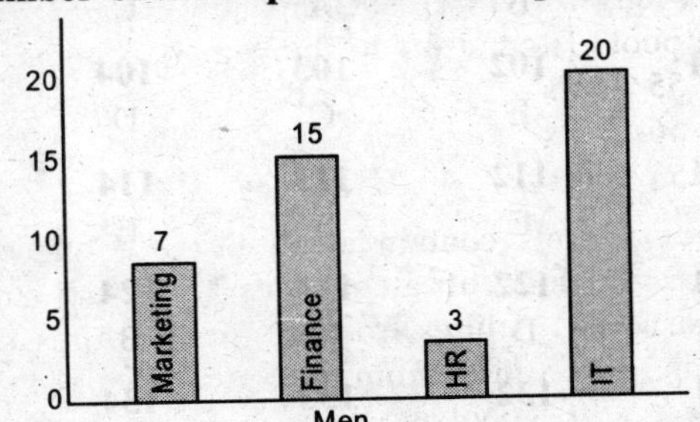

The pie charts shows the distribution of no. women preferring different specialization where the total number of women = 50.

146. If an audit is being conducted by a 10 member finance team, what is the probability that it can accommodate maximum of women?

A. 0.6 B. 0.8
C. 0.7 D. 0.9
E. 0.5

147. A prefectural board is selected comprising of 8 men or 8 women. What is the probability that equal number of men or women is selected from each department?

A. 0.001 B. 0.003
C. 0.005 D. 0.007
E. 0.009

148. What is the probability that number of women in a 20 member dancing club will have no women taking part from HR department?

A. 0.133 B. 0.833
C. 0.633 D. 0.338
E. None of these

Directions (Qs. No. 149-150): *In the following number series, only one number is incorrect. Find out the wrong number in the series.*

149. 25, 21, 30, 14, 139, 3

A. 103 B. 30
C. 25 D. 20
E. 139

150. 1000, 500, 271, 153.5, 97.75, 72.875

A. 271 B. 500
C. 153.5 D. 97.75
E. 72.875

ANSWERS

1	2	3	4	5	6	7	8	9	10
B	D	B	A	B	B	A	C	A	D
11	12	13	14	15	16	17	18	19	20
C	C	A	D	D	B	C	D	A	C
21	22	23	24	25	26	27	28	29	30
A	A	D	D	D	A	B	E	D	D
31	32	33	34	35	36	37	38	39	40
A	E	D	B	B	A	B	B	A	A
41	42	43	44	45	46	47	48	49	50
D	B	D	E	C	E	C	E	B	B
51	52	53	54	55	56	57	58	59	60
D	E	E	A	B	E	D	B	D	E
61	62	63	64	65	66	67	68	69	70
B	C	D	A	A	A	C	B	D	E
71	72	73	74	75	76	77	78	79	80
B	B	C	D	B	A	B	C	A	C
81	82	83	84	85	86	87	88	89	90
A	D	B	E	B	A	D	B	C	B
91	92	93	94	95	96	97	98	99	100
A	B	A	C	B	B	E	B	B	A
101	102	103	104	105	106	107	108	109	110
C	E	C	D	A	C	A	D	B	A
111	112	113	114	115	116	117	118	119	120
A	E	B	E	A	A	A	B	B	A
121	122	123	124	125	126	127	128	129	130
E	D	C	B	B	B	C	B	A	E
131	132	133	134	135	136	137	138	139	140
C	C	B	E	B	E	A	E	A	C
141	142	143	144	145	146	147	148	149	150
C	A	A	A	C	B	D	B	E	B

EXPLANATORY ANSWERS

For Qs. 1-5:

- F sits third to the right of S.
- F is sixth to the right of T.
- C and D are not immediate neighbours of F, who sits second to the right of E.
- E sits at the fifth position from the right end.
- B sits fourth to the right of P, who is not the immediate neighbour of U.
- There are two persons between U and A.
- There are two persons between D and Q.
- S is not an immediate neighbour of A.
- C is not an immediate neighbour of D and Q.

From the above statement, we conclude:

Facing North:

P	C	A	T	B	U	S	E	Q	F	R	D

For Qs. 6-10:

In row-1, J, K, L, M, N and O are seated and all of them are facing south. In row-2, C, D, E, F, G and H are seated and all of them are facing north

- M sits third to the left of J.
- The person facing M sits second to the left of H.
- Two persons are sitting between H and E.
- G is not an immediate neighbour of E.
- D does not face M.
- L and K are immediate neighbours.
- L and K do not sit at any of the extreme ends of the line.
- Only one person sits between N and L.
- The person facing K is an immediate neighbour of C.

According to above statement, we conclude:

J	K	L	M	N	O	Row 1 (Facing South)
C	D	E	F	G	H	Row 2 (Facing North)

For Qs. 11-15:

Month	Person
January (31)	Q
February (28/29)	P
March (31)	-
April (30)	A
May (31)	S
June (30)	-
July (31)	M
August (31)	C
September (30)	-
October (31)	K
November (30)	R
December (31)	-

For Qs. 16-20:

Students	Subjects	Standard
D	Chemistry	VIII
H	English	VIII
E	Biology	VII
A	Marathi	VII
G	Math	VII
C	Economics	VI
F	Physics	VI
B	Geography	VI

For Qs. 21-25:

Floor	Boy	Girl	City
9	Rohit	Amita	Lucknow
8	Vikash	Sanjana	Chennai
7	Sanjay	Anita	Varanasi
6	Kamal	Surabhi	Agra
5	Amit	Komal	Mathura
4	Sunil	Susheela	Noida
3	Anit	Saroj	Allahabad
2	Saurabh	Kumkum	Mirzapur
1	Sushil	Suhana	Patna

26. I. $A > X \rightarrow$ True (as $A \geq P = S > T > X$)

II. $P < B \rightarrow$ False

Hence, only conclusion I follows.

27. I. $S < Z \rightarrow$ False (as $S > U < Z$)

II. $X > Y \rightarrow$ True (as $Y < U < Z < X$)

Hence, only conclusion II follows.

28. I. $V < S \rightarrow$ True (as $V = P < X < Y < S$)

II. $T > R \rightarrow$ True (as $T > Y > X > P = V > R$)

Hence, both conclusions follow.

29. I. $H < C \rightarrow$ False (as there is no relation between H and C)

II. $H > D \rightarrow$ False (as $H \geq I = E \leq D$)

Hence, no conclusion follows.

30. I. $P < B \rightarrow$ False (as $P \geq Q > E \geq F > B$)

II. $S > A \rightarrow$ False (as $P \geq Q > E = S \geq F > B \leq A$)

Hence, no conclusion follows.

31.

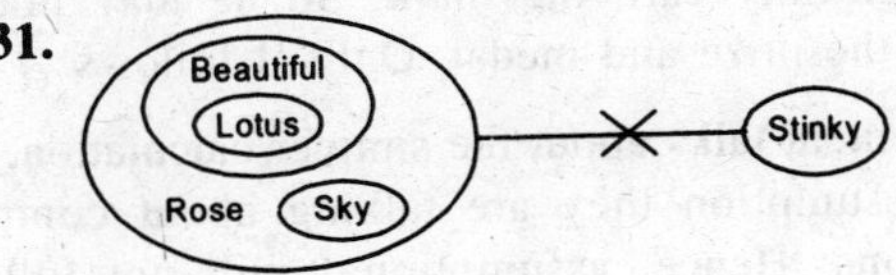

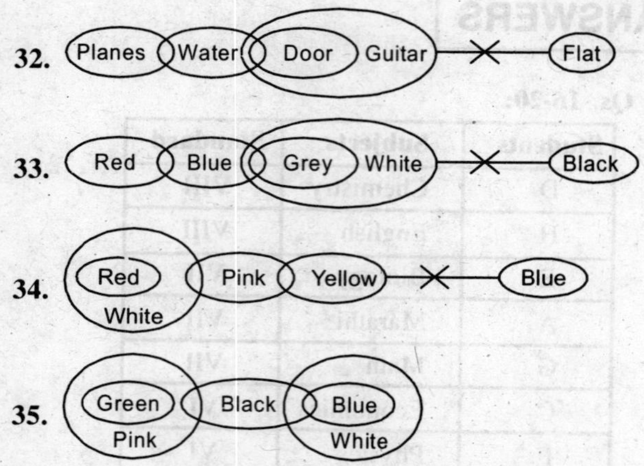

36. It is necessary for the banks to promote the modern banking techniques and embrace the new system so as to provide comfortable banking options for their customers.

37. Reporting the student to principal on such pity matters is simply a waste of his time. Therefore teacher should leave him with a final warning and should accept his sheet.

38. Here only II follows as it was the IT Company itself that hired them in the first place. They should train them instead of firing them.

39. The given situation presents a situation, a solid conclusion for which cannot be drawn without a proper investigation. Thus, only I follows. Though the statement by the police sounds far-fetched, a fair judgment can only be made after a sound investigation. Thus, option A is the correct answer.

40. An allegation does not prove the army officials guilty. There should be proper investigation before branding the army officials as guilty of arms smuggling. So (I) is clearly a course of action. If they are found guilty then proper action can be taken. (II) is not a proper course of action as it brands the officials guilty without giving them a chance to prove their innocence.

41. The statement says that the high pressure boilers are **hazardous** and that's why they are strictly regulated with special laws. Conclusion 1 talks about availability although the statement does not relate to the availability. Conclusion 2 talks about the rarity of high pressure boilers although the statement does not mention it anywhere.

42. Only people who rightfully earned the marks will get medal. Kevin was found to be cheating and hence he didn't rightfully earn the mark. So he may not be awarded the prize and medal. Only II follows.

43. The statement talks about the simpler calculation, but in the assumption they are talking about complex calculations. Hence, assumption I will not follow. I can be an inference but not an assumption. Complex calculations can be done even without a calculator. Hence, conclusion II will also not follow. Hence, option C is the correct response.

44. As Easy Air will pay all the expenses of holiday to Bangkok, which means Flight tickets are available with the given airline. Hence, conclusion I will follow. It is given in the statement that travel to Meerut by our airlines and get a chance to win an all-expenses-paid holiday to Bangkok', which implies the city of Meerut has an airport. Hence, conclusion II will also follow.

45. As per the statement, one can make out that the situation in Myanmar is not good. Ms. Suu Kyi might not want to make things bad and this is what brings us to the conclusion 1. Her not challenging the officials also proves the conclusion 2. Hence, option C is the correct option.

46. From statement II, T is the husband of W *i.e.,* T and W are a married couple. From Statement III, Out of 3 children of T, one is a boy *i.e.,* he has two daughters and one son. By combining Statements II and III, W has two daughters. So, Statements II and III are sufficient to answer the question.

47. From I, $A \geq B < C = D > E \geq F = G$

We can't compare B and F.

From II, $A \leq B = C > D > E < F < G$

We can't compare B and F.

From III, $A > B > C = D \geq E > F < G$

Clearly B is greater to F.

So, Only III is sufficient. Hence, option C.

48. From I, T ⟶ G ⟵ H, G ↓ M

From II, N is between G and H.

From III,

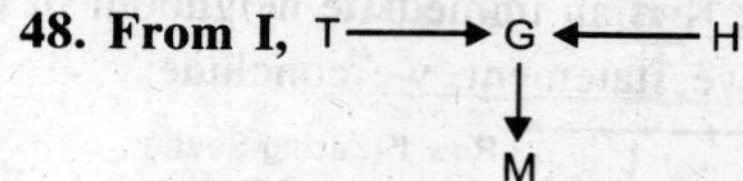

From I and II,

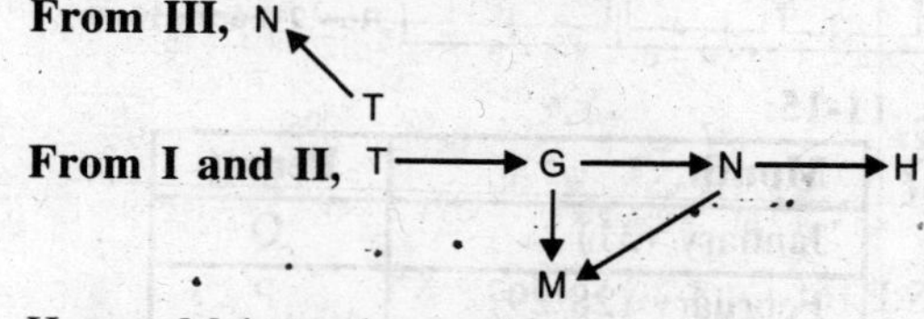

Hence, M is to the south-west of N.

From I and III,

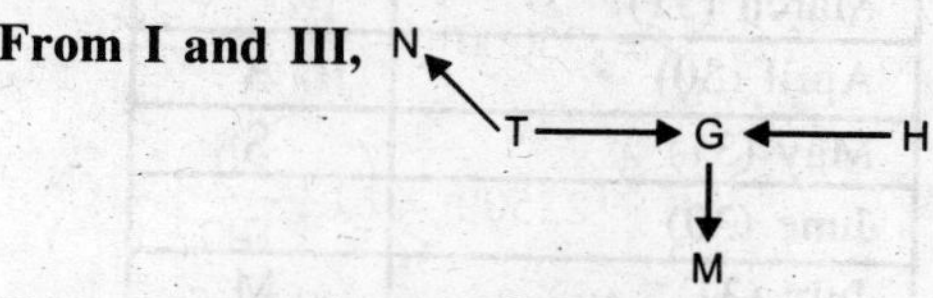

Thus, M is to the south-east of N.

So answer can be found by using I and either II or III.

49. From I, (writer)(cover)—(page)

In this only 'writer' is given nothing information about 'word'.

From II,

In this only 'writer' is given nothing information about 'word'.

From III,

No information about 'writer'

From II and III,

If we combine both II and III we can get that 'no writer is word'.

So, both II and III will be answer.

50. From I. Neha > Mahi > Nitesh

From II. – > – > – > Rita > – > –

Now combining all the statements, we have

Neha > Mahi > Nitesh > Rita > – > –

Thus, Neha is the tallest.

101. 51   60   42   78   [6]   150

+9   −18   +36   −72   +144

102. 82   [187]   286   373   436   451

+105   +99   +87   +63   +15

−6   −12   −24   −48

103. 20   32   30   [80]   105   360   577.5

×1.5   ×3.5   ×5.5

×2.5   ×4.5

104. 49   193   766   3055   12208   [48817]

× 4 – 3   × 4 – 6   × 4 – 9   × 4 – 12   × 4 – 15

105. 21   27   64   204   [828]   4150

× 1 + (1 × 6)   × 2 + (2 × 5)   × 3 + (3 × 4)   × 4 + (4 × 3)   × 5 + (5 × 2)

106. S.P. of Lenovo sold by X

$$= 25000\left(1-\frac{10}{100}\right) = 22500$$

$$\text{S.P.} = 22500 = \left(1+\frac{20}{100}\right) \times (\text{CP})_{\text{Lenovo}}$$

$\Rightarrow$ C.P. of Lenovo = 18750

$$\text{S.P. of Oppo sold by Y} = 16000\left(1+\frac{30}{100}\right) = 20800$$

$$\text{M.P. (Oppo)} \times \left(1-\frac{20}{100}\right) = 28000$$

M.P. (Oppo) = 26000

$$\text{Desired \%} = \frac{(26000-18750)}{26000} \times 100$$

= 27.88%.

107.

$$\text{Desired ratio} = \frac{\text{C.P. of Apple phone by X}}{\text{C.P. of MI by Y}}$$

$$\text{M.P. of Apple phone} = \left(1+\frac{44}{100}\right) \times 25000 = 36000$$

$$\text{C.P. of Apple phone} = 36000 \times \frac{100}{120} = 30000$$

$$\text{M.P. of MI phone} = 16000\left(1+\frac{30}{100}\right) \times \left(1+\frac{56.25}{100}\right)$$

$$= 16000 \times \frac{130}{100} \times \frac{156.35}{100}$$

= 32500

$$\text{C.P. of MI} = 32500 \times \frac{100}{125} = 26000$$

$$\text{Desired ratio} = \frac{30000}{26000} = \frac{15}{13}.$$

108. $$\text{M.P. after 20\% discount} = 28000\left(1-\frac{20}{100}\right) = 22400$$

C.P. = 22400 – 2400 = 20000

or, M.P. after 30% discount

$$= 28000\left(1-\frac{30}{100}\right) = 19600$$

C.P. = 19600 + 400 = 20000

Net profit = 2 × 2400 – 6 × 400 = 2400

$$\text{Profit \%} = \frac{2400}{(8 \times 20000)} \times 100$$

= 1.5%.

109. $$\text{S.P. of Lenovo by Y} = 28000 \times \frac{3}{4} = 21000$$

C.P. of Lenovo bought by X

$$= 25000 \times \frac{90}{100} \times \frac{100}{120} = 18750$$

C.P. of Lenovo bought by

$$= 21000 \times \frac{100}{112} = 18750$$

$$\text{Desired average} = \frac{(2 \times 18750 + 6 \times 18750)}{8} = 18750.$$

110. Let, C.P. of Apple phone = x

C.P. of Oppo = y

According to question,

$$\frac{(x+y)}{2} = 14000$$

$$x + y = 28000 \quad ...(i)$$

$$\frac{x*1.2 + y*1.35}{2} = 18000$$

$$1.2x + 1.35y = 36000 \quad ...(ii)$$

On solving (i) and (ii) $y = 16000$; $x = 12000$

Desired difference = 16000 − 12000 = 4000.

111. (i)

$$2x^2 - 31x + 84 = 0$$
$$2x^2 - 24x - 7x + 84 = 0$$
$$2x(x - 12) - 7(x - 12) = 0$$
$$(x - 12)(2x - 7) = 0$$
$$x = 12, \frac{7}{2}$$

(ii)

$$3y^2 + y - 2 = 0$$
$$3y^2 + 3y - 2y - 2 = 0$$
$$3y(y + 1) - 2(y + 1) = 0$$
$$(y + 1)(3y - 2) = 0$$
$$y = -1, \frac{2}{3}$$

$x > y$.

112. (i)

$$6x^2 + 14x - 12 = 0$$
$$6x^2 + 18x - 4x - 12 = 0$$
$$6x(x + 3) - 4(x + 3) = 0$$
$$(x + 3)(6x - 4) = 0$$
$$x = -3, \frac{2}{3}$$

(ii)

$$6y^2 + 11y + 4 = 0$$
$$6y^2 + 8y + 3y + 4 = 0$$
$$2y(3y + 4) + 1(3y + 4) = 0$$
$$y = -\frac{4}{3}, -\frac{1}{2}$$

No relation.

113. (i)

$$x^2 - 30x + 216 = 0$$
$$x(x - 12) - 18(x - 12) = 0$$
$$(x - 18)(x - 12) = 0$$
$$x = 18, 12$$

(ii)

$$y^2 - 21y + 108 = 0$$
$$y^2 - 12y - 9y + 108 = 0$$
$$y(y - 12) - 9(y - 12) = 0$$
$$(y - 9)(y - 12) = 0$$
$$y = 9, 12$$

$x \geq y$.

114. (i)

$$8x^2 + 21x - 9 = 0$$
$$8x^2 + 24x - 3x - 9 = 0$$
$$8x(x + 3) - 3(x + 3) = 0$$
$$x = 3/8, -3$$

(ii)

$$3y^2 + 28y + 25 = 0$$
$$3y^2 + 3y + 25y + 25 = 0$$
$$3y(y + 1) + 25(y + 1) = 0$$

$y = -1, -\frac{25}{3} \Rightarrow$ No relation.

115. (i)

$$4x^2 - 15x + 14 = 0$$
$$4x^2 - 8x - 7x + 14 = 0$$
$$4x(x - 2) - 7(x - 2) = 0$$
$$(x - 2)(4x - 7) = 0$$
$$x = 2, 7/4$$

(ii)

$$3y^2 - 6y + 3 = 0$$
$$3y^2 - 3y - 3y + 3 = 0$$
$$3y(y - 1) - 3(y - 1) = 0$$
$$(y - 1)(3y - 3) = 0$$
$$y = 1, 1 \Rightarrow x > y.$$

116. Amount invested in scheme Q is 30% of Amount invested in scheme R.

$$Q = \left(\frac{30}{100}\right) \times R \Rightarrow \frac{Q}{R} = \frac{3}{10}$$

Let the amount invested in scheme P = P

Ratio = P : Q : R = P : 3 : 10

Let, P = Px, Q = 3x, R = 10x

Rate in scheme P = 21%

Rate in scheme Q = 39%

Rate in scheme R = 13%

$$\text{Rate in scheme Q and R} = \left(\frac{3}{13}\right) \times 39\% + \left(\frac{10}{13}\right) \times 13\%$$
$$= 19\%$$

Time = 2 years

Simple interest in 2 years = 4000

Simple interest in 1 year = 2000

Principal = 10000

$$\text{Rate in 3 schemes} = 2000 \times \frac{100}{10000}$$

Now, By allegation method:

P		Q + R
21%		19%
	20%	
1		1

$$\text{Amount invested by P} = \frac{(10000 \times 1)}{2} = ₹\ 5000.$$

117. Rate of interest for a period of 9 years

= (10 × 2 + 12 × 3 + 4 × 4)% = 72%

Hence, the amount is returning 72% in the form of S.I. according to the new plan of bank.

Now, 72% of P = 11520 ⇒ P = ₹ 16000

Now the person invested same amount in 2nd scheme which offers C.I.,

$$\text{Effective rate} = 10+10+10\times\frac{10}{100} = 21\%$$

$$\text{C.I.} = 21\% \text{ of } 16000 = ₹\ 3360.$$

118. Let three cooks are x, y and z. And they bake number of cakes in 1 minute $\frac{1}{x}, \frac{1}{y}, \frac{1}{z}$ respectively.

Now, it is given that they can bake 20 cakes in a minute when they work together.

$$\left(\frac{1}{x}+\frac{1}{y}+\frac{1}{z}\right) = 20 \quad ...(i)$$

Now let cook x works for K minutes and K > 2

So, $$K\left(\frac{1}{x}\right) = 20 \quad ...(ii)$$

And y and z complete remaining work.
They complete the whole work in 8 minutes.

$$(8-K)\left(\frac{1}{y}+\frac{1}{z}\right) = 60 \quad ...(iii)$$

By equation (*i*), (*ii*) and (*iii*),

$$x = \frac{1}{5}, \frac{1}{10}$$

If we take $x = \frac{1}{10}$ then K = 2 and is equal to 2

So, we will take $x = \frac{1}{5}$

Now x bakes 1 cake in $= \frac{1}{5}$ minute.

$$160 \text{ cake in} = \frac{1}{5}\times 160 = 32 \text{ minutes.}$$

119.

←200 m→ G₁ D₁ ←300 m→ D₂ G₂

Time gap passing D_1D_2 and D_2G_1 = 30 sec

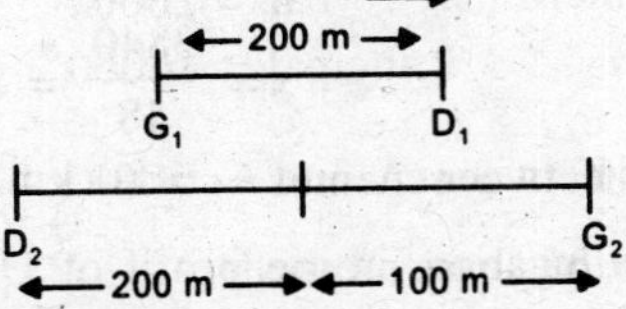

Let Speed of train is x m/s

$$T_{D_1D_2} = \frac{200+200}{x+x} = \frac{400}{2x}$$

$$T_{D_2G_1} = \frac{500}{2x}$$

$$\therefore \quad T_{D_2G_1} - T_{D_1G_2} = 30 \text{ sec}$$

$$\frac{500}{2x} - \frac{400}{2x} = 30$$

$$\frac{100}{2x} = 30 \Rightarrow x = \frac{100}{60}$$

$$2x = \frac{10}{3} \text{ m/s}$$

∵ Speed of both the train is same

←200 m→ G₁ D₁ D₂ G₂ ←300 m→

$$T_{D_1G_2} = \frac{300-200}{2x} = \frac{100}{2x} = \frac{100}{(10/3)} = \frac{100\times 3}{10} = 30 \text{ sec.}$$

120. Let the original average of the marks of all the candidates = x
The highest marks = a
The least marks = b
Then, according to the question,

$$98\% \text{ of } x = \frac{76x-a}{75}$$

$$98\% \text{ of } 75x + a = 76x \quad ...(i)$$

$$\text{And } 103\% \text{ of } x = \frac{76x-b}{75}$$

$$103\% \text{ of } 75x + b = 76x \quad ...(ii)$$

From equation (*i*) and equation (*ii*),

$$98\% \text{ of } 75x + a = 103\% \text{ of } 75x + b$$

$$5\% \text{ of } 75x = a - b$$

According to the question,

$$a - b = 33$$

So, $$5\% \text{ of } 75x = 33$$

$$5\times\frac{75x}{100} = 33$$

By solving, $$x = 8.8$$

121. 62.5% of 18920 + ?% of 5325 = 16827

⇒ 11825 + ?% of 5325 = 16827

$$\Rightarrow \quad ?\times\frac{5325}{100} = 5002$$

⇒ ? = 94%.

122. $(14.989)^2 + (121.012)^3 + 2090 = ?$

225 + 1771561 + 2090 = 1773876.

123. 61.99% of 2004.85+ 69.99% of 1706.03 = ?

$$\frac{(2005\times 62)}{100}+\frac{(1706\times 70)}{100} = ?$$

1243 + 1194 (Approx) = 2437.

124. $$\frac{(9000)^{1/3}\times(10/9)}{(40\% \text{ of } 120)} = \frac{?}{8\% \text{ of } 600}\times\left(\frac{100}{81}\right)^{1/2}$$

? = 20.80 = 21.

125. $$16^2+19^2-\frac{29}{100}\times 800$$

$$= 256+361-\frac{30}{100}\times 800$$

= 617 − 240 = 377.

For Qs. No. 126-130:

Workers	Percentage of Word Done	Time taken (hours)
Mahendra	37.5%	9
Rampal	20%	3.2
Vijay	125%	35
Ramesh	25%	9
Suresh	150%	27

Time taken by Mahendra to complete 37.5% of the work = 9 hours

Time taken by Mahendra to complete the whole work

$$= \frac{9}{37.5} \times 100 = 24 \text{ hours}$$

Time taken by Rampal to complete 20% of the work = 3.2 hours

Time taken by Rampal to complete the whole work

$$= \frac{3.2}{20} \times 100 = 16 \text{ hours}$$

Time taken by Vijay to complete 125% of the work = 35 hours

Time taken by Vijay to complete the whole work

$$= \frac{35}{125} \times 100 = 28 \text{ hours}$$

Time taken by Ramesh to complete 25% of the work = 9 hours

Time taken by Ramesh to complete the whole work

$$= \frac{9}{25} \times 100 = 36 \text{ hours}$$

Time taken by Suresh to complete 150% of the work = 27 hours

Time taken by Suresh to complete the whole work

$$= \frac{27}{150} \times 100 = 18 \text{ hours.}$$

126. As, Rampal takes the minimum number of hours to complete the work, therefore, he has the highest efficiency.

127. So, time taken by Mahendra and Ramesh to complete the work if they are working together

$$= \frac{24 \times 36}{24+36} = \frac{72}{5} \text{ hours}$$

So, time taken by Ramesh and Suresh to complete the work if they are working together

$$= \frac{18 \times 36}{18+36} = 12 \text{ hours}$$

So, time taken by Mahendra and Rampal to complete the work if they are working together

$$= \frac{24 \times 16}{24+16} = \frac{48}{5} \text{ hours}$$

So, time taken by Mahendra and Suresh to complete the work if they are working together

$$= \frac{24 \times 18}{24+18} = \frac{72}{7} \text{ hours}$$

So, time taken by Vijay and Rampal to complete the work if they are working together

$$= \frac{28 \times 16}{28+16} = \frac{112}{11} \text{ hours.}$$

128. So, one hour work done by Mahendra, Ramesh and Suresh if working together $= \frac{1}{24} + \frac{1}{36} + \frac{1}{18} = \frac{1}{8}$

Therefore, number of hours taken by Mahendra, Ramesh and Suresh if working together = 8 hours.

129. Let the time taken by Ajay to complete the work $= x$ days

Therefore, $\frac{1}{24} + \frac{1}{16} + \frac{1}{x} = \frac{1}{8}$

On solving, we get, $x = 48$ hours

Therefore, ratio of their efficiency

$$= \frac{1}{24} : \frac{1}{16} : \frac{2}{48} = 2:3:1$$

Therefore, share of Ajay $= \frac{1}{2+3+1} \times 12000$

$= ₹\, 2000.$

130. So, $\frac{16 \times (100+x)}{100} = 28$

On solving, we get, $x = 75$.

131. A —x— C —(180 − x)— B

$$\frac{2x+5}{11} = \frac{2(180-x)-5}{13}$$

$$26x + 65 = 22\,(180) - 22x - 55$$

$$48x = 3840$$

$$\therefore \quad x = \frac{3840}{48} = 80 \text{ km}$$

Distance between A and C = 80 km.

132. The ratio of share in the profit of Dev and Eshan is 3 : 5

Menka's share is double than Eshan's share and Nishu receives ₹ 10500 out of the total profit of ₹ 37500

Let Eshan's share be x,

So Menka's would be $2x$ and Dev's share would be $\frac{3x}{5}$

$$\text{Nishu's share} = \frac{10500}{37500} = \frac{7}{25}$$

So, the share of Menka, Dev and Eshan would be

$$= 1 - \frac{7}{25} = \frac{18}{25}$$

So, $x+2x+\frac{3x}{5} = \frac{18}{25}$

On solving, we get, $x = \frac{1}{5}$

So, Eshan's share = $\frac{1}{5}$

Menka's share = $\frac{2}{5}$

Dev's share = $\frac{3}{25}$

So the required ratio = $\frac{2}{5} : \frac{7}{25} : \frac{3}{25} : \frac{1}{5}$

So, the ratio in which the profit will be shared among Menka, Nishu, Dev and Eshan = 10 : 7 : 3 : 5.

133. Length of the pool = $\frac{7}{10} \times 40$ = 28 m

Breadth of the pool = $\frac{2}{10} \times 40$ = 8 m

Height of the pool = $\frac{1}{10} \times 40$ = 4 m

Volume of the pool = $l \times b \times h$

= 28 × 8 × 4 = 896000 litres

Quantity needed to be emptied

= $\left(\frac{1}{500}\right) \times 896000$ = 1792 litres

Portion emptied in the 1st 2 hours

= (12 + 15) + (15 + 25)

= 27 + 40 = 67 litres

So, portion emptied in the 1st 53 hours

= 26 × 67 + (12 + 15)

= 1742 + 27 = 1769 litres

Remaining quantity to be emptied

= 1792 − 1769 = 23 litres

This can be emptied by A and B in (23/40) hours

= 0.575 hours

So, total time taken = 53.575 hours = 54 hours.

134. The concentration of alcohol in the resulting mixture

$= \frac{4\times0.25+6\times0.5+8\times0.75}{4+6+8} = \frac{10}{18} = \frac{5}{9}$

Ratio of Alcohol : Water = 5 : 4.

135. According to the question,

$\frac{450}{40+y} + \frac{450}{40-y} = 24$

$\frac{80}{1600-y^2} = \frac{24}{450}$

$1600 - y^2 = 1500$

$100 = y^2$

$y = 10$ km/hr

$\frac{320}{x+20} + \frac{320}{x-20} = 12$

$\frac{2x}{x^2-400} = \frac{12}{320}$

$3x^2 - 160x - 1200 = 0$

On solving, we get x = 60 km/hr

So, $x + y$ = 60 + 10 = 70 km/hr.

137. Let the length of the largest piece be x

From statement I:

$x + x - 2 + x - 2 = 40$

$3x - 4 = 40$

$3x = 44$

$x = \frac{44}{3}$ m

From statement II:

Let the length of shorter piece be y m

$y + y + x = 40$

Here the value of y is unknown. Hence, statement I alone is sufficient to answer this question.

138. From statement I:

Only weights are given, H = 7 (history)

E = 10 (english)

Hn = 13 (hindi)

From statement II: $\frac{(H+E)}{2} = 150$

H + E = 300

$\frac{(E+Hn)}{2} = \frac{150}{2}$

E + Hn = 150

Weighted average = $\frac{(7H+10E+13Hn)}{(7+10+13)}$

Here the individual marks are unknown.

Hence, Both the statements together are not sufficient.

141. Let the marked price of an article be 100

Then, selling price with tax

= 100 + 20% of 100 = 120

New selling price = 100 − 5 = 95

Effective discount = 120 − 95 = 25

At selling price of ₹ 95, he get discount of ₹ 25

At selling price of ₹ 1, he get discount of $\left(\frac{25}{95}\right)$

At selling price of ₹ 2280, he get discount of

$\left(\frac{25}{95}\right) \times 2280 = 600.$

15. _____; for any node *n*, every descendant node's value in the left sub tree of *n* is less than the value of *n* and every descendant node's sub tree is greater than the value *n*.
A. Binary tree B. Binary search tree
C. AVL tree D. Binary heap tree
E. None of these

16. Which of the following is not an Advantage of Garbage Collection in Java?
A. It makes Java memory efficient because garbage collector removes the unreferenced objects from heap memory.
B. It is automatically done by the garbage collector (a part of JVM) so we don't need to make extra efforts.
C. Both A and B
D. None of these
E. Either A or B

17. 'Aging Registers' are _________.
A. Counters which indicate how long ago their associated pages have been referenced.
B. Registers which keep track of when the program was last accessed.
C. Counters to keep track of last accessed instruction.
D. Counters to keep track of the latest data structures referred.
E. None of these

18. Which of the following correctly accesses the seventh element stored in arr, an array with 100 elements?
A. Arr[6] B. arr[7]
C. arr[5] D. arr[8]
E. None of these

19. A circular list can be used to represent:
A. A queue B. B-tree
C. B++ tree D. Stack
E. Recursion

20. Help Menu is available at which button?
A. End B. Start
C. Turn off D. Restart
E. Reboot

21. Frequency band definition and Wireless signal encoding are functions of which layer?
A. Physical Layer B. Logic Link Control Layer
C. Medium Access Layer D. None of these
E. Both A and B

22. The web standard allows programmers on many different platforms to dispersed format and display the information server. These programs are called:
A. Web browsers B. HTML
C. Internet Explorer D. SDML
E. None of these

23. In Reverse Polish notation, expression A*B+C*D is written as _____
A. AB*CD*+ B. A*BCD*+
C. AB*CD+* D. A*B*CD+
E. None of these

24. The height of a tree is the length of the longest root-to-leaf path in it. The maximum and minimum number of nodes in a binary tree of height 5 is:
A. 63 and 6 respectively B. 64 and 5 respectively
C. 32 and 6 respectively D. 31 and 5 respectively
E. None of these

25. A company is developing an advance version of their current software available in the market, what model approach would they prefer?
A. RAD
B. Iterative Enhancement
C. Both RAD and Iterative Enhancement
D. Spiral
E. None of these

26. What is correct with respect to size of the data types?
A. char > int > float B. int > char > float
C. char > int > double D. double > char > int
E. None of these

27. What does the following declaration mean?
Int (*ptr)[10]
A. Ptr is an array of pointers to 10 integers
B. Ptr is a pointer to an array of 10 integers
C. Ptr is an array of 10 integers
D. Ptr is a pointer to array
E. None of these

28. Which of the following is a best data structure to check an arithmetic expression has balanced parenthesis?
A. Queue B. Stack
C. Tree D. List
E. Graph

29. In which type of cryptography same key is used as encryption and decryption?
A. Symmetric Cryptography
B. Asymmetric Cryptography
C. Key Cryptography
D. Encryption
E. None of these

30. In which database model the rule of Normalization can apply?
A. Network model B. Hierarchical model
C. Relational model D. Document model
E. Context model

31. The number of usable host addresses on a subnet with mask 255.255.255.0 is:
A. 32 B. 254
C. 65534 D. 8
E. 14

32. What is the most common security stance employed on firewalls?
A. Allowing by default
B. Custom configuring of access based on user account
C. Caching internet content
D. Denying by default, allowing by exception
E. Using best available path

33. Which of the following is a set of flip flops integrated together?
A. Adder B. Memory
C. Counter D. Register
E. Clock

34. What is the output of this program?

```
#include<iostream>
Using namespace std;
Int main()
{
    Int a = 10;
    If (a < 10) {
        For (I = 0; i < 10; i++)
            Cout << i;
    }
    Else {
        Cout <<i;
    }
    Return 0;
}
```

A. 0123456789 B. 123456789
C. 0 D. error
E. 1234098765

35. Which of the following is a subject-oriented, integrated, time-variant, non-volatile collection of data in support of management decisions?
A. Data Mining B. Data Warehousing
C. Web Mining D. Text Mining
E. None of these

36. The key size in DES (Data Encryption Standard) is:
A. 24 bit B. 32 bit
C. 56 bit D. 64 bit
E. 8 bit

37. What is ICMP protocol?
A. A protocol used to dynamically bind a high level IP Address to a low-level physical hardware address
B. A protocol for transferring files from one machine to another
C. A protocol used to monitor computers
D. A protocol that handles error and control messages
E. A protocol that is used for internet access

38. "CREATE TABLE...." Command is used to create which type of table in Mysql?
A. Permanent Tables B. Virtual Tables
C. Temporary Tables D. Both B and C
E. All of the above

39. Data mining is used to aid in:
A. Analyzing current decisions made by managers
B. Operational management
C. Retrieving archival data
D. Analyzing past decisions made by managers
E. Detecting patterns in operational data

40. Which of the following is not a Class A host address?
A. 128.4.5.6 B. 117.4.5.1
C. 117.0.0.0 D. 117.8.0.0
E. 111.4.3.1

41. Which of the following is a systematic evolution of the network security in an organization?
A. Authorization B. Evolution
C. Security Audit D. Data Management
E. Authentication

42. Bit stuffing technique is used in which of the following method?
A. Checking error B. Flow control
C. Framing D. Route finding
E. Update Anomaly

43. If memory access takes 20 ns with cache and 110 ns without it, then the ratio (cache uses a 10 ns memory) is
A. 0.93 B. 0.9
C. .88 D. .87
E. None of these

44. Suppose that a bus has 16 data lines and requires 4 cycles of 250 nsecs each to transfer data. The bandwidth of this bus would be 2 Megabytes/sec. If the cycle time of the bus was reduced to 125 nsecs and the number of cycles required for transfer stayed the same what would be the bandwidth of the bus?
A. 1 Megabyte/sec B. 4 Megabytes/sec
C. 8 Megabytes/sec D. 2 Megabytes/sec
E. None of these

45. What is the difference between turnaround time and response time?
A. Turnaround time is the interval between the submission of a job and its completion. Response time is the interval between submission of a request and the first response to that request.
B. Response time is the interval between the submission of a job and its completion. Turnaround time is the interval between submission of a request and the last response to that request.
C. None of these
D. Response time is the interval between the submission of a job and its completion. Turnaround time is the interval between submission of a request and the first response to that request.
E. Both A and B

46. A hash function guarantees integrity of a message. It guarantees that message has not been _______ .
A. replaced B. over view
C. changed D. violated
E. None of these

47. What is the process of defining a method in terms of itself, that is a method that calls itself?
A. Polymorphism B. Abstraction
C. Encapsulation D. Recursion
E. Inheritance

48. Which of the following is used to convert infix notations to postfix notation in data structure?
A. Branch B. Queue

C. Tree
D. Stack
E. List

49. What is the use of "AS" clause in SQL?
A. Selection Operation
B. Rename Operation
C. Join Operation
D. Projection Operation
E. Union Operation

50. IPsec uses standards suite protocol that provides integrity, authentication and security. It is standardized by which organization?
A. IETF
B. EMFT
C. IKE
D. ISA
E. ISE

51. Which of the following is the complexity of the selection sort?
A. O(n)
B. $O(n^2)$
C. O(1)
D. O(n log n)
E. O(n + 1)

52. Deadlocks are possible only when one of the transactions wants to obtain a(n) ______ lock on a data item.
A. Binary
B. Exclusive
C. Shared
D. Complete
E. None of these

53. Each node in a linked list must contain at least?
A. Three fields
B. Five fields
C. Four fields
D. One fields
E. Two fields

54. Which message denotes the request has been fulfilled and a new source is created?
A. 202
B. 201
C. 403
D. 404
E. 302

55. Which arithmetic operator is used in Java for string concatenation?
A. (+)
B. (–)
C. (*)
D. (/)
E. (%)

56. Which of the following cloud deployment are owned and operated by a third-party cloud service provider, which deliver their computing resources like servers and storage over the Internet?
A. Public Cloud
B. Private Cloud
C. Hybrid Cloud
D. Both A and B
E. PaaS

57. Which HTTP request method are used to submits data to be processed to a specified resource?
A. GET
B. POST
C. HEAD
D. PUT
E. OPTIONS

58. What is the output of the following program?

```
#include<iostream>
using namespace std;
main ()
{
    int x = 1;
    switch (x)
    {
        default: cout <<"Hello";
        case 1: cout << "Hi"; break;
    }
}
```

A. Hello
B. Hi
C. HelloHi
D. Compile error
E. None of these

59. Common Gateway Interface (CGI) is which of the following?
A. An interface that accepts and returns data that may be written in SQL.
B. A small program that executes within other application and is stored on the server.
C. A small program that executes within other application and is stored on the client.
D. A small program that executes within other application and is stored on the client or the server.
E. An interface that accepts and returns data that may be written in any language that produces executable file.

60. Which SQL is used to avoid the selection of duplicate rows?
A. UNIQUE
B. DISTINCT
C. EXCLUSIVE
D. DISCRETE
E. None of these

ANSWERS

1	2	3	4	5	6	7	8	9	10
B	B	C	D	A	B	C	C	B	A
11	**12**	**13**	**14**	**15**	**16**	**17**	**18**	**19**	**20**
C	C	D	C	B	D	A	A	A	B
21	**22**	**23**	**24**	**25**	**26**	**27**	**28**	**29**	**30**
A	A	A	A	C	E	B	B	A	C
31	**32**	**33**	**34**	**35**	**36**	**37**	**38**	**39**	**40**
B	D	D	D	B	C	D	B	E	B
41	**42**	**43**	**44**	**45**	**46**	**47**	**48**	**49**	**50**
C	C	B	D	A	C	D	D	B	A
51	**52**	**53**	**54**	**55**	**56**	**57**	**58**	**59**	**60**
B	B	E	B	A	A	B	B	E	B

Previous Paper (Solved)

Institute of Banking Personnel Selection

IBPS–Specialist (IT) Officer Scale-I

Preliminary & Main Exam 2017-2018

Preliminary Exam held on 30-12-2017

Main Exam held on 28-01-2018

PRELIMINARY EXAM

REASONING

1. In the past, consumers would rarely walk into an ice cream store and order low-fat ice cream. But that isn't the case today. An increasing health consciousness combined with a much bigger selection of tasty low-fat foods in all categories has made low-fat ice cream a very profitable item for ice cream store owners.

Which of the following best support the statement?

A. low-fat ice cream produces more revenue than other low-fat foods.

B. ice cream store owners would be better off carrying only low-fat ice cream.

C. ice cream store owners no longer think that low-fat ice cream is an unpopular item.

D. low-fat ice cream is more popular than other kinds of ice cream.

E. consumers are fickle and it is impossible to please them.

2. Cause: All the major rivers in the state have been flowing way over the danger level for the past few weeks.

Which of the following is/are possible effect(s) of the above cause?

(*a*) Many villages situated near the river banks are submerged forcing residents to flee.

(*b*) Government has decided to provide alternate shelter to all the affected villagers residing near the river banks.

(*c*) The entire state has been put on high flood alert.

A. Only (*a*) B. Only (*a*) and (*b*)

C. Only (*b*) and (*c*) D. All (*a*), (*b*) and (*c*)

E. None of these

Directions (Qs. Nos. 3-6) : *In these questions, relationship between different elements is shown in the statements. These statements are followed by two conclusions. Study the conclusions based on the given statement and select appropriate answer.*

Give answer—

A. If either conclusion I or II follows

B. If neither conclusion I nor II follows

C. If only conclusion II follows

D. If both conclusions I and II follow

E. If only conclusion I follows

3. Statements : $C \geq V \leq R = N \geq T > Q;$ $Y \geq N < A$

Conclusions : I. $Q > V$ II. $Q < Y$

4. Statements : $C \geq V \leq R = N \geq T > Q;$ $Y \geq N < A$

Conclusions : I. $Q \geq Y$ II. $A > Q$

5. Statements : $P \geq R < U \leq M < V;$ $T \leq U; L < M$

Conclusions : I. $T < L$ II. $L > V$

6. Statements : $P \geq R < U \leq M < V;$ $T \leq U; L < M$

Conclusions : I. $V > T$ II. $L \leq P$

Direction (Qs. No. 7): *Study the given information carefully and answer the given question.*

Following are the observations of an experiment on 'sleep and memory' conducted on 18 healthy young adults (ages 18 to 25) and 18 healthy older adults (ages 61 to 81).

(*a*) The recall after 8 hours of sleep in younger adults was 65% more than that in the older adults.

(*b*) Night-sleep had higher negative impact on all of the participants as compared to that of day-sleep of equal duration.

(*c*) If a given set of words is memorised immediately before going to sleep, its recall after waking up was found to be better in younger adults than in the older adults.

7. Which of the following can be concluded from the given findings of the research?

I. As per the experiment, there is some correlation between sleep and memory.

II. The part of brain involved in memory is more active during the day as compared to that during the night.

* *Based on Memory*

III. A sleep of more than 8 hours can improve the memory in older adults.

IV. Memorising something immediately after waking up from an 8-hour long sleep will yield better results than memorising before sleep.

A. Only IV
B. All the given statements can be concluded from the given findings of the research.
C. Both I and III
D. Both II and IV
E. Only II

8. In this question, two statements I and II are given. These statements may be either independent causes or may be effects of independent causes or a common cause. One of those statements may be the effect of the other statement. Read both the statements and decide which of the given answer choice correctly depicts the relationship between these two statements.

Statements :

I. Company ABC, a leading automobile company in country G has decided to merge all its subsidiary companies into the parent company last week.

II. Company XYZ, a subsidiary of automobile company ABC, has opened five new branches in country F in the previous financial year.

A. Both the statements I and II are effects of some common cause.
B. Both the statements I and II are independent causes.
C. Statement II is the cause, and statement I is its effect.
D. Statement I is the cause and Statement II is its effect.
E. Both the statements I and II are effects of independent causes.

9. If all the letters in the word 'REGULATION' are arranged in English alphabetical order from left to right and then all the vowels are changed to the next alphabet in the English alphabetical series and all the consonants are changed to the previous alphabet in English alphabetical series, how will the word be written?

A. BFFJKOQQSV B. ZFFJKONSSV
C. ZDHHMONSUT D. BFHUKMPORV
E. BFFJKMPQSV

10. In Country A, it is mandatory for all government organizations to provide transportation facilities (home pick-up and drop) to employees if 75% or more number of total employees working in the organization reside more than 15 km away from office. The same, however, does not apply to XY enterprises as only 1500 of their employees travel more than 15 km to work.

Which of the following can be inferred from the given statement?

(*a*) The total number of employees in XY enterprises is definitely more than 2000.

(*b*) Only 25% employees of XY enterprises travel less than 15 km to office.

(*c*) If 25 new recruits who travel more than 15 km join XY enterprises, the XY enterprises will be definitely have to provide transportation facilities.

(*d*) XY enterprises is definitely not a government enterprise

A. Only (*a*) B. Only (*c*)
C. Both (*b*) and (*d*) D. Only (*d*)
E. (*a*), (*b*) and (*c*)

Directions (Qs. Nos. 11-15) : *Study the given information carefully to answer the given questions.*

Seven people — J, K, L, M, N, O and P have an interview on seven different days of the same week, starting from Monday and ending on Sunday, but not necessarily in the same order. Each one of them also likes different subjects namely — Statistics, Zoology, Sociology, English, Mathematics, Psychology and Economics, but not necessarily in the same order.

Only four people have their interview between N and the one who likes Zoology. Neither N nor the one who likes Zoology has an interview on Sunday. P has an interview immediately after the one who likes Zoology. Only two people have their interviews between P and J. The one who likes Psychology has an interview on one of the days before J but not on Wednesday. Neither N nor P likes Psychology. Only two people have their interviews between the one who likes Psychology and the one who likes Statistics. The one who likes Economics has an interview immediately before the one who likes Statistics. The number of people having interview between P and the one who likes Economics is same as that of the number of people between J and the one who likes English. N does not like English. Only one person has an interview between the one who likes English and K. The one who likes Sociology has an interview immediately after O. L has an interview on one of the days after M.

11. Four of the following five are alike in a certain way based on the given arrangement and hence form a group. Which of the following does not belong to the group?

A. K-English
B. Wednesday-K
C. Mathematics-Wednesday
D. Sociology-Statistics
E. Friday-L

12. How many people have their interviews between L and M?

A. Two B. Three
C. None D. One
E. More than three

13. Which of the following statements is TRUE as per the given arrangement?

A. None of the given statements is true
B. Only one person has an interview between K and J.

C. O likes Psychology.
D. M has an interview on Friday.
E. The one who likes Zoology has an interview on one of the day after M.

14. Who has an interview immediately after K?
A. M
B. The one who likes Zoology
C. The one who likes Statistics
D. J
E. P

15. How many people have their interview before the one who likes Mathematics?
A. One B. More than three
C. None D. Two
E. Three

Directions (Qs. Nos. 16-20) : *Study the following information and answer the given questions.*

Seven people namely, J, K, L, M, N, O and P like seven different movies namely, Twilight, Gladiator, Wanted, Dread, Hero, Jumanji and Signs but not necessarily in the same order. Each person also works in the same office but in a different department (on the basis of experience) namely Administration, Production, Marketing, HR, Finance, R & D and Client relations (CR), not necessarily in the same order.

(Please Note: Each person has been allocated to a department as per increasing order of experience with the one in Administration being the least experienced whilst the one in Client Relations (CR) being the most experienced).

Only two persons have less experience than K. P works in R & D. The one who likes Wanted has more experience than K but less than one who likes Jumanji. P neither likes Wanted nor Jumanji. The one who likes Wanted does not work in Finance.

J, who is more experienced than K, likes Twilight. The person who works in Production is less experienced than the person who likes Hero. K does not like Hero. The person who works in HR is more experienced than both L and N. N is not the least experienced person. The one who likes Signs has more experience than N. M is more experienced than J. L does not like Dread.

16. Four of the following five are alike in a certain way based on the given arrangement and so form a group. Which is the one that does not belong to that group?
A. MO B. NK
C. PK D. NJ
E. LO

17. Which combination represents the department in which O works and the movie he likes?
A. CR-Signs B. CR-Gladiator
C. HR-Gladiator D. Marketing-Wanted
E. HR-Wanted

18. Which of the following movies does M like?
A. Jumanji B. Hero
C. Gladiator D. Signs
E. Dread

19. As per the given arrangement, HR is related to Signs and CR is related to Hero in a certain way. To which of the following is Production related to in the same way?
A. Dread B. Jumanji
C. Wanted D. Gladiator
E. Twilight

20. Which of the following pairs represent the respective people who have more experience than J and less experience than K?
A. M, N B. P, O
C. O, J D. L, N
E. P, M

21. *Read the given information and answer the question.*
'Despite spending huge amount of money, we have not yet been able to find life on other planets. I am personally of the opinion that such research should stop with immediate effect as it is a waste of time and money as no good will ever come out of it. Instead it would be better to use this money to research other elements in space' Statement by a Scientist from Space Institute of Country X.

Which of the following does not weaken the statement of the scientist of space institute of country X?
A. Although life on other planets has not been discovered yet, such research has widened our knowledge and under-standing about other planets and has led to growth and development in science.
B. According to space scientists, if such efforts are continued, the probability of finding life in at least one other planet is much higher as compared to not finding life at all.
C. Various other research projects taken up by the said institute in the past have also failed despite spending huge amount of time as well as money on them.
D. With the amount of time and money that has already been invested in this research, shutting it now would lead to a greater loss than continuing the search.
E. None of the above

22. This question consists of information and two statements numbered I and II given below it. You have to decide which of the given statements weaken(s) or strengthen(s) the information and decide the appropriate answer. In order to discourage crowd built-up at railway station X, the platform ticket (charged to all such priced at ₹ 10 should be increased to ₹ 20.
I. The price of ticket from X to nearest railway station is ₹ 12.

II. On an average, every railway station generates ₹ 24 lacs revenue by charging ₹ 10 for platform ticket while X generates ₹ 28 lacs.

A. Both statement I and statement II weaken the information.
B. Statement I weakens the information while Statement II is a neutral statement.
C. Statement I strengthens the information while statement II weakens the information.
D. Statement I weakens the information while Statement II strengthens the information.
E. Both statements I and II strengthen the information

23. Which of the following expressions will be definitely false if the given expression 'G > H = I ≥ V ≤ Y ≤ Z ≤ T is definitely true?

A. I < G
B. T < V
C. Y ≤ T
D. Z ≥ V
E. V < G

Directions (Qs. Nos. 24-28) : *A word and number arrangement machine when given an input line of words and numbers rearranges them following a particular rule in each step. The following is an illustration of input and rearrangement. (All the numbers are two-digit numbers.)*

Input: 42 prey burn 78 21 melt gulp 96 83 head
Step I : ban 23 42 prey 78 melt gulp 96 83 head
Step II : gap 44 ban 23 prey 78 melt 96 83 head
Step III : had 80 gap 44 ban 23 prey melt 96 83
Step IV : mat 85 had 80 gap 44 ban 23 prey 96
Step V : pay 98 mat 85 had 80 gap 44 ban 23

Step V is the last step of the above arrangement as the intended output of arrangement is obtained.

As per the rules followed in the given steps, find the appropriate steps for the given input.

Input: 61 rust 33 colt 86 four torn 28 49 leap

24. Which of the following is the fourth to the left of the eighth element from the left end of step II?

A. cat
B. far
C. 35
D. rust
E. 30

25. Which of the following represents the element that is fifth to the right of 'cat' in step III?

A. torn
B. 63
C. lap
D. far
E. 86

26. In step III, how many elements are there between '86' and the third element from the left end?

A. More than three
B. One
C. Three
D. None
E. Two

27. What is the difference between the third element from the right end in step V and the fifth element from the left end in step II?

A. 31
B. 55
C. 26
D. 5
E. 16

28. 'torn' is related to 'rust' in step I in the same way as 'lap' is related to 'tan' in step V. Following the same pattern to which element is '86' related to in step IV?

A. cat
B. 51
C. 35
D. far
E. 30

29. The question consists of a statement followed by two courses of action numbered I and II given below it. A course of action is an administrative decision to be taken for improvement, follow-up or further action in regard to the problem, policy etc. You have to assume everything in the statement to be true and then decide which of the suggested courses of action logically follow(s) from the given statement.

Statement: Most of the people looking for buying/ renting properties these days complain of being taken to the same property by more than 6-7 brokers. So, even after contracting multiple agents, they end up having usually the same options.

Courses of action :

I. All the owners should strictly give the responsibility of their properties to only one.
II. The brokers should be instructed to mandatorily disclose the list of all the properties they will be showing the customers on a particular day before taking them to the actual site.

A. Both I and II follow
B. Only II follows
C. Only I follows
D. Neither I nor II follows
E. Either I or II follows

Directions (Qs. Nos. 30-34) : *Study the following information to answer the given questions.*

In a certain code language,
'economy and work related' is written as 'oj my bx st'
'work and employment today' is written as 'pk bx oj dy'
'employment for growth only' is written as 'el pk fd zn'
'growth is related today' is written as 'el dy gm my'
(All codes are two letter codes only)

30. If the code for 'related people only' is 'ld my xd' then what may be the code for 'people for decision' in the given code language?

A. to xd my
B. zn xd fd
C. zn xd dy
D. zn kz xd
E. kz fd xd

31. What does the code 'pk' stand for in the given code language?
A. growth B. employment
C. only D. economy
E. today

32. What may be the code for 'economy is boosting' in the given code language?
A. gm rc st B. zn gm st
C. ye st el D. cp st rc
E. st bx gm

33. Which of the following additional statements is required to definitely find the code of 'and' in the given code language?
A. 'work and prosper now' is written as 'bx yp jn oj'
B. 'work today also important' is written as 'iv en oj dy'
C. No additional statement is required to find the code
D. 'and more work today' is written as 'z1 oj dy bx'
E. 'related only for employment' is written as 'mv zn fd pk'

34. What is the code for 'growth today' in the given code language?
A. fd el B. dy fd
C. pk dy D. dy el
E. an fd

Directions (Qs. Nos. 35-39) : *Study the following information carefully to answer the given question:*

Ten persons from different companies viz Samsung, Bata, Microsoft, Google, Apple, HCL, ITC, Reliance, Airtel and Vodafone are sitting in two parallel rows containing five people each, in such a way that there is an equal distance between adjacent persons. In row 1-B, C, D, E and F are seated and all of them are facing south. In row-2 R, S, T, U and V are seated and all of them are facing north. Therefore, in the given seating arrangement, each member seated in a row faces another member of the other row. (All the information given above does not the order of seating as in give the final arrangement.)

- There people sit between R and the person from Apple. The person from Reliance is an immediate neighbour of the one who faces the person from Apple. V sits to the immediate left of the one who faces the person from Reliance.
- Only one person sits between V and T. The person from Bata sits second to the right of the one who faces T. F sits second to the left of the person from Google. The person from Google does not sit at an extreme end of the line.
- Only two people sit between F and D. The person from Samsung faces an immediate neighbour of D. U is an immediate neighbour of the person from Microsoft. V is not from Microsoft. B sits second to the left of C.
- The person from ITC is an immediate neighbour of the person from Vodafone. Neither V nor F is from ITC. The person from ITC faces the person from HCL.

35. F is related to ITC in the same way as T is related to HCL, based on the given arrangement. To who amongst the following is D related to following the same pattern?
A. Microsoft B. Samsung
C. Apple D. Bata
E. Reliance

36. Which of the following is true regarding E?
A. E is from ITC.
B. E is an immediate neighbour of the person from Samsung.
C. E sits at an extreme end of the line.
D. The person from Airtel faces E.
E. None of the given options is true.

37. Who amongst the following sit at extreme end of the rows?
A. The person from Apple and F.
B. V, E
C. The person from Samsung and C.
D. The person from HCL and Bata
E. R and the person from Reliance.

38. Four of the following five are alike in a certain way based on the given arrangement and so form a group. Which is the one that does not belong to that group.
A. R B. V
C. C D. F
E. B

39. Who amongst the following faces the person from Airtel?
A. The person from Google
B. B
C. The person from Reliance
D. E
E. The person from Bata

40. Which of the following symbols should replace the question mark (?) in the given expression in order to make the expressions 'H < R' as well as 'D ≥ M' definitely true ?

D ≥ I ≥ H = S ? M < P ≤ R

A. ≥ B. ≤
C. < D. >
E. =

41. T is the father of M and P. P is the only daughter of V. M is married to N. A and B are children of M. How is V related to B?
A. Grandmother B. Uncle
C. Aunt D. Sister
E. Grandfather

42. A severe cyclonic storm hit the Eastern coastline last month resulting in huge loss of life and property on the entire east coast and the Government had to disburse a considerable amount for relief activities through the district administration machineries.

Which of the following may possibly be a follow up measure to be taken by the Government?

A. The Government may set up a task force to review the post relief scenario in all districts and also to confirm proper end user receipt of the relief supplies.

B. The Government may set up a committee for proper disbursement' of relief supplies in future.

C. The Government may empower the District magistrates to make all future disbursements of relief.

D. The Government may send relief supplies to the affected, people in future only after proper assessment of the damage caused by such calamities.

E. The government may need not to activate any follow up measure.

Directions (Qs. Nos. 43-47) : *These questions consist of a question and two statements numbered I and II given below it. You have to decide whether the data provided in the statements are sufficient to answer the question. Read both the statements and mark the appropriate answer.*

Give answer:

A. The data even in both statements I and II together are not sufficient to answer the question.

B. The data in statement I alone are sufficient to answer the question while the data in statement II alone are not sufficient to answer the question.

C. The data either in statement I alone or in statement II alone are sufficient to answer the question.

D. The data in both statements I and II together are necessary to answer the question.

E. The data in statement II alone are sufficient to answer the question while the data in statement I are not sufficient to answer the question.

43. In a building, the ground floor is numbered one, first floor is numbered two and so on till the topmost floor is numbered five. Amongst five people—M, N, O, P and Q, each living on a different floor, but not necessarily in the same order, on which floor does Q live?

I. O lives on an odd numbered floor. M lives immediately below O. Only two people live between M and P. N lives neither immediately below M nor immediately below P.

II. N lives on an even numbered floor. Only two people live between N and O. Only one person lives between O and Q.

44. Among people A, B, C, D, E and F, each having a different height, who is the second shortest?

I. Only two people are taller than A. E is taller than both B and C. F is shorter than E. F is taller than C.

II. Only two people are shorter than D. A is taller than D but shorter than E. F is neither the tallest nor the shortest. B is taller than C.

45. How many people are standing between A and D (Note: All are standing in a straight line facing north)?

I. K stands second from the left end of the line. Only four people stand between K and T. Y is an immediate neighbour of T. A stands second to the right of Y. As many people stand between K and D as between A and D.

II. A stands second from the right end of the line. Z stands third from the left end of the line. D stands exactly in the centre of the line. As many people stand between A and T as between D and Z.

46. How far and in which direction is Point M from Point S?

I. Point E is 2 m to the east of Point S. Point B is 4 m to the south of Point E. Point L is 10 m to the east of Point B. Point L forms a midpoint of the vertical straight line of 8 m formed by joining points Q and D. Point M is 5 m to the west of Point Q.

II. Point M is 8 m to the north of Point A. Point M forms the midpoint of the horizontal straight line formed by joining points O and F. Point F is 8 m to the west of Point O. Point S is 4 m to the west of Point F.

47. Amongst six people—P, Q R, S, T and U standing around a circle, some facing the centre while some facing outside (*i.e.*, opposite to the centre) but not necessarily in the same order, what is the position of T with respect to U ?

I. P stands second to the right of R. R faces the centre. Q stands second to the left of P. Q is an immediate neighbour of both U and T. U and P face opposite directions (*i.e.*, if U faces the centre then P faces outside and vice-versa.) Only two people stand between P and T.

II. Only two people stand between R and U. P stands to the immediate left of U. P faces outside. R is an immediate neighbour of T.

Directions (Qs. Nos. 48-50) : In these questions, two/three statements followed by two conclusions numbered I and II are given. You have to take the given statements to be true even if they seem to be at variance from commonly known facts and then decide which of the given conclusions logically follows from the given statements disregarding commonly known facts.

Give answer:
A. If either conclusion I or II follows
B. If neither conclusion I nor II follows
C. If only conclusion II follows
D. If both conclusions I and II follow
E. If only conclusion I follows

48. Statements : Some coffee is tea. All tea is water. All water is milk.
Conclusions :
I. All coffee being water is a possibility.
II. All milk is tea.

49. Statements : No sea is a sky. Some skies are kites. All kites are balloons.
Conclusions :
I. Some balloons are seas.
II. All balloons being skies is a possibility.

50. Statements : Some stars are planets. Some planets are galaxies. Some galaxies are suns.
Conclusions :
I. All suns being galaxies is a possibility.
II. Some galaxies are stars.

QUANTITATIVE APTITUDE

51. A can complete a project in 20 days and B can complete the same project in 30 days. If A and B start working on the project together and A quits 10 days before the project is completed, in how many days will the project be completed?
A. 18 days B. 27 days
C. 26.67 days D. 16 days
E. 12 days

52. A runs 25% faster than B and is able to allow B a lead of 7 metres to end a race in dead heat. What is the length of the race?
A. 10 metres B. 25 metres
C. 45 metres D. 15 metres
E. 35 metres

53. A train travelling at 100 kmph overtakes a motorbike travelling at 64 kmph in 40 seconds. What is the length of the train in metres?
A. 1777 metres B. 1822 metres
C. 400 metres D. 1111 metres
E. 520 metres

Directions (Qs. Nos. 54-58): *Study the following graph and table to answer the given questions.*

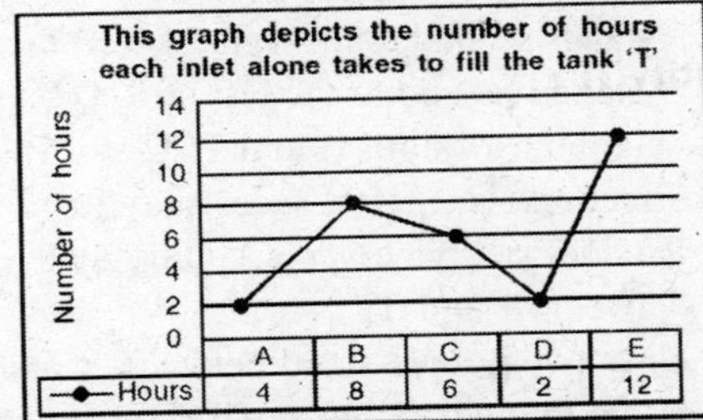

This table depicts the number of hours taken by each outlet alone to empty the full tank 'T'

Outlets	*Number of hours*
W	–
X	34
Y	–
Z	30

54. The time taken to fill the empty tank completely when inlet A and outlet X were opened together was 6 hours 40 minutes less than that taken by inlet B and outlet W together. How much time will outlet W alone take to completely empty the full tank? (in hours)
A. 26 B. 28
C. 20 D. 48
E. 24

55. When the tank was completely full, outlets X and Y were opened together for 8 hours 30 minutes. Both were then closed and inlet A was opened which filled the tank completely in 3 hours 30 minutes. In how much time (in hours) will outlet Y alone empty the full tank?
A. 15 hours B. 13.6 hours
C. 13 hours D. 14 hours
E. 15.5 hours

56. When the tank was completely full, outlets X and Z were opened together for 'H' hours. Had outlet Z been open alone, it would have taken 'H + 10' hours to empty the same quantity of water from the tank. What is the value of 'H'?
A. 10 B. 18
C. $11\frac{1}{3}$ D. $18\frac{1}{3}$
E. $10\frac{2}{3}$

57. Inlet E was open for 2 hours and then closed. If the remaining tank was filled by inlets B and C together, what was the total time (in hours) taken to fill the tank completely?
A. $5\frac{1}{7}$ B. $5\frac{4}{7}$
C. $4\frac{3}{7}$ D. $4\frac{6}{7}$
E. $5\frac{6}{7}$

58. When the tank was completely empty, inlets A, D and E were opened for one hour each and then closed. If after that outlet Z was opened, how much time (in hours) will it take to empty the tank completely?

A. $15\frac{2}{5}$ B. 18
C. 17 D. 20
E. 25

59. A boat running upstream takes 8 hours 48 minutes to cover a certain distance, while it takes 4 hours to cover the same distance running downstream. What is the ratio between the speed of the boat in still water and speed of the water current respectively?

A. 2 : 1 B. 3 : 2
C. 8 : 3 D. 3 : 5
E. 8 : 2

60. A, B and C jointly thought of engaging themselves in a business venture. It was agreed that A would invest ₹ 6,500 for 6 months, B, ₹ 8,400 for 5 months and C, ₹ 10,000 for 3 months. A wants to be the working member for which, he was to receive 5% of the profits. The profit earned was ₹ 7,400. What is the share of B in the profit?

A. ₹ 1,900 B. ₹ 2,660
C. ₹ 2,800 D. ₹ 2,840
E. ₹ 2,900

61. How much time will it take for an amount of ₹ 900 to yield ₹ 81 as interest at 4.5% per annum of simple interest?

A. 2 years B. 3 years
C. 1 year D. 4 years
E. 5 years

62. Mr. Thomas invested an amount of ₹ 13,900 divided in two different schemes A and B at the simple interest rate of 14% per annum and 11% per annum respectively. If the total amount of simple interest earned in 2 years be ₹ 3,508, what was the amount invested in scheme B?

A. ₹ 6,400 B. ₹ 7,200
C. ₹ 6,500 D. ₹ 7,500
E. ₹ 7,000

63. A bag contains 2 red, 3 green and 2 blue balls. Two balls are drawn at random. What is the probability that none of the balls drawn is blue?

A. $\frac{10}{21}$ B. $\frac{11}{21}$

C. $\frac{2}{7}$ D. $\frac{5}{7}$

E. $\frac{3}{7}$

64. A can contains a mixture of two liquids A and B in the ratio 7 : 5. When 9 litres of mixture is drawn off and the can is filled with B, the ratio of A and B becomes 7 : 9. How many litres of liquid A were contained by the can initially?

A. 10 B. 20
C. 21 D. 25
E. 29

65. A circular swimming pool is surrounded by a concrete wall 4 ft. wide. If the area of the concrete wall surrounding the pool is $\frac{11}{25}$ that of the pool, then the radius of the pool is:

A. 8 ft B. 16 ft
C. 20 ft D. 30 ft
E. None of these

Directions (Qs. Nos. 66-70): *In the given questions, two quantities are given, one as Quantity I and another as Quantity II. You have to determine relationship between two quantities and choose the appropriate option.*

A. If Quantity I ≥ Quantity II
B. If Quantity I > Quantity II
C. If Quantity I < Quantity II
D. If Quantity I = Quantity II or the relationship cannot be established from the information that is given.
E. If Quantity I ≤ Quantity II

66. The boat takes total time of 4 hours to travel 14 km upstream and 36 km downstream together. The boat takes total time of 5 hours to travel 20 km upstream and 24 km downstream together?

Quantity I : Speed of the boat in still water (in km/h).
Quantity II : 16 km/h.

67. M is an integer selected at random from the set. (7, 14, 25, 27, 33, 29 and 30)

Quantity I : Probability that the average of 12, 9 and M is at least 17.
Quantity II : $\frac{1}{3}$.

68. $\left(\frac{x^2}{5}\right)+x+\left(\frac{4}{5}\right)=0$

$3y^2 + 4y + 1 = 0$

Quantity I : x
Quantity II : y

69. $mn \neq 0$

Quantity I : $m = n$
Quantity II : m/n.

70. A and B can together finish a piece of work in 20 days. If B starts working and after 15 days is replaced by A, A can finish the remaining work in 24 days.

Quantity I : Number of days taken by B alone to finish the same piece of work.

Quantity II : Number of days taken by A alone to finish the same piece of work.

Directions (Qs. Nos. 71-75): *Study the given information carefully and answer the given questions.*

The revenue of a given railway zone was collected from 4 primary sources—Offline Ticket Sales, Online Ticket Sales, Freight, Fines–during 3 Financial Years (FY 2013-14, FY 2014-15, FY 2015-16).

FY 2013-14 : Total revenue collected was ₹ 3,500 crore. Fines (₹ *x* crore) comprised $7\frac{6}{7}\%$ of the total revenue and revenue from online ticket sales was ₹ '*x* + 300' crore. Revenue from freight was 12% more than that from offline ticket sales.

FY 2014-15 : Revenue from online ticket sales increased by ₹ 25 crore over FY 2013-14. Revenue from Offline ticket sales was 40% of the total revenue in FY 2014-15. Revenue from Freight and Fines was in the respective ratio of 5 : 1.

FY 2015-16 : Revenue from fines in FY 2013-14 was $\frac{11}{16}$th of that in FY 2015-16. Revenue from online ticket sales increased by 50% over that in FY 2014-15 and that from offline ticket sales was the average of that in FY 2013-14 and 2014-15. Revenue from freight has been and will continue to increase steadily by ₹ 250 crore every financial year.

71. Revenue from fines comprised two sources—vendors and passengers. Fines from passengers (₹ *y* crore) remained constant in FY 2013-14 and FY 2014-15. If the fine from vendors in FY 2013-14 was 55% of that in FY 2014-15, what was the value of *y*?

A. 180 B. 200
C. 218 D. 208
E. 220

72. If the railway profit in FY 2014-15 was 12.5% of the total expense, what was the total expense for FY 2014-15? (in ₹ crore)

A. 2900 B. 2400
C. 3200 D. 3000
E. 3822

73. In FY 2017-18, if the revenue from fines increases by 20% over FY 2015-16, what would be the ratio between the revenues from fines and freight in FY 2017-18?

A. 2 : 3 B. 1 : 5
C. 2 : 5 D. 3 : 4
E. 4 : 5

74. If the average revenue from online ticket sales in FY 2014-15, FY 2015-16 and FY 2016-17 was ₹ 1150 crore, by what per cent did the revenue from online ticket sales increase in FY 2016-17 as compared to that in 2014-15?

A. 250 B. 150
C. 300 D. 225
E. 230

75. If the average cost of a railway ticket was ₹ 300 in FY 2014-15, how many passengers (approx) travelled by railways in FY 2014-15? (in ₹ crore)

A. 4.8 B. 6.4
C. 6.2 D. 5.4
E. 7.73

Directions (Qs. Nos. 76-80): *Refer to the pie-charts to answer the given questions.*

Data regarding five villages—A, B, C, D and E—in a district in 2015.

Total village population = 18000

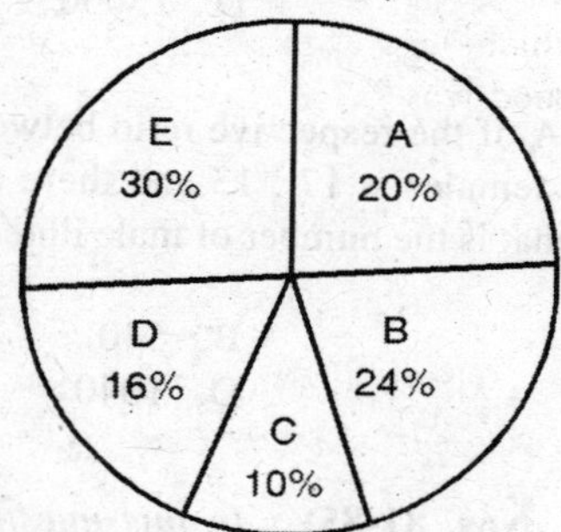

Total number of illiterates = 40% of Total village population

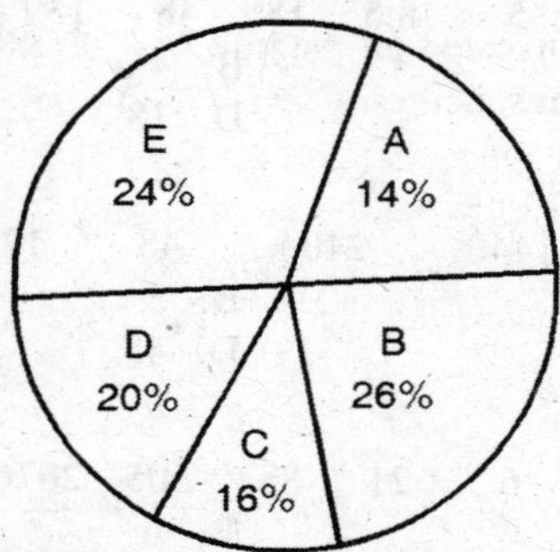

Total village population = Number of literates + Number of illiterates

76. In 2017, the population of village C remained the same as that in 2015, but the number of literates increased by '*x*'. As a result, the total number of literates became 70% of that of illiterates. What is the approximate value of '*x*'?

A. 620 B. 440
C. 680 D. 485
E. 430

77. The difference between the number of illiterates in villages D and E is approximately what per cent of that of literates in villages D and E?

A. 30% B. 20%
C. 35% D. 13%
E. 15%

78. In village D, the male to female ratio among the illiterates is 5 : 3 respectively. Out of the illiterates, if 'x' females and '$1.25x$' males work as farmers and the ratio between males and females who do not work as farmers is 5 : 2 respectively, what is the value of 'x'?

A. 240 B. 300
C. 360 D. 380
E. 280

79. The average number of illiterates in villages D, F and G is 1910. 40% and 30% of the population of villages F and G respectively are illiterates. If the ratio of the population of villages F and G is 4 : 5 respectively, what is the total population of villages F and G together?

A. 10000 B. 12000
C. 12456 D. 13000
E. 14000

80. In village A, if the respective ratio between number of males and females is 17 : 13 and there are 1000 male literates, what is the number of male illiterates in village A?

A. 480 B. 540
C. 940 D. 1040
E. 1140

Directions (Qs. Nos. 81-85) : *In this question, a number series is given. Only one number is wrong which doesn't fit in the series. Find out the wrong number?*

81. 6 4 5 8.5 18 48 139

A. 8.5 B. 4
C. 5 D. 18
E. 48

82. 10080 1440 240 48 12 3 2

A. 240 B. 3
C. 1440 D. 48
E. 12

83. 1 2 6 21 88 505 2676

A. 21 B. 6
C. 2 D. 505
E. 88

84. 18 21 25 35 52 78 115

A. 25 B. 21
C. 28 D. 35
E. 52

85. 120 137 178 222 290 375 477

A. 178 B. 137
C. 290 D. 375
E. 222

86. Area of a rectangle is 150 metre sq. When the breadth of the same rectangle is increased by 2 meter and the length decreased by 5 metre, the area of the rectangle decreases by 30 metre square. What is the perimeter of the square whose sides are equal to the length of the rectangle?

A. 76 m B. 72 m
C. 120 m D. 80 m
E. 60 m

87. A, B and C started a business with investments of ₹ 4200, ₹ 3600 and ₹ 2400 respectively. After 4 months from the start of the business, A invested ₹ 1000 more. After 6 months from the start of the business, B and C invested additional amounts in the respective ratio of 1 : 2. If at the end of 10 months they received a profit of ₹ 2820 and it's share in the profit was ₹ 1200, What was the additional amount that B invested?

A. ₹ 800 B. ₹ 200
C. ₹ 500 D. ₹ 600
E. ₹ 400

88. A vessel contains a mixture of milk and water in the respective ratio of 5 : 1. 24 litres of mixture was taken out and replaced with the same quantity of milk so that the resultant ratio between the quantities of milk and water in the mixture was 13 : 2 respectively. If 15 litres of the mixture is again taken out from the vessel, what is the resultant quantity of milk in the mixture? (in litres)

A. 97 B. 89
C. 91 D. 99
E. 84

Directions (Qs. Nos. 89-93) : *Refer to the table and answer the given question.*

Data related to performance of 6 batsmen in a tournament:

Name of the batsman	Number of matches played in the tournament	Average runs scored in the tournament	Total balls faced in the tournament	Strike rate
A	8	-	-	129.6
B	20	81	-	-
C	-	38	400	114
D	-	-	-	72
E	28	55	1280	-
F	-	-	-	66

Note:

(*i*) Strike rate = (Total runs scored/Total balls faced) * 100

(*ii*) All the given batsmen could bat in all the given matches played by them.

(*iii*) Few values are missing in the table (indicated by –). A candidate is expected to calculate the missing value, if it is required to answer the given question, on the basis of the given data and information.

89. The respective ratio between total number of balls faced by D and that by F in the tournament is 3 : 4. Total number of runs scored by F in the tournament is what per cent more than the total runs scored by D in the tournament?

A. $22\frac{2}{9}$ B. $32\frac{4}{9}$

C. $18\frac{8}{9}$ D. $24\frac{4}{9}$

E. $28\frac{2}{9}$

90. If the runs scored by E in last 3 matches of the tournament are not considered, his average runs scored in the tournament will decrease by 9. If the runs scored by E in the 26th and 27th match are below 128 and no two scores among these 3 scores are equal, what are the minimum possible runs scored by E in the 28th match?

A. 137 B. 135
C. 141 D. 133
E. 139

91. In the tournament, the total number of balls faced by batsman A is 74 less than the total number of runs scored by him. What is the average run scored by batsman A in the tournament?

A. 42.5 B. 39.5
C. 38 D. 44
E. 40.5

92. Batsman B faced equal number of balls in first 10 matches he played in the tournament and last 10 matches he played in the tournament. If his strike rate in first 10 matches and last 10 matches of the tournament are 120 and 158 respectively, what is the total number of balls faced by him in the tournament?

A. 1150 B. 1400
C. 1200 D. 1000
E. 1500

93. What is the number of matches played by batsman C in the tournament?

A. 10 B. 16
C. 12 D. 18
E. 8

94. 10 men can complete a project in 12 days, 12 children can complete the same project in 16 days and 8 women can complete the same project in 20 days. 5 men and 12 children started working on the project. If after 4 days, 8 children were replaced by 4 women. In how many days the remaining project was completed?

A. $4\frac{2}{5}$ B. $5\frac{1}{2}$

C. $7\frac{1}{2}$ D. $3\frac{5}{9}$

E. $6\frac{2}{3}$

95. In a village, 60% registered voters cast their votes in the election. Only two candidates (A & B) were contesting the election. A won the election by 600 votes. Had B received 40% more votes, the result would have been a tie. How many registered voters are there in the village?

A. 4000 B. 3500
C. 3000 D. 3250
E. 3750

96. Eight years ago, Poorvi's age was equal to the sum of the present ages of her one son and one daughter. Five years hence, the respective ratio between the ages of her daughter and her son that time will be 7 : 6. If Poorvi's husband is 7 years elder to her and his present age is three times the present age of their son, what is the present age of the daughter? (in years)

A. 15 years B. 23 years
C. 19 years D. 27 years
E. 13 years

97. Boat A travels downstream from Point X to Point Y in 3 hours less than the time taken by Boat B to travel upstream from Point Y to Point Z. The distance between X and Y is 20 km, which is half of the distance between Y and Z. The speed of Boat B in still water is 10 km/h and the speed of Boat A in still water is equal to the speed of Boat B upstream. What is the speed of Boat A in still water? Consider the speed of the current to be the same?

A. 10 km/h B. 16 km/h
C. 12 km/h D. 8 km/h
E. 15 km/h

Directions (Qs. Nos. 98-100) : *Study the following information carefully and answer the given question.*

Data regarding number of applications received for various courses in University A and that in University B in the year 2001.

(Note : Universities A and B offer courses in six courses only, namely, Commerce, Science, Engineering, Arts, Management and Law.)

- In University A, applications received for Commerce, Science and Engineering together constituted 70% of the total number of applications received (for all the given courses together). Applications received for Arts, Management and Law were 800, 750 and

400 respectively. Applications received for management were 40% less than that for engineering. Applications received for Commerce were 20% more than that for Science.

- In University B, applications received for Science were 20% less than that for Science in University A.
- In University B, applications received for Arts were 780 and they constituted 15% of the total number of applications received (for all the given courses together). Also the applications received for arts were 40% less than that received for Commerce. Total number of applications received for engineering and management together, were double the total number of applications received for arts and law together. Applications received for engineering were equal to that for management.

98. What is the respective ratio between the total number of applications received for Engineering and Science together in University A and that for the same courses together in University B?

A. 50 : 47
B. 65 : 53
C. 52 : 37
D. 55 : 42
E. 43 : 36

99. Number of applications received for only Commerce in University B is what per cent less than that in University A?

A. 30
B. $27\frac{7}{9}$
C. 20
D. 15
E. $15\frac{5}{8}$

100. $\frac{5}{8}$th of the number of applications for Arts in University A were by female students. If the number of female applicants for the same course in University B is less than that in University A by 120, what is the number of male applications for Arts in University B?

A. 500
B. 420
C. 450
D. 360
E. 400

GENERAL ENGLISH

Directions (Qs. Nos. 101-110) : *Read the following passage carefully and answer the questions based on it. Some words have been printed in* **bold** *to help you locate them while answering some of the questions.*

Gross Domestic Savings (GDS) play a vital role in the economic growth of a country since it facilitates to provide requisite financial resources to undertake various developmental and welfare programs. A high level of savings helps the economy to progress on a continuous growth path as investment is mainly financed out of savings. GDS is one of the important economic indicators to measure financial regulation and soundness of the country. Absence of required savings rate may lead to external dependence, which may **jeopardize** the interests of the Nation.

Savings habit is an in-built culture of the Indian system and it has been growing consistently over the years. The GDS percentage to GDP has shown considerable improvement from 10% in 1950 to 33.70% in 2010, which is one of the highest globally. It is interesting to note that while the share of corporate sector increased from 10% to 24% during 1950 to 2010, the share of public sector has come down to 6% from 18% during the said period. The buoyancy of corporate sector in post reform era could be one of the reasons for increased share of corporates in GDS. While there is increasing trend in saving rate, marginal decline is observed under household sector *i.e.,* 72% to 70%.

Notwithstanding the fact that the share of household savings to GDS is showing decline, still this segment is the significant contributor to GDS with 70% share. Indian households are among the most frugal in the world. However, **commensurate** capital formation has not been taking place as a lion's share of household savings are being parked in physical assets compared to financial assets.

The pattern of disposition of saving is an important factor in determining how the saved amount is utilized for productive purposes. The proportion of household saving in financial assets determines the channelisation of saving for investment in other sectors of the economy. However, the volume of investment of saving in physical assets determines the productivity and generation of income in that sector itself.

Post independence era has witnessed a significant shift in deployment of household savings especially the share of financial assets increased from 26.39% in 1950 to 54.05% in 1990 may be on account of increased bank branch network across the country coupled with improved awareness of investors on various financial/banking products. However, contrast to common expectations, the share of financial assets in total household savings has come down from 54.05% to 50.21% especially in post-reform period *i.e.,* 1990 to 2010 despite providing easy access and availability of banking facilities compared to earlier years. The increased share of physical assets over financial assets (around 4%) during the last two decades is a cause of concern requires focused attention to arrest the trend.

Traditionally, the Indians are risk-averse and prefer to invest surplus funds in physical assets such as Gold, Silver and lands. Nevertheless, considerable share of savings also flowing to financial assets, which includes, Currency, Bank

poverty will always ...(144)... and it should always be at the forefront of efforts to improve our world because it ...(145)... more than the bare minimum solution. ...(146)... this, the aid industry currently has quite a few eggs in the end poverty basket. We risk assuming that the public ...(147)... between absolute and relative poverty. It probably doesn't especially not in austere times. Just look at the ...(148)... political view on and to the middle income countries that contain hundreds of millions of desperately poor people. Too much negatively and we are ...(149)... of not making any progress with aid money, too much task of progress and aid is no longer necessary. It shouldn't be a Catch 22 situation but in ...(150)..., for some, it is.

141. A. subjected B. apprehended C. bestowed D. lifted E. labelled

142. A. spritely B. objectionably C. fatally D. continually E. probably

143. A. problem B. nature C. [illegible]ce D. being E. population

144. A. remainder B. leave C. allow D. exist E. touch

145. A. seek B. asks C. insists D. ensure E. demands

146. A. Along B. Added C. Despite D. Favouring E. Siding

147. A. understands B. distinguishes C. grasps D. separates E. draws

148. A. prevailing B. currently C. aimed D. lost E. multiple

149. A. accused B. alleged C. suspicion D. remarked E. stationed

150. A. actual B. now C. place D. reality E. form

ANSWERS

1 D	2 D	3 C	4 C	5 C	6 E	7 E	8 E	9 E	10 A
11 E	12 A	13 C	14 B	15 C	16 D	17 A	18 A	19 E	20 C
21 C	22 C	23 C	24 E	25 A	26 A	27 C	28 D	29 A	30 D
31 B	32 A	33 B	34 D	35 B	36 E	37 A	38 D	39 A	40 E
41 A	42 B	43 C	44 A	45 E	46 E	47 D	48 E	49 C	50 E
51 A	52 E	53 C	54 B	55 B	56 C	57 D	58 E	59 C	60 B
61 A	62 A	63 A	64 C	65 C	66 B	67 C	68 E	69 D	70 B
71 D	72 E	73 C	74 D	75 E	76 D	77 D	78 C	79 C	80 D
81 E	82 B	83 D	84 B	85 A	86 E	87 E	88 C	89 A	90 A
91 E	92 A	93 C	94 E	95 C	96 B	97 D	98 D	99 B	100 E
101 D	102 C	103 D	104 B	105 D	106 A	107 C	108 A	109 D	110 E
111 D	112 E	113 A	114 D	115 B	116 B	117 A	118 A	119 C	120 B

121	122	123	124	125	126	127	128	129	130
A	B	D	C	B	A	C	A	C	A
131	**132**	**133**	**134**	**135**	**136**	**137**	**138**	**139**	**140**
B	B	C	C	A	C	C	A	C	A
141	**142**	**143**	**144**	**145**	**146**	**147**	**148**	**149**	**150**
E	E	B	D	E	C	B	A	A	D

EXPLANATORY ANSWERS

51. Let the work be finished in x days

Then A's $(x - 10)$ day's work + B's x day's work = 1

$$\frac{x-10}{20}+\frac{x}{30}=1$$

$$\Rightarrow \frac{3(x-10)+2x}{60}=1$$

$$\Rightarrow 3x - 30 + 2x = 60$$

$$\Rightarrow 5x = 90 \Rightarrow x = 18$$

Hence, the project will be completed in 18 days.

52. Let B runs 100 m then A runs 125 m

$$\text{Ratio of speed} = \frac{125}{100} = \frac{5}{4}$$

$$\text{Length of the race} = \frac{7\times 1}{\left(1-\frac{4}{5}\right)}$$

$$= 7 \times 5 = 35 \text{ m}$$

53. Let length of the train = x m

Relative speed = (100 – 64) = 36 km/hr

$$= 36\times\frac{5}{18} \text{ m/s} = 10 \text{ m/s}$$

length of the train = speed × time

= 10 × 40 = 400 m.

54. A's 1 hour work = $\frac{1}{4}$

X's 1 hour work = $\frac{1}{34}$

(A + X)'s 1 hour work

$$= \frac{1}{4}-\frac{1}{34}=\frac{17-2}{68}=\frac{15}{68}$$

$\therefore$ Tank will fill in $\frac{68}{15}$ hours

Now, B's 1 hour work = $\frac{1}{8}$

W's 1 hour work = $\frac{1}{x}$

(B + W)'s 1 hour work = $\frac{1}{8}-\frac{1}{x}=\frac{x-8}{8x}$

$\therefore$ Tank will fill in $\frac{8x}{x-8}$ hours

But $\frac{8x}{x-8}=\frac{68}{15}+\frac{20}{3}$

$$\Rightarrow \frac{8x}{x-8}=\frac{68+100}{15}=\frac{168}{15}=\frac{56}{5}$$

$$\Rightarrow 56x - 448 = 40x$$

$$\Rightarrow 56x - 40x = 448$$

$$\Rightarrow 16x = 448$$

$$\Rightarrow x = \frac{448}{16}=28$$

Hence, outlet W alone empty the full tank in 28 hours.

55. A's 1 hour work = $\frac{1}{4}$

A's $\frac{1}{2}$ hour work = $\frac{1}{4\times 2}=\frac{1}{8}$ part

$$1-\frac{1}{8}=\frac{7}{8} \text{ part}$$

$\because$ $\frac{7}{8}$ part empty $(x + w)$ in $\frac{17}{2}$ hours

$\therefore$ 1 part can empty = $\frac{7}{8}\times\frac{2}{17}=\frac{7}{68}$ hours

$\therefore$ y can alone empty 1 part

$$=\frac{7}{68}-\frac{1}{34}=\frac{7-2}{68}=\frac{5}{68}$$

Hence, y can alone empty full tank in $\frac{68}{5}$ hours

$$= 13\frac{3}{5} \text{ hours} = 13.6 \text{ hours.}$$

56. (X + Z)'s 1 hour work

$$= \frac{1}{34}+\frac{1}{30}=\frac{15+17}{510}=\frac{32}{510}$$

(X + Z)'s H hour work $= \frac{32H}{510}$

Z's 1 hour work $= \frac{1}{30}$

Z's (H + 10) hour work $= \frac{(H+10)}{30}$

$$\frac{32H}{510} = \frac{H+10}{30}$$

$$32H = 17H + 170$$

$$15H = 170$$

$$H = \frac{170}{15} = \frac{34}{3} = 11\frac{1}{3}$$

Hence, value of H $= 11\frac{1}{3}$ hours.

57. E's 1 hour work $= \frac{1}{12}$

E's 2 hours work $= \frac{1}{12}\times 2 = \frac{1}{6}$

Remaining work $= 1-\frac{1}{6}=\frac{5}{6}$

(B + C)'s 1 hour work

$$= \frac{1}{8}+\frac{1}{6}=\frac{3+4}{24}=\frac{7}{24}$$

$\because$ $\frac{7}{24}$ part is filled in 1 hour

$\therefore$ $\frac{5}{6}$ part is filled in $\frac{1}{\frac{7}{24}}\times\frac{5}{6}$ hours

$$= \frac{24}{7}\times\frac{5}{6}=\frac{20}{7} \text{ hours}$$

$\therefore$ Total time taken to fill the tank completely

$$= 2+\frac{20}{7}=\frac{34}{7}=4\frac{6}{7} \text{ hours.}$$

58. (A + D + E)'s 1 hour work

$$= \frac{1}{4}+\frac{1}{2}+\frac{1}{12}=\frac{3+6+1}{12}=\frac{10}{12}=\frac{5}{6}$$

Z's 1 hour work $= \frac{1}{30}$

$\because$ $\frac{1}{30}$ part can empty in 1 hour

$\therefore$ 1 part can empty in $\frac{30}{1}$ hour

$\therefore$ $\frac{5}{6}$ part can empty $= 30\times\frac{5}{6}$ hours = 25 hr

Outlet Z can empty the tank completely in 25 hours.

59. Let the speed of the boat = x km/hr
and speed of stream = y km/hr

Let distance = d km

$$\frac{d}{x+y} = 4$$

$\Rightarrow$ $d = 4(x + y)$ ...(*i*)

$$\frac{d}{x-y} = \frac{44}{5}$$

$\Rightarrow$ $d = \frac{44(x-y)}{5}$ ...(*ii*)

From (*i*) and (*ii*)

$$4(x + y) = \frac{44(x-y)}{5}$$

$\Rightarrow$ $20x + 20y = 44x - 44y$

$\Rightarrow$ $24x = 64y$

$\Rightarrow$ $\frac{x}{y} = \frac{64}{24} = \frac{8}{3}$

$\therefore$ $\frac{\text{Speed of boat}}{\text{Speed of stream}} = 8 : 3.$

60. A : B : C = 6500 × 6 : 8400 × 5 : 10000 × 3
= 39000 : 42000 : 30000
= 39 : 42 : 30
= 13 : 14 : 10

$\because$ A is working member

$\therefore$ $\frac{5}{100}\times 7400$ = ₹ 370

Profit = 7400 − 370
= ₹ 7030

Share of B in the profit

$= \frac{14}{37}\times 7030$
= ₹ 14 × 190
= ₹ 2660.

61. Time $= \frac{\text{S.I.}\times 100}{P\times r} = \frac{81\times 100\times 2}{900\times 9}$ = 2 years.

62. Let Amount deposited in scheme A = ₹ x

$\therefore$ Amount deposited in scheme B = ₹ $13900 - x$

According to the question,

$$\frac{x \times 14 \times 2}{100} + \frac{(13900 - x) \times 11 \times 2}{100} = 3508$$

$$\Rightarrow 28x + 13900 \times 22 - 22x = 3508 \times 100$$

$$\Rightarrow 6x = 350800 - 305800$$

$$\Rightarrow 6x = 45000$$

$$\Rightarrow x = 7500$$

Hence, amount deposited in scheme B

$$= 13900 - 7500$$

$$= ₹\ 6400.$$

63. Required probability = $\frac{10}{21}$.

64. Suppose the two liquids A and B are $7x$ litres and $5x$ litres respectively.

Now, when 9 litres of mixture are taken out,

$$\text{A remains} = 7x - 9\left(\frac{7}{7+5}\right)$$

$$= 7x - \frac{63}{12} = \left(7x - \frac{21}{4}\right) l$$

$$\text{and B remains} = 5x - 9\left(\frac{5}{7+5}\right)$$

$$= 5x - \frac{45}{12} = \left(5x - \frac{15}{4}\right) l$$

When 9 litres of liquid B are added

$$\left(7x - \frac{21}{4}\right) : \left(5x - \frac{15}{4} + 9\right) = 7 : 9$$

$$\Rightarrow \frac{7x - \frac{21}{4}}{5x - \frac{15}{4} + 9} = \frac{7}{9}$$

$$\Rightarrow 63x - \frac{189}{4} = 35x - \frac{105}{4} + 63$$

$$\Rightarrow 28x = \frac{189}{4} - \frac{105}{4} + 63$$

$$= 21 + 63 = 84$$

$$\Rightarrow x = \frac{84}{28} = 3$$

$$\therefore 7x = 7 \times 3$$

$$= 21 \text{ litres.}$$

65.
$$\pi(r + 4)^2 - \pi r^2 = \frac{11}{25}\pi r^2$$

$$\Rightarrow \pi(r^2 + 8r + 16 - r^2) = \frac{11}{25}\pi r^2$$

$$\Rightarrow 8r + 16 = \frac{11}{25}r^2$$

$$\Rightarrow 200r + 400 = 11r^2$$

$$\Rightarrow 11r^2 - 200r - 400 = 0$$

$$\Rightarrow 11r^2 - 220r + 20r - 400 = 0$$

$$\Rightarrow 11r(r - 20) + 20(r - 20) = 0$$

$$(r - 20)(11r + 20) = 0$$

$$\Rightarrow r = 20$$

or $r = \frac{-20}{11}$

Hence, radius of the swimming pool

$$= 20 \text{ feet.}$$

66.
$$\frac{14}{x-y} + \frac{36}{x+y} = 4$$

$$\frac{20}{x-y} + \frac{24}{x+y} = 5$$

$$36a + 14b = 4 \quad] \times 2$$

$$24a + 20b = 5 \quad] \times 3$$

$$72a + 28b = 8$$

$$72a + 60b = 15$$

$$- \quad - \quad -$$

$$32b = 7 \Rightarrow b = \frac{7}{32}$$

$$24a + 20 \times \frac{7}{32} = 5$$

$$\Rightarrow 24a = 5 - \frac{140}{32}$$

$$= \frac{160 - 140}{32} = \frac{20}{32}$$

$$\Rightarrow a = \frac{20}{32 \times 24} = \frac{5}{192}$$

$$\frac{1}{x+y} = \frac{5}{192}$$

$$\Rightarrow 5x + 5y = 192 \quad] \times 7$$

$$\frac{1}{x-y} = \frac{7}{32}$$

$$\Rightarrow 7x - 7y = 32 \quad] \times 5$$

$$35x + 35y = 1344$$

$$35x - 35y = 160$$

$$70x = 1504$$

$$x = \frac{1504}{70} = 21 \text{ km/hr}$$

II speed of boat = 16 km/hr

$\therefore$ Quantity I > Quantity II

Hence, option (B) is correct.

68. $$\frac{x^2}{5} + x + \frac{4}{5} = 0$$

$\Rightarrow$ $x^2 + 5x + 4 = 0$

$\Rightarrow$ $x^2 + 4x + x + 4 = 0$

$\Rightarrow$ $x(x + 4) + 1(x + 4) = 0$

$\Rightarrow$ $(x + 4)(x + 1) = 0$

either $x = -4$ or $x = -1$

$3y^2 + 4y + 1 = 0$

$\Rightarrow$ $3y^2 + 3y + y + 1 = 0$

$\Rightarrow$ $3y(y + 1) + 1(y + 1) = 0$

$\Rightarrow$ $(3y + 1)(y + 1) = 0$

either $y = -1$ or $y = -\frac{1}{3}$

Quantity I $\leq$ Quantity II

Hence, option (E) is correct.

69. Quantity I $\geq$ Quantity II

Hence, option (D) is correct.

81. 6, 4, 5, 8.5, 18, 48 [46], 139

$\times\frac{1}{2}+1$, $\times 1 + 1$, $\times\frac{3}{2}+1$, $\times 2 + 1$, $\times\frac{5}{2}+1$, $\times 3 + 1$

Hence, wrong number is 48.

82. 10080, 1440, 240, 48, 12, 3 [4], 2

$\div 7$, $\div 6$, $\div 5$, $\div 4$, $\div 3$, $\div 2$

Hence, wrong number is 3.

83.

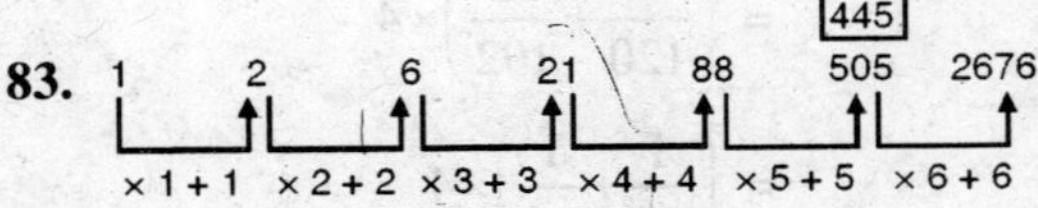

1, 2, 6, 21, 88, 505 [445], 2676

$\times 1 + 1$, $\times 2 + 2$, $\times 3 + 3$, $\times 4 + 4$, $\times 5 + 5$, $\times 6 + 6$

Hence, wrong number is 505.

84. 18, 21 [20], 25, 35, 52, 78, 115

+ 2, + 5, + 10, + 17, + 26, + 37

+ 3, + 5, + 7, + 9, + 11

+ 2, + 2, + 2, + 2

Hence, wrong number is 21.

85. 120, 137, 178 [171], 222, 290, 375, 477

+ 17, + 34, + 51, + 68, + 85, + 102

↓ ↓ ↓ ↓ ↓ ↓

17 × 1, 17 × 2, 17 × 3, 17 × 4, 17 × 5, 17 × 6

Hence, wrong number is 178.

86. $\because$ Area of rectangle = 150 m^2

$\Rightarrow$ $xy = 150$

$\Rightarrow$ $x = \frac{150}{y}$ ...(*i*)

Now, $(x - 5)(y + 2) = 120$

$\Rightarrow$ $xy + 2x - 5y - 10 = 120$

$\Rightarrow$ $150 + 2x - 5y - 10 = 120$

$\Rightarrow$ $2x - 5y = -20$

$\Rightarrow$ $2\left(\frac{150}{y}\right) - 5y = -20$

$\Rightarrow$ $300 - 5y^2 = -20y$

$\Rightarrow$ $5y^2 - 20y - 300 = 0$

$\Rightarrow$ $y^2 - 4y - 60 = 0$

$\Rightarrow$ $(y - 10)(y + 6) = 0$

$\Rightarrow$ $y = 10$ or $y = -6$

which is not possible

$\therefore$ Breadth of rectangle = 10 m

Length of rectangle = 15 m

Side of square = 15 m

[$\because$ Length of rectangle = side of square given]

$\therefore$ Perimeter of square = 15 × 4 = 60 m.

87. Amount invested by A

= 4200 × 4 + 5200 × 6 = 48000

Amount invested by B

= 3600 × 6 + (3600 + x) × 4

= 21600 + 14400 + 4x

= 4x + 36000

Amount invested by C

= 2400 × 6 + (2400 + 2x)4

= 14400 + 9600 + 8x

= 24000 + 8x

A : B : C = 48000 : 4x + 36000 : 8x + 24000

$$\text{A's share} = \left(\frac{48000}{48000 + 12x + 60000}\right) \times 2820$$

$$\Rightarrow \quad 1200 = \left(\frac{48000}{12x + 108000}\right) \times 2820$$

$\Rightarrow$ $12x + 108000 = 282 \times 400 = 112800$

$\Rightarrow$ $12x = 112800 - 10800 = 4800$

$$x = \frac{4800}{12} = 400$$

Hence, B invested additional amount = ₹ 400.

88. 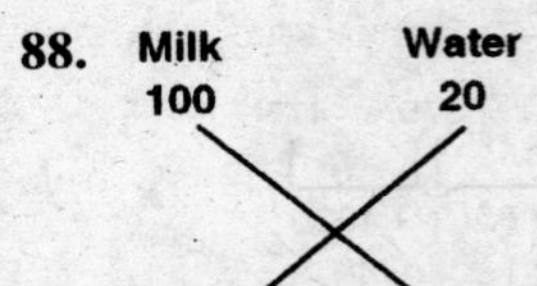

Let amount of milk = 100 l
and amount of water = 20 l
24 l mix taken out
Amount of milk in 24 l mix

$$= \frac{5}{6} \times 24 = 20 l$$

Amount of water in 24 l mix

$$= \frac{1}{6} \times 24 = 4 l$$

Now Amount of milk
= 100 l = 80 l + 24 l (added)
= 104 l
Amount of water
= 20 – 4 = 16 l
Again 15 l of mix taken out
Amount of milk in 15 l mix

$$= \frac{13}{15} \times 15 = 13\ l$$

Amount of water

$$= \frac{2}{15} \times 15 = 2\ l$$

Hence, the resultant quantity of milk in the mixture = 104 – 13 = 91 litres.

89. Let number of ball faced by D = 3x
then, number of ball faced by F = 4x
Total run scored by D = 72 × 3x
Total run scored by F = 66 × 4x
Per cent difference of run scored by F more than D

$$= \left(\frac{66 \times 4x - 72 \times 3x}{72 \times 3x}\right) \times 100$$

$$= \frac{4800}{216} = \frac{200}{9} = 22\frac{2}{9}\%.$$

90. Total run scored by E = 55 × 28 = 1540
Total run scored by E in first 25 matches
= 25 × (55 – 9) = 1150
Total run scored by E in last 3 matches
= 1540 – 1150 = 390
Minimum run scored by E in 28th match

$n \geq 390 - 127 - 126$

$n \geq 137$

$\therefore \quad n = 137.$

91. Total run scored by A = $8x$
Total ball faced = $8x - 74$

$$\text{Strike rate of A} = \left(\frac{8x}{8x - 74}\right) \times 100$$

$$\Rightarrow \quad 129.6 = \frac{8x \times 100}{8x - 74}$$

$\Rightarrow$ 129.6 × $8x$ – $8x$ × 100 = 129.6 × 74

$\Rightarrow$ $8x$(129.6 – 100) = 129.6 × 74

$$\Rightarrow \quad x = \frac{129.6 \times 74}{8 \times 29.6} = \frac{81}{2}$$

$$\Rightarrow \quad x = 40\frac{1}{2}$$

$\therefore$ Average runs scored by A = 40.5.

93. Let no. of matches played by C = x
Total runs scored = 38 x

$$\text{Strike rate} = \left(\frac{38x}{400}\right) \times 100$$

$$\Rightarrow \quad 114 = \frac{38x}{4}$$

$$\therefore \quad x = \frac{114 \times 4}{38} = 12$$

Hence, total number of matches played by batsman C = 12

94. $1 \text{ man 1 day work} = \frac{1}{10 \times 12} = \frac{1}{120}$

$1 \text{ child 1 day work} = \frac{1}{12 \times 16} = \frac{1}{192}$

$1 \text{ women 1 day work} = \frac{1}{8 \times 20} = \frac{1}{160}$

(5 men + 12 children) 4 days work

$$= \left(\frac{5}{120} + \frac{12}{192}\right) \times 4$$

$$= \left(\frac{1}{24} + \frac{1}{16}\right) \times 4$$

$$= \left(\frac{2+3}{48}\right) \times 4 = \frac{5}{12}$$

$$\text{Remaining work} = 1 - \frac{5}{12} = \frac{7}{12}$$

(5 men + 4 women + 4 children) 1 day work

$$= \left(\frac{1}{24} + \frac{4}{160} + \frac{4}{192}\right) \text{1 day work}$$